DEMOSTHENES, SPEECHES 27–38

THE ORATORY OF CLASSICAL GREECE

Translated with Notes • *Michael Gagarin, Series Editor*

VOLUME 8

DEMOSTHENES, SPEECHES 27–38

Translated by Douglas M. MacDowell

 UNIVERSITY OF TEXAS PRESS, AUSTIN

First edition, 2004

Requests for permission to reproduce material from
this work should be sent to Permissions, University
of Texas Press, Box 7819, Austin, TX 78713-7819.

⊗ The paper used in this book meets the minimum
requirements of ANSI/NISO Z39.48-1992 (R1997)
(Permanence of Paper).

Library of Congress Cataloging-in-Publication Data

Demosthenes.
    [Selections. English. 2004]
    Demosthenes, speeches 27–38 / translated by
Douglas M. MacDowell.—1st ed.
        p.   cm. — (The oratory of classical Greece ;
v. 8) Includes bibliographical references and index.
    ISBN 0-292-70253-1 (alk. paper) —
    ISBN 0-292-70254-X (pbk. : alk. paper)
    1. Demosthenes—Translations into English.
2. Speeches, addresses, etc., Greek—Translations
into English.   3. Athens (Greece)—Politics and
government—Early works to 1800.   I. Title:
Speeches 27–38.   II. Title.   III. Series.
    PA3951.E5   2004
    885′.01—dc22
                                        2003023288

CONTENTS

SERIES EDITOR'S PREFACE

This is the eighth volume in a series of translations of the Oratory of Classical Greece. The aim of the series is to make available primarily for those who do not read Greek up-to-date, accurate, and readable translations with introductions and explanatory notes of all the surviving works and major fragments of the Attic orators of the classical period (ca. 420–320 BC): Aeschines, Andocides, Antiphon, Demosthenes, Dinarchus, Hyperides, Isaeus, Isocrates, Lycurgus, and Lysias. This volume is the second to appear with Demosthenes' private speeches, and it includes the speeches he gave in his first court cases—his suits against his guardians for defrauding him of most of his father's estate.

Once again I would like to thank all those at the University of Texas Press who have worked with this volume and the others in the series, Director Joanna Hitchcock, Humanities Editor Jim Burr, Managing Editor Carolyn Wylie, and Copyeditor Nancy Moore.

—M.G.

SERIES INTRODUCTION
Greek Oratory

❦❦

By Michael Gagarin

ORATORY IN CLASSICAL ATHENS

From as early as Homer (and undoubtedly much earlier) the Greeks placed a high value on effective speaking. Even Achilles, whose greatness was primarily established on the battlefield, was brought up to be "a speaker of words and a doer of deeds" (*Iliad* 9.443); and Athenian leaders of the sixth and fifth centuries,[1] such as Solon, Themistocles, and Pericles, were all accomplished orators. Most Greek literary genres —notably epic, tragedy, and history—underscore the importance of oratory by their inclusion of set speeches. The formal pleadings of the envoys to Achilles in the *Iliad,* the messenger speeches in tragedy reporting events like the battle of Salamis in Aeschylus' *Persians* or the gruesome death of Pentheus in Euripides' *Bacchae,* and the powerful political oratory of Pericles' funeral oration in Thucydides are but a few of the most notable examples of the Greeks' never-ending fascination with formal public speaking, which was to reach its height in the public oratory of the fourth century.

In early times, oratory was not a specialized subject of study but was learned by practice and example. The formal study of rhetoric as an "art" (*technē*) began, we are told, in the middle of the fifth century in Sicily with the work of Corax and his pupil Tisias.[2] These two are

---

[1] All dates in this volume are BC unless the contrary is either indicated or obvious.　.

[2] See Kennedy 1963: 26–51. Cole 1991 has challenged this traditional picture, arguing that the term "rhetoric" was coined by Plato to designate and denigrate an activity he strongly opposed. Cole's own reconstruction is not without prob-

scarcely more than names to us, but another famous Sicilian, Gorgias of Leontini (ca. 490–390), developed a new style of argument and is reported to have dazzled the Athenians with a speech delivered when he visited Athens in 427. Gorgias initiated the practice, which continued into the early fourth century, of composing speeches for mythical or imaginary occasions. The surviving examples reveal a lively intellectual climate in the late fifth and early fourth centuries, in which oratory served to display new ideas, new forms of expression, and new methods of argument.[3] This tradition of "intellectual" oratory was continued by the fourth-century educator Isocrates and played a large role in later Greek and Roman education.

In addition to this intellectual oratory, at about the same time the practice also began of writing speeches for real occasions in public life, which we may designate "practical" oratory. For centuries Athenians had been delivering speeches in public settings (primarily the courts and the Assembly), but these had always been composed and delivered impromptu, without being written down and thus without being preserved. The practice of writing speeches began in the courts and then expanded to include the Assembly and other settings. Athens was one of the leading cities of Greece in the fifth and fourth centuries, and its political and legal systems depended on direct participation by a large number of citizens; all important decisions were made by these large bodies, and the primary means of influencing these decisions was oratory.[4] Thus, it is not surprising that oratory flourished in Athens,[5] but it may not be immediately obvious why it should be written down.

The pivotal figure in this development was Antiphon, one of the fifth-century intellectuals who are often grouped together under the

---

lems, but he does well to remind us how thoroughly the traditional view of rhetoric depends on one of its most ardent opponents.

[3] Of these only Antiphon's *Tetralogies* are included in this series. Gorgias' *Helen* and *Palamedes*, Alcidamas' *Odysseus*, and Antisthenes' *Ajax* and *Odysseus* are translated in Gagarin and Woodruff 1995.

[4] Yunis 1996 has a good treatment of political oratory from Pericles to Demosthenes.

[5] All our evidence for practical oratory comes from Athens, with the exception of Isocrates 19, written for a trial in Aegina. Many speeches were undoubtedly delivered in courts and political forums in other Greek cities, but it may be that such speeches were written down only in Athens.

name "Sophists."[6] Like some of the other sophists he contributed to the intellectual oratory of the period, but he also had a strong practical interest in law. At the same time, Antiphon had an aversion to public speaking and did not directly involve himself in legal or political affairs (Thucydides 8.68). However, he began giving general advice to other citizens who were engaged in litigation and were thus expected to address the court themselves. As this practice grew, Antiphon went further, and around 430 he began writing out whole speeches for others to memorize and deliver. Thus began the practice of "logography," which continued through the next century and beyond.[7] Logography particularly appealed to men like Lysias, who were metics, or noncitizen residents of Athens. Since they were not Athenian citizens, they were barred from direct participation in public life, but they could contribute by writing speeches for others.

Antiphon was also the first (to our knowledge) to write down a speech he would himself deliver, writing the speech for his own defense at his trial for treason in 411. His motive was probably to publicize and preserve his views, and others continued this practice of writing down speeches they would themselves deliver in the courts and (more rarely) the Assembly.[8] Finally, one other type of practical oratory was the special tribute delivered on certain important public occasions, the best known of which is the funeral oration. It is convenient to designate these three types of oratory by the terms Aristotle later uses: forensic (for the courts), deliberative (for the Assembly), and epideictic (for display).[9]

---

[6] The term "sophist" was loosely used through the fifth and fourth centuries to designate various intellectuals and orators, but under the influence of Plato, who attacked certain figures under this name, the term is now used of a specific group of thinkers; see Kerferd 1981.

[7] For Antiphon as the first to write speeches, see Photius, *Bibliotheca* 486a7–11 and [Plut.], *Moralia* 832c–d. The latest extant speech can be dated to 320, but we know that at least one orator, Dinarchus, continued the practice after that date.

[8] Unlike forensic speeches, speeches for delivery in the Assembly were usually not composed beforehand in writing, since the speaker could not know exactly when or in what context he would be speaking; see further Trevett 1996.

[9] *Rhetoric* 1.3. Intellectual orations, like Gorgias' *Helen,* do not easily fit into Aristotle's classification. For a fuller (but still brief) introduction to Attic oratory and the orators, see Edwards 1994.

THE ORATORS

In the century from about 420 to 320, dozens—perhaps even hundreds—of now unknown orators and logographers must have composed speeches that are now lost, but only ten of these men were selected for preservation and study by ancient scholars, and only works collected under the names of these ten have been preserved. Some of these works are undoubtedly spurious, though in most cases they are fourth-century works by a different author rather than later "forgeries." Indeed, modern scholars suspect that as many as seven of the speeches attributed to Demosthenes may have been written by Apollodorus, son of Pasion, who is sometimes called "the eleventh orator." [10] Including these speeches among the works of Demosthenes may have been an honest mistake, or perhaps a bookseller felt he could sell more copies of these speeches if they were attributed to a more famous orator.

In alphabetical order the Ten Orators are as follows: [11]

- AESCHINES (ca. 395–ca. 322) rose from obscure origins to become an important Athenian political figure, first an ally, then a bitter enemy of Demosthenes. His three speeches all concern major public issues. The best known of these (Aes. 3) was delivered at the trial in 330, when Demosthenes responded with *On the Crown* (Dem. 18). Aeschines lost the case and was forced to leave Athens and live the rest of his life in exile.

- ANDOCIDES (ca. 440–ca. 390) is best known for his role in the scandal of 415, when just before the departure of the fateful Athenian expedition to Sicily during the Peloponnesian War (431–404), a band of young men mutilated statues of Hermes, and at the same time information was revealed about the secret rites of Demeter. Andocides was exiled but later returned. Two of the four speeches

---

[10] See Trevett 1992.

[11] The Loeb volumes of *Minor Attic Orators* also include the prominent Athenian political figure Demades (ca. 385–319), who was not one of the Ten; but the only speech that has come down to us under his name is a later forgery. It is possible that Demades and other fourth-century politicians who had a high reputation for public speaking did not put any speeches in writing, especially if they rarely spoke in the courts (see above n. 8).

in his name give us a contemporary view of the scandal: one pleads for his return, the other argues against a second period of exile.

• ANTIPHON (ca. 480–411), as already noted, wrote forensic speeches for others and only once spoke himself. In 411 he participated in an oligarchic coup by a group of 400, and when the democrats regained power he was tried for treason and executed. His six surviving speeches include three for delivery in court and the three Tetralogies—imaginary intellectual exercises for display or teaching that consist of four speeches each, two on each side. All six of Antiphon's speeches concern homicide, probably because these stood at the beginning of the collection of his works. Fragments of some thirty other speeches cover many different topics.

• DEMOSTHENES (384–322) is generally considered the best of the Attic orators. Although his nationalistic message is less highly regarded today, his powerful mastery of and ability to combine many different rhetorical styles continues to impress readers. Demosthenes was still a child when his wealthy father died. The trustees of the estate apparently misappropriated much of it, and when he came of age, he sued them in a series of cases (27–31), regaining some of his fortune and making a name as a powerful speaker. He then wrote speeches for others in a variety of cases, public and private, and for his own use in court (where many cases involved major public issues), and in the Assembly, where he opposed the growing power of Philip of Macedon. The triumph of Philip and his son Alexander the Great eventually put an end to Demosthenes' career. Some sixty speeches have come down under his name, about a third of them of questionable authenticity.

• DINARCHUS (ca. 360–ca. 290) was born in Corinth but spent much of his life in Athens as a metic (a noncitizen resident). His public fame came primarily from writing speeches for the prosecutions surrounding the Harpalus affair in 324, when several prominent figures (including Demosthenes) were accused of bribery. After 322 he had a profitable career as a logographer.

• HYPERIDES (389/8–322) was a political leader and logographer of so many different talents that he was called the pentathlete of orators. He was a leader of the Athenian resistance to Philip and

Alexander and (like Demosthenes) was condemned to death after Athens' final surrender. One speech and substantial fragments of five others have been recovered from papyrus remains; otherwise, only fragments survive.

- ISAEUS (ca. 415–ca. 340) wrote speeches on a wide range of topics, but the eleven complete speeches that survive, dating from ca. 390 to ca. 344, all concern inheritance. As with Antiphon, the survival of these particular speeches may have been the result of the later ordering of his speeches by subject; we have part of a twelfth speech and fragments and titles of some forty other works. Isaeus is said to have been a pupil of Isocrates and the teacher of Demosthenes.

- ISOCRATES (436–338) considered himself a philosopher and educator, not an orator or rhetorician. He came from a wealthy Athenian family but lost most of his property in the Peloponnesian War, and in 403 he took up logography. About 390 he abandoned this practice and turned to writing and teaching, setting forth his educational, philosophical, and political views in essays that took the form of speeches but were not meant for oral delivery. He favored accommodation with the growing power of Philip of Macedon and panhellenic unity. His school was based on a broad concept of rhetoric and applied philosophy; it attracted pupils from the entire Greek world (including Isaeus, Lycurgus, and Hyperides) and became the main rival of Plato's Academy. Isocrates greatly influenced education and rhetoric in the Hellenistic, Roman, and modern periods until the eighteenth century.

- LYCURGUS (ca. 390–ca. 324) was a leading public official who restored the financial condition of Athens after 338 and played a large role in the city for the next dozen years. He brought charges of corruption or treason against many other officials, usually with success. Only one speech survives.

- LYSIAS (ca. 445–ca. 380) was a metic—an official resident of Athens but not a citizen. Much of his property was seized by the Thirty during their short-lived oligarchic coup in 404–403. Perhaps as a result he turned to logography. More than thirty speeches survive in whole or in part, though the authenticity of some is doubted. We also have fragments or know the titles of more than a hundred others. The speeches cover a wide range of cases, and he may have delivered one himself (Lys. 12), on the death of his brother at the hands of the Thirty. Lysias is particularly known for his vivid narratives, his *ēthopoiïa*, or "creation of character," and his prose style, which became a model of clarity and vividness.

THE WORKS OF THE ORATORS

As soon as speeches began to be written down, they could be preserved. We know little about the conditions of book "publication" (i.e., making copies for distribution) in the fourth century, but there was an active market for books in Athens, and some of the speeches may have achieved wide circulation.[12] An orator (or his family) may have preserved his own speeches, perhaps to advertise his ability or demonstrate his success, or booksellers may have collected and copied them in order to make money.

We do not know how closely the preserved text of these speeches corresponded to the version actually delivered in court or in the Assembly. Speakers undoubtedly extemporized or varied from their text on occasion, but there is no good evidence that deliberative speeches were substantially revised for publication.[13] In forensic oratory a logographer's reputation would derive first and foremost from his success with jurors. If a forensic speech was victorious, there would be no reason to alter it for publication, and if it lost, alteration would probably not deceive potential clients. Thus, the published texts of forensic speeches were probably quite faithful to the texts that were provided to clients, and we have little reason to suspect substantial alteration in the century or so before they were collected by scholars in Alexandria (see below).

In addition to the speaker's text, most forensic speeches have breaks for the inclusion of documents. The logographer inserted a notation in his text—such as *nomos* ("law") or *martyria* ("testimony")—and the

---

[12] Dover's discussion (1968) of the preservation and transmission of the works of Lysias (and perhaps others under his name) is useful not just for Lysias but for the other orators too. His theory of shared authorship between logographer and litigant, however, is unconvincing (see Usher 1976).

[13] See further Trevett 1996: 437–439.

speaker would pause while the clerk read out the text of a law or the testimony of witnesses. Many speeches survive with only a notation that a *nomos* or *martyria* was read at that point, but in some cases the text of the document is included. It used to be thought that these documents were all creations of later scholars, but many (though not all) are now accepted as genuine.[14]

With the foundation of the famous library in Alexandria early in the third century, scholars began to collect and catalogue texts of the orators, along with many other classical authors. Only the best orators were preserved in the library, many of them represented by over 100 speeches each (some undoubtedly spurious). Only some of these works survived in manuscript form to the modern era; more recently a few others have been discovered on ancient sheets of papyrus, so that today the corpus of Attic Oratory consists of about 150 speeches, together with a few letters and other works. The subject matter ranges from important public issues and serious crimes to business affairs, lovers' quarrels, inheritance disputes, and other personal or family matters.

In the centuries after these works were collected, ancient scholars gathered biographical facts about their authors, produced grammatical and lexicographic notes, and used some of the speeches as evidence for Athenian political history. But the ancient scholars who were most interested in the orators were those who studied prose style, the most notable of these being Dionysius of Halicarnassus (first century BC), who wrote treatises on several of the orators,[15] and Hermogenes of Tarsus (second century AD), who wrote several literary studies, including *On Types of Style.*[16] But relative to epic or tragedy, oratory was little studied; and even scholars of rhetoric whose interests were broader than style, like Cicero and Quintilian, paid little attention to the orators, except for the acknowledged master, Demosthenes.

Most modern scholars until the second half of the twentieth century continued to treat the orators primarily as prose stylists.[17] The

---

[14] See MacDowell 1990: 43–47; Todd 1993: 44–45.

[15] Dionysius' literary studies are collected and translated in Usher 1974–1985.

[16] Wooten 1987. Stylistic considerations probably also influenced the selection of the "canon" of ten orators; see Worthington 1994.

[17] For example, the most popular and influential book ever written on the orators, Jebb's *The Attic Orators* (1875) was presented as an "attempt to aid in giving Attic Oratory its due place in the history of Attic Prose" (I.xiii). This modern focus

reevaluation of Athenian democracy by George Grote and others in the nineteenth century stimulated renewed interest in Greek oratory among historians; and increasing interest in Athenian law during that century led a few legal scholars to read the orators. But in comparison with the interest shown in the other literary genres—epic, lyric, tragedy, comedy, and even history—Attic oratory has been relatively neglected until the last third of the twentieth century. More recently, however, scholars have discovered the value of the orators for the broader study of Athenian culture and society. Since Dover's groundbreaking works on popular morality and homosexuality,[18] interest in the orators has been increasing rapidly, and they are now seen as primary representatives of Athenian moral and social values, and as evidence for social and economic conditions, political and social ideology, and in general those aspects of Athenian culture that in the past were commonly ignored by historians of ancient Greece but are of increasing interest and importance today, including women and the family, slavery, and the economy.

GOVERNMENT AND LAW IN CLASSICAL ATHENS

The hallmark of the Athenian political and legal systems was its amateurism. Most public officials, including those who supervised the courts, were selected by lot and held office for a limited period, typically a year. Thus a great many citizens held public office at some point in their lives, but almost none served for an extended period of time or developed the experience or expertise that would make them professionals. All significant policy decisions were debated and voted on in the Assembly, where the quorum was 6,000 citizens, and all significant legal cases were judged by bodies of 200 to 500 jurors or more. Public prominence was not achieved by election (or selection) to public office but depended rather on a man's ability to sway the majority of citizens in the Assembly or jurors in court to vote in favor of a pro-

---

on prose style can plausibly be connected to the large role played by prose composition (the translation of English prose into Greek, usually in imitation of specific authors or styles) in the Classics curriculum, especially in Britain.

[18] Dover (1974, 1978). Dover recently commented (1994: 157), "When I began to mine the riches of Attic forensic oratory I was astonished to discover that the mine had never been exploited."

posed course of action or for one of the litigants in a trial. Success was never permanent, and a victory on one policy issue or a verdict in one case could be quickly reversed in another.[19] In such a system the value of public oratory is obvious, and in the fourth century, oratory became the most important cultural institution in Athens, replacing drama as the forum where major ideological concerns were displayed and debated.

Several recent books give good detailed accounts of Athenian government and law,[20] and so a brief sketch can suffice here. The main policy-making body was the Assembly, open to all adult male citizens; a small payment for attendance enabled at least some of the poor to attend along with the leisured rich. In addition, a Council of 500 citizens, selected each year by lot with no one allowed to serve more than two years, prepared material for and made recommendations to the Assembly; a rotating subgroup of this Council served as an executive committee, the Prytaneis. Finally, numerous officials, most of them selected by lot for one-year terms, supervised different areas of administration and finance. The most important of these were the nine Archons (lit. "rulers"): the eponymous Archon after whom the year was named, the Basileus ("king"),[21] the Polemarch, and the six Thesmothetae. Councilors and almost all these officials underwent a preliminary examination (*dokimasia*) before taking office, and officials submitted to a final accounting (*euthynai*) upon leaving; at these times any citizen who wished could challenge a person's fitness for his new position or his performance in his recent position.

---

[19] In the Assembly this could be accomplished by a reconsideration of the question, as in the famous Mytilenean debate (Thuc. 3.36–50); in court a verdict was final, but its practical effects could be thwarted or reversed by later litigation on a related issue.

[20] For government, see Sinclair 1988, Hansen 1991; for law, MacDowell 1978, Todd 1993, and Boegehold 1995 (Bonner 1927 is still helpful). Much of our information about the legal and political systems comes from a work attributed to Aristotle but perhaps written by a pupil of his, *The Athenian Constitution* (*Ath. Pol.*—conveniently translated with notes by Rhodes 1984). The discovery of this work on a papyrus in Egypt in 1890 caused a major resurgence of interest in Athenian government.

[21] Modern scholars often use the term *archōn basileus* or "king archon," but Athenian sources (e.g., *Ath. Pol.* 57) simply call him the *basileus*.

There was no general taxation of Athenian citizens. Sources of public funding included the annual tax levied on metics, various fees and import duties, and (in the fifth century) tribute from allied cities; but the source that figures most prominently in the orators is the Athenian system of liturgies (*leitourgiai*), by which in a regular rotation the rich provided funding for certain special public needs. The main liturgies were the *chorēgia*, in which a sponsor (*chorēgos*) supervised and paid for the training and performance of a chorus which sang and danced at a public festival,[22] and the trierarchy, in which a sponsor (trierarch) paid to equip and usually commanded a trireme, or warship, for a year. Some of these liturgies required substantial expenditures, but even so, some men spent far more than required in order to promote themselves and their public careers, and litigants often tried to impress the jurors by referring to liturgies they had undertaken (see, e.g., Lys. 21.1–n5). A further twist on this system was that if a man thought he had been assigned a liturgy that should have gone to someone else who was richer than he, he could propose an exchange of property (*antidosis*), giving the other man a choice of either taking over the liturgy or exchanging property with him. Finally, the rich were also subject to special taxes (*eisphorai*) levied as a percentage of their property in times of need.

The Athenian legal system remained similarly resistant to professionalization. Trials and the procedures leading up to them were supervised by officials, primarily the nine Archons, but their role was purely administrative, and they were in no way equivalent to modern judges. All significant questions about what we would call points of law were presented to the jurors, who considered them together with all other issues when they delivered their verdict at the end of the trial.[23] Trials were "contests" (*agōnes*) between two litigants, each of whom presented his own case to the jurors in a speech, plaintiff first, then de-

---

[22] These included the productions of tragedy and comedy, for which the main expense was for the chorus.

[23] Certain religious "interpreters" (*exēgetai*) were occasionally asked to give their opinion on a legal matter that had a religious dimension (such as the prosecution of a homicide), but although these opinions could be reported in court (e.g., Dem. 47.68–73), they had no official legal standing. The most significant administrative decision we hear of is the refusal of the Basileus to accept the case in Antiphon 6 (see 6.37–46).

fendant; in some cases each party then spoke again, probably in rebuttal. Since a litigant had only one or two speeches in which to present his entire case, and no issue was decided separately by a judge, all the necessary factual information and every important argument on substance or procedure, fact or law, had to be presented together. A single speech might thus combine narrative, argument, emotional appeal, and various digressions, all with the goal of obtaining a favorable verdict. Even more than today, a litigant's primary task was to control the issue—to determine which issues the jurors would consider most important and which questions they would have in their minds as they cast their votes. We only rarely have both speeches from a trial,[24] and we usually have little or no external evidence for the facts of a case or the verdict. We must thus infer both the facts and the opponent's strategy from the speech we have, and any assessment of the overall effectiveness of a speech and of the logographer's strategy is to some extent speculative.

Before a trial there were usually several preliminary hearings for presenting evidence; arbitration, public and private, was available and sometimes required. These hearings and arbitration sessions allowed each side to become familiar with the other side's case, so that discussions of "what my opponent will say" could be included in one's speech. Normally a litigant presented his own case, but he was often assisted by family or friends. If he wished (and could afford it), he could enlist the services of a logographer, who presumably gave strategic advice in addition to writing a speech. The speeches were timed to ensure an equal hearing for both sides,[25] and all trials were completed within a day. Two hundred or more jurors decided each case in the popular courts, which met in the Agora.[26] Homicide cases and certain other religious trials (e.g., Lys. 7) were heard by the Council of the Areopagus or an associated group of fifty-one Ephetae. The Areopagus was composed of all former Archons—perhaps 150–200 members at most

---

[24] The exceptions are Demosthenes 19 and Aeschines 2, Aeschines 3 and Demosthenes 18, and Lysias 6 (one of several prosecution speeches) and Andocides 1; all were written for major public cases.

[25] Timing was done by means of a water-clock, which in most cases was stopped during the reading of documents.

[26] See Boegehold 1995.

times. It met on a hill called the Areopagus ("rock of Ares") near the Acropolis.

Jurors for the regular courts were selected by lot from those citizens who registered each year and who appeared for duty that day; as with the Assembly, a small payment allowed the poor to serve. After the speakers had finished, the jurors voted immediately without any formal discussion. The side with the majority won; a tie vote decided the case for the defendant. In some cases where the penalty was not fixed, after a conviction the jurors voted again on the penalty, choosing between penalties proposed by each side. Even when we know the verdict, we cannot know which of the speaker's arguments contributed most to his success or failure. However, a logographer could probably learn from jurors which points had or had not been successful, so that arguments that are found repeatedly in speeches probably were known to be effective in most cases.

The first written laws in Athens were enacted by Draco (ca. 620) and Solon (ca. 590), and new laws were regularly added. At the end of the fifth century the existing laws were reorganized, and a new procedure for enacting laws was instituted; thereafter a group of Law-Givers (*nomothetai*) had to certify that a proposed law did not conflict with any existing laws. There was no attempt, however, to organize legislation systematically, and although Plato, Aristotle, and other philosophers wrote various works on law and law-giving, these were either theoretical or descriptive and had no apparent influence on legislation. Written statutes generally used ordinary language rather than precise legal definitions in designating offenses, and questions concerning precisely what constituted a specific offense or what was the correct interpretation of a written statute were decided (together with other issues) by the jurors in each case. A litigant might, of course, assert a certain definition or interpretation as "something you all know" or "what the lawgiver intended," but such remarks are evidently tendentious and cannot be taken as authoritative.

The result of these procedural and substantive features was that the verdict depended largely on each litigant's speech (or speeches). As one speaker puts it (Ant. 6.18), "When there are no witnesses, you (jurors) are forced to reach a verdict about the case on the basis of the prosecutor's and defendant's words alone; you must be suspicious and examine their accounts in detail, and your vote will necessarily be cast on the basis of likelihood rather than clear knowledge." Even the testimony of witnesses (usually on both sides) is rarely decisive. On the other hand, most speakers make a considerable effort to establish facts and provide legitimate arguments in conformity with established law. Plato's view of rhetoric as a clever technique for persuading an ignorant crowd that the false is true is not borne out by the speeches, and the legal system does not appear to have produced many arbitrary or clearly unjust results.

The main form of legal procedure was a *dikē* ("suit") in which the injured party (or his relatives in a case of homicide) brought suit against the offender. Suits for injuries to slaves would be brought by the slave's master, and injuries to women would be prosecuted by a male relative. Strictly speaking, a *dikē* was a private matter between individuals, though like all cases, *dikai* often had public dimensions. The other major form of procedure was a *graphē* ("writing" or "indictment") in which "anyone who wished" (i.e., any citizen) could bring a prosecution for wrongdoing. *Graphai* were instituted by Solon, probably in order to allow prosecution of offenses where the victim was unable or unlikely to bring suit himself, such as selling a dependent into slavery; but the number of areas covered by *graphai* increased to cover many types of public offenses as well as some apparently private crimes, such as *hybris*.

The system of prosecution by "anyone who wished" also extended to several other more specialized forms of prosecution, like *eisangelia* ("impeachment"), used in cases of treason. Another specialized prosecution was *apagōgē* ("summary arrest"), in which someone could arrest a common criminal (*kakourgos,* lit. "evil-doer"), or have him arrested, on the spot. The reliance on private initiative meant that Athenians never developed a system of public prosecution; rather, they presumed that everyone would keep an eye on the behavior of his political enemies and bring suit as soon as he suspected a crime, both to harm his opponents and to advance his own career. In this way all public officials would be watched by someone. There was no disgrace in admitting that a prosecution was motivated by private enmity.

By the end of the fifth century the system of prosecution by "anyone who wished" was apparently being abused by so-called sykophants (*sykophantai*), who allegedly brought or threatened to bring false suits against rich men, either to gain part of the fine that would be levied or to induce an out-of-court settlement in which the accused would pay to have the matter dropped. We cannot gauge the true extent of this problem, since speakers usually provide little evidence to support their claims that their opponents are sykophants, but the Athenians did make sykophancy a crime. They also specified that in many public procedures a plaintiff who either dropped the case or failed to obtain one-fifth of the votes would have to pay a heavy fine of 1,000 drachmas. Despite this, it appears that litigation was common in Athens and was seen by some as excessive.

Over the course of time, the Athenian legal and political systems have more often been judged negatively than positively. Philosophers and political theorists have generally followed the lead of Plato (427–347), who lived and worked in Athens his entire life while severely criticizing its system of government as well as many other aspects of its culture. For Plato, democracy amounted to the tyranny of the masses over the educated elite and was destined to collapse from its own instability. The legal system was capricious and depended entirely on the rhetorical ability of litigants with no regard for truth or justice. These criticisms have often been echoed by modern scholars, who particularly complain that law was much too closely interwoven with politics and did not have the autonomous status it achieved in Roman law and continues to have, at least in theory, in modern legal systems.

Plato's judgments are valid if one accepts the underlying presuppositions, that the aim of law is absolute truth and abstract justice and that achieving the highest good of the state requires thorough and systematic organization. Most Athenians do not seem to have subscribed to either the criticisms or the presuppositions, and most scholars now accept the long-ignored fact that despite major external disruptions in the form of wars and two short-lived coups brought about by one of these wars, the Athenian legal and political systems remained remarkably stable for almost two hundred years (508–320). Moreover, like all other Greek cities at the time, whatever their form of government, Athenian democracy was brought to an end not by internal forces but by the external power of Philip of Macedon and his son Alexander. The legal system never became autonomous, and the rich sometimes complained that they were victims of unscrupulous litigants, but there is no indication that the people wanted to yield control of the legal process to a professional class, as Plato recommended. For most Athe-

nians—Plato being an exception in this and many other matters—
one purpose of the legal system was to give everyone the opportunity
to have his case heard by other citizens and have it heard quickly and
cheaply; and in this it clearly succeeded.

Indeed, the Athenian legal system also served the interests of the
rich, even the very rich, as well as the common people, in that it provided a forum for the competition that since Homer had been an important part of aristocratic life. In this competition, the rich used the
courts as battlegrounds, though their main weapon was the rhetoric of
popular ideology, which hailed the rule of law and promoted the ideal
of moderation and restraint.[27] But those who aspired to political lead-
ership and the honor and status that accompanied it repeatedly entered
the legal arena, bringing suit against their political enemies whenever
possible and defending themselves against suits brought by others
whenever necessary. The ultimate judges of these public competitions
were the common people, who seem to have relished the dramatic
clash of individuals and ideologies. In this respect fourth-century oratory was the cultural heir of fifth-century drama and was similarly ap-
preciated by the citizens. Despite the disapproval of intellectuals like
Plato, most Athenians legitimately considered their legal system a hallmark of their democracy and a vital presence in their culture.

THE TRANSLATION OF GREEK ORATORY

The purpose of this series is to provide students and scholars in all
fields with accurate, readable translations of all surviving classical Attic oratory, including speeches whose authenticity is disputed, as well
as the substantial surviving fragments. In keeping with the originals,
the language is for the most part nontechnical. Names of persons and
places are given in the (generally more familiar) Latinized forms, and
names of officials or legal procedures have been translated into English
equivalents, where possible. Notes are intended to provide the necessary historical and cultural background; scholarly controversies are
generally not discussed. The notes and introductions refer to scholarly
treatments in addition to those listed below, which the reader may
consult for further information.

---

[27] Ober 1989 is fundamental; see also Cohen 1995.

Cross-references to other speeches follow the standard numbering system, which is now well established except in the case of Hyperides (for whom the numbering of the Oxford Classical Text is used).[28] References are by work and section (e.g., Dem. 24.73); spurious works are not specially marked; when no author is named (e.g., 24.73), the reference is to the same author as the annotated passage.

ABBREVIATIONS

Aes.	= Aeschines
And.	= Andocides
Ant.	= Antiphon
Arist.	= Aristotle
Aristoph.	= Aristophanes
Ath. Pol.	= *The Athenian Constitution*
Dem.	= Demosthenes
Din.	= Dinarchus
Herod.	= Herodotus
Hyp.	= Hyperides
Is.	= Isaeus
Isoc.	= Isocrates
Lyc.	= Lycurgus
Lys.	= Lysias
Plut.	= Plutarch
Thuc.	= Thucydides
Xen.	= Xenophon

NOTE: The main unit of Athenian currency was the drachma; this was divided into obols and larger amounts were designated minas and talents.

1 drachma	= 6 obols
1 mina	= 100 drachmas
1 talent	= 60 minas (6,000 drachmas)

It is impossible to give an accurate equivalence in terms of modern currency, but it may be helpful to remember that the daily wage of

---

[28] For a listing of all the orators and their works, with classifications (forensic, deliberative, epideictic) and rough dates, see Edwards 1994: 74–79.

some skilled workers was a drachma in the mid-fifth century and 2–2½ drachmas in the later fourth century. Thus it may not be too misleading to think of a drachma as worth about $50 or £33 and a talent as about $300,000 or £200,000 in 1997 currency.

BIBLIOGRAPHY OF WORKS CITED

Boegehold, Alan L., 1995: *The Lawcourts at Athens: Sites, Buildings, Equipment, Procedure, and Testimonia.* Princeton.

Bonner, Robert J., 1927: *Lawyers and Litigants in Ancient Athens.* Chicago.

Carey, Christopher, 1997: *Trials from Classical Athens.* London.

Cohen, David, 1995: *Law, Violence and Community in Classical Athens.* Cambridge.

Cole, Thomas, 1991: *The Origins of Rhetoric in Ancient Greece.* Baltimore.

Dover, Kenneth J., 1968: *Lysias and the Corpus Lysiacum.* Berkeley.

———, 1974: *Greek Popular Morality in the Time of Plato and Aristotle.* Oxford.

———, 1978: *Greek Homosexuality.* London.

———, 1994: *Marginal Comment.* London.

Edwards, Michael, 1994: *The Attic Orators.* London.

Gagarin, Michael, and Paul Woodruff, 1995: *Early Greek Political Thought from Homer to the Sophists.* Cambridge.

Hansen, Mogens Herman, 1991: *The Athenian Democracy in the Age of Demosthenes.* Oxford.

Jebb, Richard, 1875: *The Attic Orators,* 2 vols. London.

Kennedy, George A., 1963: *The Art of Persuasion in Greece.* Princeton.

Kerferd, G. B., 1981: *The Sophistic Movement.* Cambridge.

MacDowell, Douglas M., 1978: *The Law in Classical Athens.* London.

———, ed. 1990: *Demosthenes, Against Meidias.* Oxford.

Ober, Josiah, 1989: *Mass and Elite in Democratic Athens.* Princeton.

Rhodes, P. J., trans., 1984: *Aristotle, The Athenian Constitution.* Penguin Books.

Sinclair, R. K., 1988: *Democracy and Participation in Athens.* Cambridge.

Todd, Stephen, 1993: *The Shape of Athenian Law.* Oxford.

Trevett, Jeremy, 1992: *Apollodoros the Son of Pasion*. Oxford.

———, 1996: "Did Demosthenes Publish His Deliberative Speeches?" *Hermes* 124: 425–441.

Usher, Stephen, 1976: "Lysias and His Clients," *Greek, Roman and Byzantine Studies* 17: 31–40.

———, trans., 1974–1985: *Dionysius of Halicarnassus, Critical Essays*. 2 vols. Loeb Classical Library. Cambridge, MA.

———, 1999: *Greek Oratory: Tradition and Originality*. Oxford.

Wooten, Cecil W., trans., 1987: *Hermogenes' On Types of Style*. Chapel Hill, NC.

Worthington, Ian, 1994: "The Canon of the Ten Attic Orators," in *Persuasion: Greek Rhetoric in Action*, ed. Ian Worthington. London: 244–263.

Yunis, Harvey, 1996: *Taming Democracy: Models of Political Rhetoric in Classical Athens*. Ithaca, NY.

DEMOSTHENES, SPEECHES 27–38

INTRODUCTION TO DEMOSTHENES

By Michael Gagarin

Since antiquity Demosthenes (384–322 BC) has usually been judged the greatest of the Attic orators. Although the patriotic and nationalistic tenor of his message has been more highly regarded in some periods of history than in others, he is unique in his mastery of so many different rhetorical styles and his ability to blend them into a powerful ensemble.

LIFE

Demosthenes was born into an old wealthy Athenian family. His father Demosthenes owned workshops that made swords and furniture. His maternal grandfather, Gylon, had been exiled from Athens and lived in the Crimea, where his mother Cleobule was born (perhaps to a Scythian mother). When Demosthenes was seven, his father died leaving his estate in the trust of several guardians. According to Demosthenes' own account, the guardians mismanaged and defrauded the estate to the point that when he turned eighteen, the age of majority, he received almost nothing. He devoted the next several years to recovering his property, first studying forensic pleading and then bringing a series of suits against the guardians to recover his patrimony (speeches 27–31). He won the first case (27, *Against Aphobus I*), but then had to bring several more suits in order to collect the amount awarded him by the court. In the course of these trials he gained a reputation as a successful speaker, became sought after by others, and began to write speeches for a wide range of private suits, including inheritance, shipping loans, assault, and trespass. His clients included one of the richest men in Athens, the banker Phormio; the speech *For Phormio* (36) involves a dispute over twenty talents (equivalent to several million dollars today). Demosthenes' vivid characterization of the honest, hard-working Phormio and his malicious and extravagant opponent proved so convincing that the jurors reportedly refused to listen to the other side and took the highly unusual step of voting immediately for Phormio.

In 355 Demosthenes became involved in his first major public case (22, *Against Androtion*). By this time it was common for ambitious or influential citizens to bring legal charges against their political opponents on matters of public interest. Charges of proposing an illegal decree (the *graphē paranomōn*) were particularly common; these involved the indictment of the proposer of a decree on the ground that it conflicted with existing law.[1] Although these speeches addressed the specific issue of a conflict between laws, it was generally accepted that the merits of the decree, and of its proposer, were also relevant factors, and these cases formed a major arena for the ongoing political struggles between leading figures in the city.

About the same time Demosthenes also began to publish speeches on public issues which he delivered in the assembly, and after 350, although he continued from time to time to write speeches for private disputes, he turned his attention primarily to public policy, especially relations between Athens and the growing power of Macedon under King Philip. Demosthenes' strategy throughout was to increase Athens' military readiness, to oppose Philip's expansion and to support other Greek cities in their resistance to it. Most notable in support of these objectives were the three *Olynthiacs* (1–3) in 349 unsuccessfully urging support for the city of Olynthus (which soon afterwards fell to Philip) and the four *Philippics* (4, 6, 9, 10) in 351–341 urging greater opposition to Philip. But Philip continued to extend his power into Greece, and in 338 he defeated a combined Greek force (including Athens) at the battle of Chaeronea in Boeotia, north of Attica. This battle

---

[1] One might compare the U.S. procedure of challenging the constitutionality of a law in court. Differences include the fact that today no charge is brought against the proposer of the law and that the case is heard by a small panel of professional judges, not the hundreds of untrained jurors who would have heard the case in Athens.

is usually taken to mark the end of the Greek cities' struggle to remain independent.

After Chaeronea Demosthenes continued to urge resistance to Philip, but his efforts were largely ineffectual and his successes and failures are more a matter of internal Athenian politics. His most prominent opponent during this period was Aeschines, who had been acquitted earlier (343) when Demosthenes brought a suit against him in connection with a delegation to Philip on which both men had served (19, cf. Aeschines 2). After Chaeronea, when a minor ally of Demosthenes named Ctesiphon proposed a decree awarding a crown to Demosthenes in recognition of his service to the city, Aeschines brought a *graphē paranomōn* against Ctesiphon (Aeschines 3). The suit, which was not tried until 330, raised legal objections to the proposed decree but also attacked the person and career of Demosthenes at considerable length. Demosthenes responded with his most famous speech *On the Crown* (18), often known by its Latin name *De Corona.* The verdict was so one-sided that Aeschines was fined for not receiving one-fifth of the votes and went into exile. This was Demosthenes' greatest triumph. The last years of his life, however, resulted in notable defeats, first in the rather shadowy Harpalus affair (324–323), from which no speech of his survives (but see Dinarchus 1). Shortly afterwards he was condemned to death at the instigation of pro-Macedonian forces and committed suicide.

WORKS

Sixty-one speeches and some miscellaneous works, including a collection of letters, have come down to us under Demosthenes' name. The authenticity of many of these has been challenged, often because of the allegedly poor quality of the work; but this reason is less often accepted today, and most of the public speeches and many of the private speeches are now thought to be authentic. Among the main exceptions are a group of private speeches (45, 46, 49, 50, 52, 53, 59 and possibly 47 and 51) that were delivered by Apollodorus and are now commonly thought to have been composed by him (Trevett 1992).

Apart from a funeral oration (60) and collections of proems and letters, Demosthenes' works fall into two groups, the assembly speeches (1–17) and the court speeches (18–59); the latter can be further divided into public and private speeches, though these are not formal legal categories. Notable among the public forensic speeches are *Against Meidias* (21), which has recently drawn attention for its pronouncements on Athenian public values, and his last surviving speech, *On the Crown* (18), generally recognized as his masterpiece. In this speech he uses his entire repertory of rhetorical strategies to defend his life and political career. He treats the legal issues of the case briefly, as being of minor concern, and then defends his conduct during the past three decades of Athenian history, arguing that even when his policy did not succeed, on each occasion it was the best policy for the city, in contrast to Aeschines' policies, which, when he ventured to propose any, were disastrous. Demosthenes' extensive personal attack on Aeschines' life and family may be too harsh for modern taste, but the blending of facts, innuendoes, sarcasm, rhetorical questions, and other devices is undeniably effective.

Demosthenes' private speeches have recently begun to attract more interest from scholars, who draw from them insight into Athenian social, political, and economic life. Only the speeches concerned with recovering his inheritance (27–31) were delivered by Demosthenes himself; the rest were written for delivery by other litigants. We have already noted *For Phormio,* which is one of several having to do with banking. *Against Conon* (54) alleges an assault by several young rowdies spurred on by their father, and *Against Neaera* (59), delivered and probably written by Apollodorus, recounts the life of a former slave woman and her affairs with different Athenian men.

STYLE

Demosthenes is a master of Greek prose style; he paid careful attention to style, and to the oral delivery of his speeches. His Roman counterpart, Cicero, modeled his oratorical style (and some other features of his work) in part on Demosthenes' Greek. Although Demosthenes' style varied considerably over the course of time and among the different types of speeches, later assessments of his style are based primarily on the public forensic speeches, and especially the last of these, *On the Crown.* Long and sometimes elaborate sentences are one feature of his style, but Demosthenes' true greatness is his ability to write in many styles and to vary his style, mixing different features together both to suit the topic and to give variety and vigor to his speeches. The final product required great skill and practice to deliver effectively, and the stories about Demosthenes' rigorous training in delivery (see in general Plutarch, *Life of Demosthenes* 6–7), even if not literally true, accurately reflect his priorities. Indeed, only by reading aloud sections of *On the Crown* in Greek can one truly appreciate the power and authority of his prose.

SIGNIFICANCE

Demosthenes played a vital role in Athenian public affairs for some thirty years. His advocacy of the vigilant defense of Greece against foreign invaders, though ultimately unsuccessful in preserving Greek freedom, inspired his fellow Athenians with patriotic loyalty, and has similarly inspired many others in later times. In recent times political rhetoric has not been so widely admired as in the past, and Demosthenes is less read today than he used to be. But he still represents the greatest achievement of Greek oratory and stands as one of the greatest orators of any age.

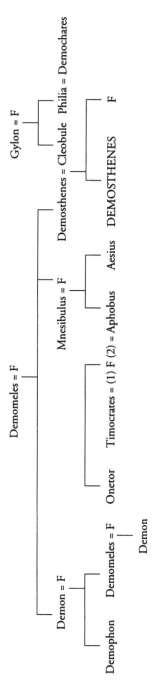

Gylon = F

Demomeles = F

Demosthenes = Cleobule   Philia = Demochares

F

Mnesibulus = F

Timocrates = (1) F (2) = Aphobus   Aesius   DEMOSTHENES

Onetor

Demon = F

Demophon   Demomeles = F

Demon

F denotes a woman whose name is unknown.
= denotes marriage.
In the case of brothers and sisters, the order of names from left to right does
not necessarily indicate the order of age, which is generally not known.

INTRODUCTION TO THIS VOLUME

By Douglas M. MacDowell

DEMOSTHENES AND HIS GUARDIANS

The first five speeches in this volume (Orations 27–31) are the earliest of all Demosthenes' speeches, written soon after he came of age in 366 BC. They were directed against the men who had been his guardians since the death of his father, and particularly against his cousin Aphobus, who was one of the guardians, and Aphobus' brother-in-law Onetor, who was alleged to have been assisting Aphobus.[1]

According to Demosthenes' own account, his father, also named Demosthenes, was a rich man when he died in 376. His property, listed in the first speech, included a workshop with slaves making knives, another workshop with slaves making beds, and several substantial sums of money deposited in banks or lent at interest, besides cash, jewelry, and other effects, to a total value of about 14 talents.[2] Before his death he called his family around him and made various dispositions. His son, Demosthenes, was only seven years old, and his daughter was five. He therefore appointed three men to be guardians of the children and the property until the boy should come of age about ten years later.[3] The guardians were his sister's son Aphobus, his

---

[1] The relatives mentioned in these speeches are shown in the genealogy on p. 8. For detailed discussion of the ramifications of the family, see Davies 1971: 113–159 (no. 3597). See also Cox 1998: 18–20.

[2] For Athenian money, see the Series Introduction, p. xxv.

[3] The scrutiny called *dokimasia*, when a young man was examined at the age of eighteen and registered as a citizen, was held in the summer, at the beginning of the Athenian year. It is not certain that the man had to have passed his eighteenth birthday; those in their eighteenth year (aged seventeen) may also have been reg-

brother Demon's son Demophon, and an old friend named Therippides. He bequeathed his wife, Cleobule, to be married to Aphobus with
a substantial dowry,[4] and Aphobus was to have his house to live in for
the ten years of Demosthenes' minority. His daughter was to be married, when she was old enough, to Demophon, who himself was probably still quite young, with an even bigger dowry. Therippides was to
have a large interest-free loan for the ten-year period. Demosthenes
senior also recommended, his son says, that the rest of his property
should be leased out, so that the rent paid for it would produce a fixed
regular income to support the boy, with a surplus to be paid over to
him when he came of age.

If we can believe Demosthenes—and we probably can believe him
in general terms, even if there is doubt about some of the details—the
guardians turned out to be so negligent, greedy, and contemptuous[5]
that they transgressed most of these instructions and kept large parts
of the property for themselves. Aphobus did not marry the widow,
and Demophon did not marry the daughter, but they both kept the
dowries. They sold many of the slaves and got back the loans. When
Demosthenes came of age in 366, Aphobus did vacate the house and
give back the remaining slaves with some cash, but Demosthenes estimates that the total value of what he was given was no more than
70 minas (somewhat over 1 talent). If they had handed over honestly the whole of what was due, including return of the two dowries,
the total amount of the property with ten years' accumulated income
should, he claims, have been around 30 talents.

Some time was taken up by abortive negotiations about the dis-

---

istered. Thus Demosthenes may have come of age when he was still under eighteen; alternatively he may have been aged seven years and some months when his
father died and the guardianship may have lasted ten years and some months,
making eighteen altogether.

[4] This is a striking example of the ability of an Athenian man to dispose of his
wife to a new husband, passing on the dowry which he had received with her. The
remarriage of Pasion's wife was similar; see p. 155, note 16. For a general discussion
of the role of Cleobule in the whole affair, see Hunter 1989.

[5] Burke 1998 suggests that one of their motives was the ideological contempt
of traditional landowners for a man whose wealth was based on manufacturing
and commerce.

pute, and Demosthenes must also have had to spend some time in military training as an ephebe. After failing to obtain satisfaction, he began legal proceedings against each of the three guardians in 364/3, claiming 10 talents from each of them. Each of the three prosecutions had to be considered first by a public arbitrator. At least in the case of Aphobus, the arbitrator gave a verdict in favor of Demosthenes, against which his opponent appealed, so that the case then went to a trial by jury; probably the same happened in the other two cases.

The first two texts that we have (Orations 27 and 28) are Demosthenes' speeches for the trial of Aphobus. Demosthenes won this case, and in the later part of the trial, for deciding the amount of the compensation to be paid to him by Aphobus, he successfully persuaded the jury to accept his proposal that it should be 10 talents, rather than 1 talent as Aphobus proposed. He also won the cases against Demophon and Therippides. But Aphobus' scheming was not yet exhausted. He next accused one of Demosthenes' witnesses at the trial, named Phanus, of giving false evidence and so causing him to lose the case. If he had succeeded in getting Phanus convicted, probably (though this is not known for certain) Phanus would then have been required to make the payment of 10 talents which Aphobus had incurred. The third speech we have (Oration 29) is Demosthenes' defense of Phanus. Aphobus' other scheme was to pretend that his farm no longer belonged to him but had been taken over by his brother-in-law, Onetor, in substitution for the dowry of his wife, Onetor's sister; Aphobus asserted that the woman was now divorced from him, so that her dowry had to be returned to her brother and Demosthenes could not claim it as part of the payment due to him from Aphobus. Demosthenes believed that Onetor had not in fact given Aphobus a dowry for his sister and also that there had been no divorce. He therefore prosecuted Onetor, bringing a case of ejectment (*dikē exoulēs*) to compel him to relinquish the farm to Demosthenes. The last two texts in this group (Orations 30 and 31) are Demosthenes' speeches for the prosecution of Onetor. They were written in 362 or 361.

As far as we know, Demosthenes was successful in all these cases. That was a remarkable triumph for a young and inexperienced speaker. But he never succeeded in getting from his guardians the entire sum of 30 talents, which may well have been a greater sum than they actually possessed.

COUNTER-INDICTMENT (*PARAGRAPHĒ*)

The other seven speeches in this volume (Orations 32–38) were written at various times in Demosthenes' life, but are traditionally grouped together because they all concern cases under the legal procedure called *paragraphē*.[6] This may be translated "contrary prosecution" or "counter-indictment." It was a procedure for objecting that a prosecution was inadmissible—not because the accusation was untrue but because the prosecution itself was in some way contrary to law. It initiated a separate trial in which the original prosecutor was himself prosecuted for bringing a prosecution that was not allowed. Thus the order in which the litigants spoke was reversed: the man who was the defendant in the original case was the prosecutor in the *paragraphē* trial and therefore spoke first. The original case was postponed until the *paragraphē* case had been decided; the result of the *paragraphē* trial settled whether the original case should proceed to a straight trial (*euthydikia*). Whoever lost the *paragraphē* case had to pay a penalty to his opponent for taking up time over the legal question; the penalty was a payment of one-sixth of the amount of money or property in dispute (*epōbelia,* 1 obol per drachma).

The *paragraphē* procedure was first used in 400 BC by a man who claimed that he could not legally be prosecuted for an offense committed before the amnesty of 403 (Isoc. 18.1–3). In various other cases an accused man claimed that the prosecution was inadmissible because it had been submitted to the wrong magistrate (Lys. 23; cf. Dem. 37.33), or because the time allowed for prosecutions of that type had expired (Dem. 38.17), or because the dispute had already been decided by a court or by private arbitration or by a formal discharge by the prosecutor (Dem. 36.25, 37.1). It was not a procedure for deciding whether the defendant had committed the alleged offense or wrong, which would be the subject of a straight trial; it was for deciding whether a straight trial should be held. Nevertheless, speakers often

---

[6] Isoc. 18 and Lys. 23 provide earlier examples of the same procedure. The definitive modern work on it, in German, is Wolff 1966. For shorter accounts in English, see Isager and Hansen 1975: 123–131; MacDowell 1978: 214–219; Todd 1993: 135–139.

confuse these two questions by talking about both of them together in a *paragraphē* speech.[7]

MERCANTILE CASES (*DIKAI EMPORIKAI*)

Four of these speeches (Orations 32–35) concern maritime loans. Laws enacted in the middle of the fourth century BC prescribed legal procedures for mercantile cases (*dikai emporikai*).[8] These were cases involving a skipper (*nauklēros*, commanding a merchant ship, possibly but not necessarily its owner) or a merchant (*emporos*, exporting and importing goods by sea). They were "monthly" cases,[9] but to be acceptable under the mercantile procedure they had to fulfill certain conditions. The ground of prosecution had to be that a written agreement[10] existed between the disputants which, the prosecutor alleged, the defendant had failed to fulfill. The agreement must either have been made in the Athenian port (*emporion*, the wholesale market at Piraeus) or concern a voyage to or from the Athenian port.[11]

A common type of transaction was for a lender, who had money available for investment, to lend a sum to a merchant; the merchant used the money to buy goods in Athens, transported them to another city, sold them there at a profit, used the proceeds to buy other goods there, which he transported back to Athens and sold at a further profit, and finally repaid the loan with interest to the original lender while still having some profit for himself. The merchant might share

---

[7] An alternative view is that the *paragraphē* and the original accusation were both judged at the same trial. That view is now generally rejected, but it has recently been reaffirmed by Carawan 2001: 29–31.

[8] On mercantile cases, see Cohen 1973. On maritime loans, see Millett 1991: 188–196; Cohen 1992: 111–189.

[9] See 33.23 with note.

[10] The Greek words are not always clearly defined or distinguished from one another, but I use "contract" to translate *symbolaion*, "written agreement" to translate *syngraphē*, and "terms" to translate *synthēkai*.

[11] On the commercial port, see Garland 1987: 83–95. I use "port" to translate *emporion*, the area at Piraeus where ships were loaded and unloaded and wholesale transactions took place. I use "market" to translate *agora*, the area for retail selling and buying in the center of Athens.

the expenses and profits with the skipper of the ship which he used; the goods, and sometimes the ship itself, served as security for the lender in case the loan was not repaid. The written agreement could be quite detailed, specifying not only the rate of interest payable but the goods which were to be purchased with the money lent and the port or ports to which they were to be conveyed. There is an example in 35.10–13. It usually also contained a clause stating that, if the ship was wrecked and the goods lost on the voyage, the loan need not be repaid. The whole system was used especially to support the importation of grain from Sicily and from the Black Sea area, and made a vital contribution to the maintenance of Athens' food supplies.[12]

THE AUTHENTICITY OF THE TEXTS

The speeches against Aphobus and Onetor (Orations 27–31) are obviously written for Demosthenes himself to deliver in court, and the same may, less certainly, be true of the speech for Phormion (Oration 36). The other speeches in this volume are written for delivery by various other men. Questions of authenticity therefore arise. Did Demosthenes actually write all these texts? And, whoever wrote them, are they accurate records of what was actually said in court?

Neither question can be answered with absolute certainty. We can only estimate the probabilities. On the first question, whether Demosthenes wrote all these speeches, we have to bear in mind several considerations which point in different directions. One is that, if a man with little or no experience in public speaking found that he had to make a speech because he had become involved in a legal case, it was quite common to ask an expert speaker to compose a speech for him; thus Demosthenes in the course of his life may well have written many speeches for other men to deliver. But a second consideration is that in Hellenistic or Roman times librarians and booksellers, on finding a copy of a fourth-century Attic speech with no author's name attached, might easily, but wrongly, assume that it was the work of the most famous orator of that period. There is also the possibility that in

---

[12] On the Athenian grain trade in the fourth century BC, see Garnsey 1988: 134–164; Whitby 1998; Rosivach 2000.

the days of the Roman empire, when rhetoric was a standard part of higher education, some pastiches of Demosthenes written by teachers or students may have been so convincing that they were mistakenly believed to be the real thing.

It is sometimes possible to detect a spurious text by anachronisms or other statements which could not have been written in the circumstances to which it purports to belong. But that does not apply to any of the twelve speeches in this volume. None of them can be dismissed on grounds of historical inaccuracy.[13] The only other criterion we can use is the style of writing. Since the nineteenth century, scholars have formed their impressions of Demosthenes' style on the basis of those speeches of which the authenticity has never been doubted and have then tried to judge which of the disputed texts are in the same style. Perhaps the greatest expert in this field was the German scholar Friedrich Blass, and his judgments have been widely accepted, though they remain subjective.[14] More recently, an attempt has been made to compile statistics of the frequency of various features of style,[15] but not all stylistic features lend themselves to arithmetical measurement. It may anyway be unsafe to assume that an author's style never varies.

The problem cannot be fully discussed here, and so I simply state my personal opinion: of the twelve speeches in this volume, there is none which could not have been written by Demosthenes, but the ones about which I (like Blass and others) have some doubts are those against Apaturius, Phormion, and Lacritus (Orations 33–35). Even those, however, are surely genuine texts of the fourth century BC and can safely be used as evidence for the social and legal conditions of that time.

As for the other question, whether the extant texts record what was actually said in court, we must try to imagine how the texts are likely to have been used. In most cases, what we have is probably (passed on through successive copies for more than two thousand years) the draft which the writer (whether Demosthenes or someone else) wrote out beforehand in preparation for the trial. The speaker (whether this was

---

[13] The only one which has been seriously attacked on this ground is the third speech against Aphobus (Oration 29); see the introduction to that speech.

[14] Blass 1893.

[15] McCabe 1981.

the same man as the writer or not) will then have tried to memorize the draft, so as to make a speech which would seem spontaneous in the court. But he would be unlikely to remember every word of it exactly, and he might depart from it quite substantially, either because he forgot parts of it, or because he misjudged the length and ran out of time, or because he suddenly thought of further points which he wished to add. Thus the text we have may be regarded as being what the speaker intended to say, but not necessarily what he actually said.

Sometimes, however, especially if the speaker won the case, he (or the writer, if that was someone different) may have been so pleased with his speech that he decided to make copies of it for distribution to friends or purchasers after the trial. If so, he may have revised the text so as to include points which he had made in court extemporaneously or to improve it in other ways. This may be indicated by a passage referring to something which the opposing speaker has said in the course of the trial; on the face of it, that could not have been written before the trial but must have been added afterwards. Such passages occur in the second speeches against Aphobus and Onetor (28.1, 31.6). Yet perhaps it was easy to guess in advance what Aphobus and Onetor would say; for example, Demosthenes knew that Aphobus was likely to allude to his grandfather's debt, which had already been mentioned at the arbitration, and so he may have planned beforehand what he would say in reply if that matter came up (28.1–4). Likewise, although he claims to have been taken by surprise when Aphobus raised the matter of his guardianship again at the trial of Phanus (29.28), that may be disingenuous; it was probably obvious that Aphobus would return to that topic. On balance, therefore, I think it likely that what we have are the drafts written before the trials for all these twelve speeches.

TEXTS AND COMMENTARIES

The Greek texts translated in this volume are those of the Oxford Classical Text of Demosthenes, volume 2, part 2, edited by William Rennie (Oxford, 1921), except where some departure from it is mentioned in the notes.

The following editions of the Greek texts provide notes in English:

Orations 27, 28, 30, 31, 32, 36: Lionel Pearson, *Demosthenes: Six Private Speeches* (Norman, Oklahoma, 1972).
Orations 34, 35, 36, 37: F. A. Paley and J. E. Sandys, *Select Private Orations of Demosthenes* (two volumes, third edition, Cambridge, 1896–1898).
Oration 34: F. C. Doherty, *Three Private Speeches of Demosthenes* (Oxford, 1927).
Oration 37: C. Carey and R. A. Reid, *Demosthenes: Selected Private Speeches* (Cambridge, 1985).

The following include discussion of the subjects and arguments:

All the orations: Stephen Usher, *Greek Oratory: Tradition and Originality* (Oxford, 1999).
Orations 27, 28, 29, 30, 31: David C. Mirhady, "Demosthenes as Advocate," in Ian Worthington (ed.), *Demosthenes: Statesman and Orator* (London, 2000) 181–204.
Orations 32, 33, 34, 35, 36, 37, 38: Signe Isager and Mogens Herman Hansen, *Aspects of Athenian Society in the Fourth Century B.C.* (Odense, 1975).
Oration 34: Wesley E. Thompson, "An Athenian Commercial Case: Demosthenes 34," *Tijdschrift voor Rechtsgeschiedenis* 48 (1980) 137–149.
Orations 35, 37: Christopher Carey, *Trials from Classical Athens* (London, 1997).

27. AGAINST APHOBUS I

INTRODUCTION

The dispute between the young Demosthenes and his guardians is outlined in the introduction to this volume (pages 9–11). This first speech opens his prosecution of one of the guardians and contains the principal statement of his case against them. It was delivered in 364/3 BC, when he was twenty years old.

He begins by professing his inexperience and his reluctance to go to law—a common type of excuse at the beginning of prosecution speeches, but in this case justified. He then gives an outline of his family situation and of the dispositions made by his dying father, including the appointment of the three guardians. He claims that when he came of age they handed over to him only about 70 minas' worth of property, although they had themselves registered the estate as being of a much higher value for the purpose of payment of the tax called *eisphora*.

The next part of the speech is the most important: the listing of all the elements of Demosthenes senior's estate, including the value of each item and the amounts of income produced. For us, this makes a significant contribution to our understanding of Athenian society and economics. Demosthenes' estimates of the value of the various items are given in Table I.[1] (To facilitate calculation all the sums are converted to drachmas in this table.)

Demosthenes claims that by the time he came of age the estate, including ten years' accumulated income, ought to have been worth

---

[1] The figures are discussed by Davies 1971: 126–131.

TABLE I

Income-producing assets	
Slaves making knives	19,000
Slaves making beds	4,000
Money on loan	6,000
Non-income-producing assets	
Ivory, iron, wood	8,000
Dye, copper	7,000
House	3,000
Contents of house	10,000
Cash	8,000
Loan to Xuthus	7,000
Deposit at Pasion's bank	2,400
Deposit at Pylades' bank	600
Loan to Demomeles	1,600
Other loans	6,000
Total assets	82,600
Annual income from those assets	
Manufacture of knives	3,000
Manufacture of beds	1,200
Interest on loans	720
Total annual income	4,920

about 30 talents, but it is difficult for us to check this claim. He calls for the testimony of witnesses to be read out to confirm many of his figures, but, as often in Athenian speeches, those statements have not been preserved, and we cannot be sure how conclusive their confirmation was.[2] He does seem to press some of his points rather hard, especially where the income is concerned; for example, he assumes that the manufacture of knives and of beds produced the same amount of profit every year and makes no allowance for difficulties in production or changes in market conditions from time to time. Thus his case

---

[2] Demosthenes' use of evidence in this speech is discussed by Mirhady 2000a: 186–190.

may be overstated to some extent; nevertheless it does appear to be a strong one.

The later part of the speech deals with some subsidiary points, including the guardians' failure to produce Demosthenes senior's written will, their failure to let the estate on lease, which would have absolved them from responsibility for its administration, and the absurd story that Demosthenes senior left the large sum of 4 talents hidden away in the keeping of his wife. Demosthenes concludes with a passage of pathos, pointing out that he, with his mother and sister, will be left in poverty if he loses the case. The speech as a whole is a remarkably accomplished debut by the young orator.

27. AGAINST APHOBUS FOR GUARDIANSHIP I

[1] If Aphobus had been willing to do the right thing, men of the jury, or to refer the disputed questions to our relatives, there would have been no need of trials or proceedings; it would have been enough to abide by their verdict, and I would have had no dispute with him. But since he would not let any decision about our affairs be made by those who are well acquainted with them,[3] and has resorted to you who have no accurate knowledge of them, I am forced to try to obtain justice from him in your court. [2] Now, I know, men of the jury, that it's not an easy matter to contend for the whole of my property against men who are competent speakers and also have powers of manipulation,[4] when because of my youth I'm completely without experience of legal business. Nevertheless, although I'm at a great disadvantage, I have high hopes that I shall obtain justice in your court, and also that, at least to the extent of narrating the events, my own speech will be adequate, so that you won't be left in ignorance of any detail of the facts, and you'll understand the issues on which you will have to vote. [3] I request you, men of the jury, to give me a favorable hearing and, if you decide that I've been treated wrongfully, to give me the support I de-

---

[3] At first Demosthenes and Aphobus agreed to submit their dispute to arbitration by three friends. But when those three gave Aphobus the hint that, if they delivered a verdict under oath (as was normal in private arbitrations), it would be a verdict against him, he promptly withdrew from the arrangement. Cf. 29.58, 30.2.

[4] This phrase hints at bribery of witnesses.

serve. I shall make my speech as brief as I can; so I'll try to explain it all to you beginning from the point which will make it easiest for you to understand it.

[4] Demosthenes, my father, men of the jury, left property worth about 14 talents, together with myself, who was aged seven, my sister, who was five, and also our mother, who had brought 50 minas into the house.[5] When he was close to death, he took thought for us and entrusted everything to this man Aphobus and to Demophon son of Demon, both of whom were his nephews, one being the son of his brother and the other of his sister, and also to Therippides of Paeania,[6] who was not a relative but had been his friend since childhood. [5] To the latter he gave the use of 70 minas of my property for the period until I was passed[7] as an adult, so that he might not be induced by desire for money to mismanage any of my affairs; to Demophon he gave my sister and 2 talents for immediate possession;[8] and to Aphobus himself he gave my mother with a dowry of 80 minas, the house for his residence, and the use of my furniture. He believed that, if he made these men even more closely related to me, their guardianship of me would be none the worse for the addition of this relationship. [6] But after receiving those sums of money for themselves at the beginning, and after managing all the other property and being my guardians for ten years, they have misappropriated all the rest and handed over only the house, fourteen slaves, and 30 minas in cash, amounting to about 70 minas in all.[9]

[7] That's a summary of their offenses, stated as concisely as pos-

---

[5] This means that 50 minas was the amount of her dowry when she was married.

[6] Paeania was an Athenian deme (political district) to the east of Mount Hymettus. This was Demosthenes' own deme.

[7] The Greek word refers to *dokimasia*, the formal procedure for acceptance of a young man as a citizen at the age of eighteen. In effect, Therippides was given an interest-free loan of 70 minas for ten years.

[8] Demophon was to receive the dowry immediately, although the marriage would not take place until the girl was old enough; cf. 29.43.

[9] Demosthenes later gives the original value of the house as 30 minas, and of the slaves as between 6 and 3 minas each (27.9–10). It is not clear how he reaches the total of 70 minas: possibly the house and the slaves had sharply deteriorated in value, or the total does not include the house (and he reckons the slaves at only 3 minas each), or else there is something wrong with the text.

sible, men of the jury. That this was the total amount of the property which he left, they themselves are my best witnesses; for they arranged on my behalf to make to the symmory contributions of 500 drachmas in each 25 minas,[10] as much as Timotheus son of Conon[11] and men with the highest assessments contributed. But you must hear the details of the items which were producing income and those which were not, and how much each was worth. When you know those exactly, you'll realize that there have never been any guardians who have plundered more shamelessly or more openly than these men have plundered my property.

[8] So first I'll provide witnesses of the fact that they agreed on my behalf to the assessment of this contribution of *eisphora* to the symmory, and next that my father did not leave me poor or possessing property worth 70 minas, but such a large estate that even those men themselves couldn't conceal it from the city because of its extent. [*To the clerk*] Please take and read this testimony.

[TESTIMONY]

[9] So from that too the size of the estate is clear. Out of 15 talents, the assessment was 3 talents; that's the *eisphora* which they thought it right to contribute.[12]

---

[10] The richer Athenian citizens and metics were required from time to time to pay *eisphora*, which was a tax on property. For this purpose they were divided into groups called symmories. Details of the system at this time (before Demosthenes came of age in 366) are obscure, but it is likely that, on each occasion when *eisphora* was demanded, each symmory was required to pay the same total amount, but the amounts paid by individuals differed according to the value of their property. Demosthenes seems to mean here that his guardians registered his estate as being of such a high value that, for each sum of 25 minas payable by the symmory as a whole, he had to pay 500 drachmas (= 5 minas), one-fifth of the total, which was the maximum ever required from one individual. In each symmory, the person who paid the most was called the leader of the symmory; cf. 28.4.

[11] Conon and Timotheus were both well-known generals. Though rich at this time, Timotheus later got into debt; see 36.53n.

[12] Because the text of the testimony is not preserved, the meaning of this sentence is obscure to us and has been much disputed. The value of the estate could have been estimated at 15 talents, for Demosthenes says that it was actually about 14 talents; cf. 27.11. But 3 talents can hardly be the total amount of *eisphora* paid

You'll understand even more exactly when you hear what the estate actually was. My father, men of the jury, left two workshops, each engaged in a not unimportant craft: one with thirty-two or thirty-three knife-makers, worth 5 or 6 minas each, or in some cases at least 3 minas, from whom he was getting a net income of 30 minas a year; the other with twenty bed-makers, who were security for a loan of 40 minas and who brought him a net income of 12 minas; also about a talent of silver, lent at a drachma,[13] on which the interest amounted to more than 7 minas every year. [10] Those were the income-producing assets he left, as these men themselves will agree. Their total capital value amounted to 4 talents 5,000 drachmas, and the income from them to 50 minas a year. Besides those, he left ivory and iron used in the manufacturing and wood for beds worth about 80 minas, and dye and copper purchased for 70 minas; also a house worth 3,000 drachmas,[14] and furniture, cups,[15] gold jewelry, and clothes, my mother's trousseau, all those together worth about 10,000 drachmas, and 80 minas in silver in the house. [11] He left all that at home. In maritime assets[16] he left 70 minas on loan to Xuthus, 2,400 drachmas at Pasion's bank, 600 at Pylades', 1,600 with Demomeles son of Demon,[17] and various loans of 200 or 300 amounting to about a talent. The total sum of this money comes to more than 8 talents 50 minas.[18] You'll find if you check it that the grand total is about 14 talents.[19]

[12] That's the amount of property he left, men of the jury. How

---

out of it, which is said later in the speech to have been 18 minas or at any rate not more than 30 minas; cf. 27.37.

[13] This phrase refers to a standard rate of interest on loans: a drachma per mina per month, equivalent to 12 percent per annum.

[14] The workshops in which knives and beds were made are not listed as separate buildings and must have been in rooms which formed part of the house.

[15] The cups were evidently valuable items, probably silver.

[16] Money which Demosthenes senior used for making loans to merchants (of the kind which we see in Orations 32–35).

[17] Xuthus is mentioned again in 29.36, but he is not otherwise known. On Pasion, see p. 150. Pylades was evidently another banker, but he is not mentioned elsewhere. Demomeles was a nephew of Demosthenes senior.

[18] The manuscripts say "80 talents 30 minas," but this is generally emended to fit with the other figures in the text.

[19] The figures given actually amount to 13 talents 46 minas.

much of it has been stolen, and how much each of them has taken individually, and how much they are all misappropriating jointly, cannot all be stated in the same allocation of water;[20] it's necessary to take each of them separately. So it will be sufficient to explain what parts of my property Demophon and Therippides have kept at the time when I deliver my prosecutions against them, but I shall speak to you now about what they reveal Aphobus has and what I know he has taken. First, I'll show you that he has kept the dowry of 80 minas, and afterwards the other matters, as briefly as I can.

[13] Immediately after my father's death, Aphobus entered the house and took up residence in accordance with his will, and he took my mother's gold jewelry and the cups which had been left. He kept possession of those, to the value of about 50 minas, and he also received from Therippides and Demophon the proceeds of sale of the slaves[21] to make up the amount of the dowry, 80 minas. [14] Once he had those things, when he was about to sail away to Corcyra as a trierarch,[22] he gave Therippides a written statement that he had them and acknowledged that he had received the dowry. In the first place, Demophon and Therippides, his fellow-guardians, are witnesses of that; besides, Demochares of Leuconoeum,[23] my aunt's husband, and many others have attested that he acknowledged that he had them. [15] For, since he didn't provide my mother with maintenance, although he kept her dowry,[24] and since he refused to lease the estate but thought fit to manage it with the other guardians,[25] Demochares spoke to him

---

[20] In one speech timed by the water-clock.

[21] Half of the slaves making knives were purchased from the estate by Therippides and Demophon; cf. 27.18, 27.61.

[22] This means that Aphobus, as a rich man, had been appointed to maintain and command a trireme for the year. The Athenian force sent to Corcyra in 375 was led by Timotheus.

[23] The location of this Athenian deme is uncertain.

[24] Whoever held a woman's dowry was legally required to pay for her keep. Demochares' complaint probably means that Cleobule was now living in his house, having moved in with her sister. (The view of Cox 1998: 147, that Cleobule resided with Aphobus without being married to him, is unlikely to be correct; if that had been so, Aphobus would hardly have been accused of failing to maintain her.)

[25] A guardian who did not want to manage his ward's estate himself had the option of letting it to a lessee, so that the rent would be the ward's income.

about these matters. Aphobus listened to him, and didn't deny that he had the dowry or express indignation at not having received it, but acknowledged it and said that he still had a little disagreement with my mother about some small items of jewelry; when he had got that straightened out, he would deal with her maintenance and the other matters in such a way that everything would be satisfactory for me. [16] But if it becomes clear that he made these acknowledgments to Demochares and the other men who were present, and that he received from Demophon and Therippides the proceeds from the slaves to make up the dowry, and that he himself gave a written statement to his fellow-guardians that he had the dowry, and that he took up residence in the house as soon as my father died, surely it will be obvious, since the matter is agreed by everyone, that he obtained the dowry of 80 minas and that his denial that he received it is quite shameless. [17] [*To the clerk*] To prove that I am telling the truth, take the testimonies and read them.

[TESTIMONIES]

So in this way he received the dowry and has kept it. But if he didn't marry my mother, the law requires him to owe interest on the dowry at the rate of 9 obols; but I'll reckon it at only a drachma.[26] If you add together the principal and the income for ten years, it comes to about 3 talents. [18] That sum I can thus prove to you he received and has kept, because he acknowledged it in the presence of all those witnesses. In addition, he has kept 30 minas, which he received as the income from the workshop[27] and has attempted to misappropriate in the most shameless possible way. My father left me an income of 30 minas from the slaves; after these men sold half of them, I should have got 15 minas proportionately. [19] Therippides, who had charge of the slaves for seven years, reported 11 minas a year, 4 minas less each year than he should have done in proportion. Aphobus, who had charge of them for the first two years, reports nothing at all, but sometimes

---

[26] Interest of 9 obols per mina per month = 18 percent per annum; 1 drachma per mina per month = 12 percent per annum. At this rate, the total of principal and interest for ten years comes to 2 talents 56 minas.

[27] The next sentences show that this means the slaves making knives.

he says that the workshop was not operating, and sometimes that he wasn't in charge of them himself but the man in charge, Milyas, our freedman, managed them and I should get an account from him. If he tells any of those stories again today, it will be easy to prove that he's lying. [20] If he says it wasn't operating: he himself has rendered accounts of expenditure, not on food for the men but on work, ivory for the workmanship and knife-handles and other supplies; this presumes that the craftsmen were working. He also calculates that he paid Therippides a fee for three slaves he had in my workshop. Yet, if no work was done, Therippides should not have received a fee, and I should not have had this expenditure in the accounts. [21] If on the other hand he says that work was done but there was no sale for the products, surely he ought at least to show that he handed over the products to me and to provide as witnesses the men in whose presence he handed them over. If he hasn't done any of this, he must have kept two years' income from the workshop, 30 minas, since it's so clear that the work was done. [22] If on the other hand he doesn't say any of this but ·asserts that Milyas managed it all, how can he be believed when he says that he himself paid out the expenditures, more than 500 drachmas, while any profit was kept by Milyas? It seems to me that the opposite would have happened if Milyas had in fact managed it: Milyas would have paid out the expenditures, and Aphobus would have taken the profits, to judge by the rest of his behavior and his impudence. [*To the clerk*] Take these testimonies and read them to them.

[TESTIMONIES]

[23] So he has kept those 30 minas from the workshop, and eight years' interest on them, which you'll find, if you reckon it at a drachma,[28] is another 30 minas. He, alone and individually, has taken that, and if you add it to the dowry, it makes about 4 talents, including the principal. Now I'll explain to you, one by one, the amounts which he's plundered jointly with the other guardians, and some which he has claimed were not left by my father at all.

[24] First about the bed-makers, whom my father left and these men are making away with: they were security for a loan of 40 minas,

---

[28] See 27.17n.

and they were twenty in number. I will prove to you that these men are robbing me of them quite shamelessly and openly. They all agree that those slaves were left in our house, and they say that they brought in 12 minas every year for my father; but they themselves report that no profit, not the least bit, came in for me from them in ten years, while Aphobus calculates that the total expenditure on them was nearly 1,000 drachmas; that's how shameless he is. [25] At no point have they handed over to me the men themselves, on whom he says this money was spent. Instead, they tell the emptiest of stories: that the man[29] who gave my father the slaves as security is the biggest scoundrel in the world, and that he has welshed on a large number of friendly loans[30] and defaulted on debts; and they have called a considerable number of witnesses to testify to these facts against him. But who it is who has got the slaves, or how they left the house, or who took them away, or against whom they lost a case about them, they cannot say. [26] Yet, if their story were sound, they would not be producing witnesses of that man's wickedness, which I should not be concerned with at all; instead, they'd be getting hold of the slaves and pointing out the abductors and not letting any of them go. But as it is, in the most high-handed manner possible, although they acknowledge that the slaves were left and they took possession of them and enjoyed the profits from them for ten years, they are now utterly making away with the whole workshop. [*To the clerk*] To prove that what I say is true, please take the testimonies and read them.

[TESTIMONIES]

[27] Now, Moeriades was not without resources, nor was it a foolish mistake of my father's to make that agreement secured on the slaves, as a very strong proof will show you. After Aphobus took possession of this workshop, as you heard yourselves from the witnesses, he, being a guardian, ought to have prevented anyone else who wished to make an agreement secured on them; but in fact he himself made Moeriades a loan of 500 drachmas secured on those slaves—a loan which he has acknowledged he rightly and properly recovered from

---

[29] The man was named Moeriades (27.27), but he is not otherwise known.

[30] The Greek word (*eranos*) refers to interest-free loans among friends.

him. [28] Yet surely it's a terrible thing if I, whose agreement was made earlier, besides getting no profit from them, have lost the security as well, while the man who made a loan secured on my property and recovered it so much later has obtained both interest and principal out of my property and has suffered no loss. [*To the clerk*] But to prove that I'm telling the truth, take the testimony and read it.

[TESTIMONY]

[29] So just think how much money these men are stealing in the matter of the bed-makers: 40 minas is the actual principal, and ten years' produce from them is 2 talents, for they were getting 12 minas every year in income from them. Is that a small sum, from an obscure source and easy to miscalculate? Isn't it quite obvious that it's nearly 3 talents that they've plundered? Since they've purloined it jointly, I think I should recover one-third of it from Aphobus.

[30] And in fact, men of the jury, what they've done in connection with the ivory and iron which were left is similar to that; they don't report those either. Yet, since my father owned so many bed-makers and also owned knife-makers, he can't have failed to leave iron and ivory. Those must have existed; if they hadn't existed, what work would have been done? [31] A man who owned more than fifty slaves and supervised two trades, in one of which easily 2 minas' worth of ivory a month was used for beds, while the knife-factory used at least as much again together with iron—they say he left none of those materials! That's how impudent they've become. [32] Their story is incredible, as it's easy to see from what they themselves say. The quantity[31] left by my father was so large that it was sufficient not only for his own workers' use but also for anyone else who wished to buy it, as is clear from the fact that he himself used to sell it during his lifetime, and after his death Demophon and Aphobus sold it to customers from my house. [33] Yet what amount must be assumed to have been left, when it was evidently sufficient for such large numbers of workers and besides was being sold by my guardians? A small amount? Or much more than is included in the charge? [*To the clerk*] Take these testimonies and read them to them.

---

[31] The following sentences show that this refers only to ivory, not iron.

[TESTIMONIES]

That ivory amounts to more than a talent, but they haven't made available to me either the ivory itself or the proceeds; they've completely made away with that too.

[34] In addition, men of the jury, in accordance with the accounts they have rendered, I shall prove to you from their own acknowledgments of what they received that the three of them have kept more than 8 talents of my money, and that of this Aphobus individually has taken 3 talents 1,000 drachmas. I shall reckon their expenditures separately, at a higher rate than they do, and I shall deduct what they have paid me from these amounts, to show you that their actions display no small degree of impudence. [35] The amounts of my money which they acknowledge receiving are: Aphobus, 108 minas apart from what I shall now prove he has kept; Therippides, 2 talents; Demophon, 87 minas. That makes 5 talents 15 minas. Of this, the amount which was not received all at once—the income from the slaves[32]—is nearly 77 minas, and the amount they received immediately is a little less than 4 talents. If you add to that the ten years' interest at a rate of only a drachma, you'll find that with the principal it comes to 8 talents 1,000 drachmas.[33] [36] The cost of maintenance[34] is to be reckoned against the 77 minas coming from the workshop. Therippides paid 7 minas each year for this purpose, and I acknowledge receiving it. So, since they expended 70 minas on my maintenance in ten years, I am giving them additional credit for the extra 700 drachmas, reckoning

---

[32] The profits made in the course of ten years from the manufacture of knives.

[33] At this point the arithmetic is not quite right. On the figures given, the principal (without the income from the slaves) and ten years' interest on it amount to at least 8 talents 4,000 drachmas, and Reiske (the eighteenth-century editor) emended the text here accordingly. Yet in 27.37 Demosthenes takes the amount as only 8 talents. So it seems likely that 8 talents 1,000 drachmas is what he wrote in 27.35; that is, the text is not corrupt but he committed an error in his calculation.

[34] Food, clothing, and other expenses such as schooling for Demosthenes himself during his boyhood. (Maintenance for his mother and sister should have been paid for by their prospective husbands, Aphobus and Demophon respectively, using the dowries which the elder Demosthenes left for them.)

the expenditure at a higher rate than they do. What they handed over to me when I was passed[35] as an adult and the sum they contributed as *eisphora* to the city[36] has to be deducted from the amount of more than 8 talents. [37] The sum paid me by Aphobus and Therippides was 31 minas, and they calculate that the contributions of *eisphora* were 18 minas. I'll overestimate this at 30 minas, to leave them no room to dispute it. If you deduct this talent from the 8 talents, 7 talents is left, and, from their own acknowledgments of what they received, that's what they must have kept. So, even if they misappropriate everything else and deny having it, they should have repaid that amount, since they acknowledge getting those sums from my property. [38] But, in fact, what do they do? They report no interest from the money and say they have spent the whole of the principal too, along with the 77 minas; and Demophon has recorded that I owe him money in addition! Isn't that huge and blatant effrontery? Isn't it the extreme of terrible avarice? What in the world does count as terrible, if such extreme behavior is not considered so? [39] Aphobus for his own part acknowledges receiving 108 minas, and he has kept both that amount and ten years' income from it, about 3 talents 1,000 drachmas. [*To the clerk*] To prove that what I say is true, and in the accounts of the guardianship each of them acknowledges receiving that sum and calculates that it was all spent, take the testimonies and read them.

[TESTIMONIES]

[40] On this matter, men of the jury, I think you understand well enough the extent of the thefts and crimes of each of these men. You would have still more exact knowledge if they'd been willing to hand over to me the will which my father left. It records, my mother tells me, all that my father left, and the property from which these men were to receive what was given to them,[37] and instructions to lease the estate.[38] [41] When I ask for it, however, they acknowledge that a will

---

[35] See 27.5n.

[36] See 27.7n.

[37] The sums listed in 27.5.

[38] See 27.15n.

was left, but they don't produce it. They do that because they don't want to reveal the size of the property which was left, and which they've plundered, and to conceal their possession of the legacies—as if they weren't going to be easily shown up by the facts themselves. [*To the clerk*] Take for the jury the testimonies of the men in whose presence they gave their answers, and read them.

[TESTIMONIES]

[42] He[39] says that there was a will, and he testifies that the 2 talents were given to Demophon and the 80 minas to Aphobus; but he does not say that the will also included the 70 minas which Therippides got, nor the size of the property which was left, nor the instructions to lease the estate, for it's not to his advantage to acknowledge those things too. [*To the clerk*] Now take this man's answer.

[TESTIMONY]

[43] He[40] too says that there was a will and that the cash raised from the copper and the dye was paid to Therippides—which the latter doesn't mention—and the 2 talents to Demophon; but as for what was given to himself, he says it was specified[41] but that he himself didn't assent to it—so that people won't think he received it. He also does not report that the size of the property as a whole was specified, nor the leasing of the estate; to acknowledge those too is not to his advantage either. [44] So, although they omit the property from the will, nonetheless their respective statements about how much money was given to the others make it plain what amount was left. If my father spent 4 talents 3,000 drachmas on giving two of them 3 talents 2,000 drachmas as dowries and the other the use of 70 minas, it's obvious to everyone, I suppose, that the property he was leaving to me, from which he took those sums, was not a small one but more than double that amount. [45] I don't suppose he wanted to leave me, his

---

[39] Therippides. Presumably the testimonies just read reported the answers which had been given by Demophon and by Therippides to questions posed perhaps at the public arbitrations of their respective cases; cf. 27.49n.

[40] Aphobus, whose answer must have been reported in this testimony.

[41] In the will.

son, poor, while desiring to make these men, who were rich, still richer; rather, it was because of the large amount that was being left to me that he gave Therippides so much money and Demophon the 2 talents to use although he wasn't going to marry my sister yet, so as to ensure one or other of two things: either he would encourage them to perform their duties as guardians better because of the gifts or, if they turned out to be bad guardians, you would show them no mercy when, after being given so much, they wronged me in this way. [46] And then Aphobus himself, besides the dowry, got some female slaves[42] and was residing in the house, and when he should have given an account of these, he says it's his own business; and he's become so avaricious that he has even deprived my teachers of their fees and has failed to make some of the payments of *eisphora*—though he charges them to me. [*To the clerk*] Take and read these testimonies to the jury too.

[TESTIMONIES]

[47] How, then, could one prove more clearly that he has plundered everything, not keeping his hands off even small items, than by proving in this manner, with so many witnesses and arguments, that he acknowledged that he received the dowry and gave the guardians a written statement that he had it; that he had the use of the workshop and didn't report the income; [48] that some of the other property he sold and didn't hand over the proceeds, while some he kept for himself and concealed it; besides, that he committed so many thefts which were proved in accordance with the accounts he himself rendered; and in addition, that he concealed the will, sold the slaves, and managed everything else in a manner that not even my worst enemies would have done? I don't know how one could prove it more clearly.

[49] Before the arbitrator[43] he had the audacity to say that he used

---

[42] Along with Demosthenes' house, Aphobus evidently took over the domestic servants in it.

[43] Most private cases were referred first to a public arbitrator. (Such arbitrators were ordinary citizens, not professional judges; every citizen was required to serve as an arbitrator in his sixtieth year of age.) The arbitrator heard the evidence and arguments, and gave a verdict. If both litigants accepted that verdict, it was final;

the money on my behalf to pay a large number of debts to his fellow-guardians Demophon and Therippides[44] and that they took much of my property; but he could not prove either of those statements. He did not show in the written accounts that my father left me in debt, and did not produce as witnesses the men to whom he said the money had been paid; nor was the amount of money he ascribed to his fellow-guardians equal to the sum he himself had evidently received, but a great deal less. [50] When he was questioned by the arbitrator about this in detail, and was asked whether he managed his own property from the profits or by spending the capital, and whether, if he had been a ward, he would have accepted this account from his guardians or would have wanted to get back the capital with the accrued income, he gave no answer to that, but he made an offer: he said that he was ready to show that the value of my property was 10 talents, and that if there was any shortfall he would make up the difference himself. [51] But when I told him to show that to the arbitrator, he didn't do so. Nor did he show that his fellow-guardians had handed the property over—if he had, the arbitrator would not have decided against him—but he submitted a testimony to that effect, which he'll try to explain to you.[45] So if today too he says that I have the property, ask him who handed it over, and demand that he produce witnesses for each item.[46] [52] And if he says that I have it in the sense that he calculates what is in the hands of each of the other two guardians, it will be clear that he's giving a figure too low by double[47] and still not showing that I actually have it. For, just as I proved that he has kept that

---

if either litigant rejected it, the case went to a jury for trial. In the present case, the arbitrator's verdict was in favor of Demosthenes, and Aphobus has insisted on having a trial by jury.

[44] The sentence is ambiguous, but probably Aphobus' claim was that he handed over to Demophon and Therippides funds with which they paid off debts owed by Demosthenes senior to other men, rather than that Demophon and Therippides themselves were the creditors.

[45] Evidently this testimony just stated in general terms that Demosthenes had already received all his property, without giving details.

[46] This is merely a rhetorical flourish. After an arbitration it was not legally permitted to introduce new testimony at the trial.

[47] He will still be speaking of 10 talents, instead of the 30 talents which Demosthenes claims.

large amount, I shall also show that each of the others has kept no less
than that. So that's not what he must say; he must argue that either he
himself or his fellow-guardians have handed it over. If he doesn't show
that, how does this offer of his deserve your notice? He still doesn't
show that I have my property.

[53] Not knowing what to say about all this before the arbitrator,
and being refuted point by point, just as he is now before you, he had
the audacity to tell an absolutely terrible lie, that my father left me
4 talents buried away and put my mother in charge of it. His aim in
saying this was that if I expected him to say the same thing now, I
should spend time refuting it when I ought to be presenting other
charges against him to you, whereas if I were to pass over it on the
assumption that it wouldn't be mentioned, he would assert it now, to
make me seem rich and less deserving of your sympathy. [54] He
didn't submit any testimony of this when he dared to say it; he just
made a bare statement and assumed he would be believed without difficulty.[48] When one asks him what he spent so much of my money on,
he says he paid off debts on my behalf and tries at this point to make
me a poor man; but when he likes, he makes me a rich man, it seems,
if my father left me so much money at home. But it's not possible that
he's telling the truth, and none of this can have happened, as it's easy
to tell for many reasons. [55] If my father had distrusted these men,
obviously he would not have entrusted the rest of his property to
them, and if he'd left this money in hiding, he wouldn't have told
them. It would be strange insanity to tell them about what was hidden if he was not going to make them guardians of his known property; but if he did trust them, he surely wouldn't have put most of
his money in their hands and not given them charge of the rest. Nor
would he have given this money to my mother to look after while giving her in marriage herself to Aphobus, who was one of the guardians; it doesn't make sense to try to protect the money by means of my
mother while putting one of the men he distrusted in charge of both
her and the money. [56] Besides, if any of this were true, do you think
Aphobus would not have married her, when she was given to him by

---

[48] "Without difficulty" translates an emendation by Blass. The manuscripts
have "through them" or "by them" or "by him," none of which gives good sense,
though the last, referring to the arbitrator, could possibly be correct.

my father? He already had her dowry of 80 minas as her future husband, but then he married the daughter of Philonides of Melite.[49] If there had been 4 talents in the house in my mother's possession, as he alleges, don't you think he would have rushed to get control of it along with her? [57] He and his fellow-guardians seized so disgracefully the visible property which most of you too were aware my father had left: would he have refrained from taking, when he could, money of which you were not likely to have any knowledge? Who could believe that? It can't be so, men of the jury, it can't be. My father handed over to these men all the money he left, and Aphobus is going to tell this story to diminish your sympathy for me.

[58] I have many other accusations which I could make against him, but by mentioning one, which sums them all up, I'll dispose of all his lines of defense. He could have avoided all this trouble if he'd leased the estate in accordance with these laws. [*To the clerk*] Take the laws and read them.

[LAWS]

It was in accordance with those laws that, from an estate of 3 talents 3,000 drachmas, Antidorus in six years was paid 6 talents and more as a result of its being leased, as some of you saw; for Theogenes of Probalinthus, the lessee of the estate, counted out that sum in the Agora.[50] [59] In my case, from an estate of 14 talents in ten years, in proportion to the length of time and the lease of Antidorus' estate, more than triple the sum could reasonably be expected to have accrued; so ask him why he didn't do that. If he says it was better for the estate not to be leased, let him show not that I have received double or triple but merely that the original sum has all been paid to me. But if, out of 14 talents, they've passed over to me less than 70 minas, while one of them[51] has put down that I owe him money in addition, how can it be right to accept anything that these men say? Surely it can't be.

[60] Although such substantial property was left to me as you heard at the beginning, producing 50 minas as the income of one-third of it,

---

[49] On this marriage, see Oration 30. The deme Melite was in the western part of the town of Athens; cf. Dem. 54.7.

[50] Nothing else is known of Antidorus and Theogenes. Probalinthus was a deme in eastern Attica, near Marathon.

[51] Demophon; cf. 27.38.

and these men with their insatiable desire for money, even if they didn't want to lease the estate, could from that income, while leaving the assets just as they were, have paid both for my maintenance and for the city's taxation and have saved up the surplus from that in addition, [61] and by investing the rest of the property, which was double that amount, could have taken moderate amounts from it for themselves, if they had a desire for money, and at the same time, besides preserving my capital, could have increased my estate from the income, yet they did none of those things. Instead, by selling to one another the most valuable of the slaves[52] and making away with others[53] entirely, they deprived me of even the existing income and procured no small income for themselves out of my property. [62] After getting hold of all the rest in that disgraceful manner, they all in unison assert that over half of the money was never left to me at all, and assuming the property to have been only 5 talents, they have rendered their accounts on the basis of an estate of that size; and it's not that they fail to declare income from it and produce only the principal, but they quite impudently allege that the capital itself has been spent. And they are not at all ashamed of this audacity.

[63] What would have become of me under their guardianship if I'd been their ward for a longer time? They wouldn't be able to say. When, after a period of ten years, I've recovered such a small amount from two of them and am put down as owing money besides to the other, surely indignation is justified. It's absolutely clear: if I'd been left fatherless at the age of a year and had been their ward for six years longer, I wouldn't have received even this small amount back from them. If the sums they mention have been properly spent, what has now been handed over wouldn't have lasted for six years; either they'd have been paying for my maintenance themselves or they'd have let me die of starvation. [64] When other estates worth 1 or 2 talents have doubled or tripled in value as a result of being leased, so as to be found suitable for liturgies,[54] surely it's a terrible thing if my estate, which was accustomed to perform trierarchies and make large contributions

---

[52] Half of the slaves making knives; cf. 27.13, 27.18.

[53] The slaves making beds; cf. 27.24–29.

[54] There was no fixed property qualification for liability to the trierarchy and other liturgies, but possession of property worth about 4 talents was considered enough to make a man likely to be called on to perform those services.

of *eisphora*,[55] will be unable to make even small ones because of these men's shameless activities. What transgressions can one mention which they have not committed? They have concealed the will, expecting that that would not be noticed; they have employed the profits to administer their own property and used my money to make their capital much greater than it was before; and they have completely demolished the principal of my property, as if we[56] had done them the greatest harm! [65] Even when you convict any public offenders, you don't deprive them of all their possessions, but you take pity on their wives and children and leave something for them; but these men are so different from you that even after receiving gifts from us to encourage them to perform their duties as guardians rightly, they have treated us in this insolent way. They didn't even show respect, much less pity, for my sister, who was granted 2 talents[57] by my father but will now get none of what is due to her. They are like bitter enemies, not friends and relatives left behind by him, and they care nothing for family ties.

[66] I am the unhappiest of men, being left with no resources either to dower her for marriage or to manage the rest of my life. Besides, the city is pressing me for *eisphora*, quite justly, for my father left me sufficient property for that purpose, but these men have taken all the money which was left. [67] And now that I'm attempting to recover my property, I'm put at a very serious risk. If Aphobus gets off— as I trust he won't—I shall have to pay *epōbelia* of 100 minas.[58] If you convict him, his penalty is to be assessed, and he'll make the payment not from his own money but from mine; but that penalty for me is a fixed one, so that I shall not only lose my patrimony but be disfranchised as well, if you don't take pity on me today.

---

[55] See 27.7n.

[56] "We" may here be taken to mean Demosthenes senior and Demosthenes himself.

[57] Her dowry; cf. 27.5.

[58] In certain cases, a prosecutor who lost had to pay to his successful opponent a penalty of one-sixth of the sum he had claimed, called *epōbelia* (an obol per drachma). If he failed to pay it, he suffered disfranchisement (*atimia*), meaning loss of public rights. Demosthenes was claiming 10 talents from each of the three guardians.

[68] So I request you, men of the jury, and beg and entreat you, bearing in mind both the laws and the oaths you swore on becoming jurors, to give me the support I deserve and not to attach more importance to this man's pleas than to mine. It's right for you to sympathize not with people who commit crimes but with those who are unfortunate beyond expectation; not with those who deprive others of their property in this ruthless way but with me, who have long been deprived of what my father left me, and am insulted by these men besides, and now am in danger of disfranchisement. [69] I think my father would be deeply grieved if he could see that the dowries and gifts he gave these men have put me, his son, at risk of *epōbelia,* and that, while some other citizens before now have dowered from their own money daughters of poor men who were relatives or even just friends, Aphobus refuses even to repay the dowry he received, though it's now the tenth year.

28. AGAINST APHOBUS II

〰〰〰

INTRODUCTION

At the trials of most private cases, each of the two litigants was
allowed to make two speeches, in the order prosecutor, defendant,
prosecutor, defendant. The speeches were timed by the water-clock
(*klepsydra*), less time being allowed for the second speech than for the
first.[1] Probably a speaker would usually extemporize his second speech
to answer points just made by his opponent, but if it is right to regard
Orations 28 and 31 as drafts made by Demosthenes before the respective trials (cf. p. 16), in these two cases, perhaps because of his inexperience, he thought it worthwhile to prepare in advance some material
for use in his second speech.

The text of Oration 28 begins with a rejection of an allegation by
Aphobus about Demosthenes' maternal grandfather, Gylon. Gylon
had at some time incurred a debt to the public treasury. If he was still
in debt when he died, the debt was inherited through his two daughters by their sons, so that the young Demosthenes would have become
liable to pay half of it. It was for this reason, according to Aphobus,
that Demosthenes senior did not want his estate to be leased at a public auction after his death, since then its value would have become
known and it, or part of it, would have been liable to confiscation to
pay the debt. Demosthenes answers this allegation by insisting that

---

[1] When more than 5,000 drachmas was in dispute, the time allowed was 10 *choes*
of water for the first speech and 3 *choes* for the second. A *chous* seems to have represented about 3 minutes; thus the first speech could take 30 minutes and the second 9 minutes. The water-clock was stopped in private cases for the reading out
of testimonies and other documents, which was not subject to the time limit.

Gylon himself paid the debt long ago and by arguing that neither Demosthenes senior nor Demochares (Gylon's other son-in-law) nor Aphobus and his fellow-guardians had attempted to conceal the value of the property.

Part of the speech is taken up with a second presentation of many of the testimonies already presented in the first speech. The most impressive passage is the description of Demosthenes senior giving his instructions on his deathbed. This leads, after reference to Thrasylochus' challenge to exchange property (see notes on 28.17), to a concluding passage of pathos which makes an effective climax to Demosthenes' case.

28. AGAINST APHOBUS FOR GUARDIANSHIP II

[1] Aphobus has told you many big lies, but I shall try first to refute the part of his speech which annoyed me most. He said that my grandfather[2] owed money to the treasury, and that was why my father did not want the estate to be leased, to avoid putting it at risk.[3] That is the explanation he gives, but he did not produce any testimony that my grandfather died in debt; he did submit testimony that he incurred a debt, but waited for the last day before doing so,[4] and he has left this until his second speech, thinking that it will enable him to misrepresent the matter.[5] [2] If he does have it read out, pay close attention to it. You'll find that it does not attest that his debt exists now, but only that he incurred a debt. So I'll try to refute first this point on which he's especially confident and which I dispute. If it had been possible at the time and I had not been thus ensnared by the timing, I would have produced witnesses to testify that the money was paid and all his ob-

---

[2] Gylon, father of Demosthenes' mother.

[3] The suggestion is that, if the estate had been openly offered for lease, its value would have come to the notice of the authorities, and it, or part of it, would have been sequestered to pay off Gylon's debt.

[4] The last day before the arbitrator gave his verdict. After that it was not permitted to put in any further testimony, so that Demosthenes had no time to produce any contrary testimony on this point.

[5] The second speech for the defense would follow the second speech for the prosecution, leaving Demosthenes no opportunity to reply to it.

ligations to the city had been settled. As it is, I shall show by strong arguments that he was not in debt, and no danger to us was posed by open possession of the property.

[3] In the first place, Demochares, whose wife is my mother's sister and Gylon's daughter, has not concealed his property. He serves as a chorus-producer and a trierarch and performs the other liturgies,[6] and is not afraid of anything of that sort. Next, my father himself revealed his property, including 4 talents 3,000 drachmas which was recorded in his will and was taken by these men themselves,[7] as they have testified against one another. [4] Besides, Aphobus himself and his fellow-guardians publicly revealed the amount of the money which was left by making me the leader of the symmory, not with a low assessment but with one high enough to contribute 500 drachmas in each 25 minas.[8] But if any of this had been true, he would never have done that, but would have shown the utmost caution. As it is, it's clear that Demochares and my father and these men themselves acted openly and were not afraid of any such danger.

[5] The most absurd thing of all is that they say my father forbade leasing the estate, but they never produce the clause of the will from which that point could be verified; they make away with that important evidence and then expect you to believe them quite readily. What they ought to have done, as soon as my father died, was to call in a number of witnesses and tell them to put their seals on the will, so that, if anything turned out to be disputed, it would have been possible to return to that document and discover the truth of it all. [6] As it is, they requested the sealing of other documents in which many of the items left were not recorded but which were just memoranda, while they failed to seal or hand over the actual will which gave them authority over those sealed documents and all the rest of the money and absolved them from blame for not leasing the estate. Oh yes, you may well believe whatever they say about that!

[7] I don't understand it, myself. [*To Aphobus*] My father forbade leasing the estate or revealing the money—to me? Or to the city? You've obviously done just the opposite: you've revealed it to the city

---

[6] See 27.64n.

[7] The gifts and dowries listed in 27.5.

[8] See 27.7n.

but completely hidden it from me, and you haven't even made clear the basis of your assessment for your payments of *eisphora*. Show us what that property was, and where you handed it over to me, and who saw you do so. [8] From the 4 talents 3,000 drachmas you took away the 2 talents and the 80 minas; so you didn't include those in the assessment you made for the treasury on my behalf, because they belonged to you at that time. But on the basis of the house and the fourteen slaves and the 30 minas which you passed on to me,⁹ the *eisphora* could not have been as much as the payments you arranged to make to the symmory. [9] It's an absolute certainty that the property my father left, which was far more than that, must all be in your hands, and clearly it's because you are proved to have plundered it that you are inventing such audacious fictions. Sometimes you call on one another for corroboration; then again you give evidence against one another of having taken it. You allege that you did not receive much, and yet you have rendered accounts of large expenditures. [10] Although you were all my guardians jointly, subsequently you have each been scheming individually. You've concealed the will, from which the truth about everything could have been known, and it's plain that your statements about one another never agree.

[*To the clerk*] Take the testimonies and read them all one by one to the jury, to enable them to remember the evidence and the statements more exactly when they give their verdict.¹⁰

[TESTIMONIES]

[11] They agreed on my behalf to that assessment, appropriate to estates worth 15 talents,¹¹ but the property which the three of them have handed over to me is worth less than 70 minas. Read out the next ones.

[TESTIMONIES]

His receipt of that dowry is attested both by the guardians and by other men to whom he acknowledged that he had it, but he has paid

---

⁹ When Demosthenes came of age; cf. 27.6.

¹⁰ The testimonies read out in Oration 28 probably were, or at least included, ones which had already been read out in Oration 27.

¹¹ See 27.7.

neither the dowry itself nor the maintenance.[12] Take the other testimonies and read them.

[TESTIMONIES]

[12] After managing the workshop for two years, he paid the rent to Therippides, but he hasn't paid me the two years' income which he received, amounting to 30 minas—neither the original sum nor the interest.[13] Take another one and read it.

[TESTIMONY]

After taking for himself those slaves and the others given to us as security along with those, he has included in his calculations that large expenditure on them but no profit at all; and he's made away with the men themselves, who were bringing in 12 minas net every year.[14] Read out another one.

[TESTIMONY]

[13] After selling that ivory and iron, he denies that they were ever left by my father and robs me of the value of them too, about a talent.[15] Read out these ones.

[TESTIMONIES]

That's 3 talents 1,000 drachmas he has kept, apart from the rest.[16] So the total of the capital he has taken is 5 talents; including the interest, if one reckons it at only a drachma, he has kept more than 10 talents. Read the next ones.

[TESTIMONIES]

[14] That those amounts were written in the will, and were received by these men, is shown by their testimony against one another. Aphobus admits that he was sent for by my father, and he went to the house; but he says that he didn't go into the presence of my father who

---

[12] See 27.15.

[13] See 27.18–23.

[14] See 27.24–26.

[15] See 27.30–33.

[16] See 27.39.

had sent for him, and didn't make any agreement on these arrangements, but heard Demophon reading out a document and Therippides saying that my father had made these dispositions—although in fact he had gone in beforehand[17] and reached an agreement with my father about everything that he left in writing. [15] For, men of the jury, when my father realized that he wasn't going to recover from his illness, he called these three men together and had his brother Demon sit beside him, and he put our persons in their hands, calling us a trust. He gave my sister to Demophon with 2 talents as an immediate dowry and betrothed her to be his wife, and he entrusted me to all of them jointly together with his money, and instructed them to lease the estate and preserve his property along with me; [16] and at the same time, he gave Therippides the 70 minas and betrothed my mother to Aphobus with the dowry of 80 minas, and he placed me on Aphobus' knees. Aphobus, being the most irreverent of men, took no notice of all this once he got control of my affairs on these terms, but with his fellow-guardians he has deprived me of all the money, and will now ask you to take pity on him, although he with the other two has made repayments of less than 70 minas and then has made a plot to get back those too.

[17] Shortly before I was to come to court for the trials of these cases against them, they contrived against me a proposal to exchange property so that, if I agreed to the exchange, I should no longer be able to litigate against them because these cases too would belong to the man who had proposed the exchange, or, if I refused to do it, by paying for a liturgy out of scanty resources I should be utterly ruined.[18] The man who did them this service was Thrasylochus of Anagyrus.[19]

---

[17] Instead of "beforehand" some manuscripts say "besides."

[18] If a man appointed to perform a liturgy (a public service, in this case a trierarchy) considered that another man, being richer than himself, ought to perform it instead, he could challenge that man either (if he admitted being richer) to perform it or (if he claimed to be poorer) to accept an exchange of their entire properties. This was the procedure called *antidosis;* cf. MacDowell 1978: 161–164. If Demosthenes had carried out the exchange, his claims against his guardians would have been part of the property which he gave up.

[19] Thrasylochus happened to be appointed that year (364/3) to a trierarchy, to maintain and command a trireme jointly with one other man. He was presum-

Without thinking of those consequences at all, I agreed to the exchange with him, but I excluded him from my property in order to obtain a trial.[20] Since I didn't obtain that, and the dates[21] were imminent, so as not to be deprived of my cases I paid for the liturgy[22] by mortgaging my house and everything I had, because I wanted to come into your court for the trials of my cases against these men.

[18] Haven't I been greatly wronged from the start? Am I not still being greatly harmed by them, because I am seeking justice? Which of you would not be rightly indignant with Aphobus and sorry for me, seeing that he, in addition to his inherited property of more than 10 talents, has gained mine to the same amount, while I have not only lost my patrimony but have also been deprived by these criminals of what actually was handed over to me? Where can I turn, if you vote for any other verdict on them? To the property given as security to my creditors? But that belongs to those creditors. To what is left over? But that goes to Aphobus, if I incur the *epōbelia*.[23] [19] Please don't cause us so much distress, men of the jury. Don't leave my mother, my sister, and me to suffer undeservedly. That's not what my father hoped when he left us: he wanted my sister to be married to Demophon with a dowry of 2 talents, my mother to be married with 80 minas to this most ruthless of all men, and me to be his own successor in performing liturgies for you.

[20] So help me, help me for the sake of justice, and of yourselves,

---

ably a friend of the guardians and had agreed that, if he took over Demosthenes' property, he would not pursue the claims against them; they would then do him a good turn in some other way. Thrasylochus' brother was Meidias, and in his speech *Against Meidias* Demosthenes describes how the two brothers burst into his house assuming that they were taking it over (21.78–80). Anagyrus was a deme in the south of Attica, midway between Piraeus and Sunium.

[20] The Greek word is *diadikasia,* meaning a form of trial for deciding between claimants. In a case of *antidosis,* if no exchange of property took place but the man challenged still refused to perform the liturgy, the challenger could demand a *diadikasia* to decide which of them should perform it.

[21] The dates fixed for the trials of the guardians.

[22] The cost was 20 minas, the amount for which Thrasylochus had already hired a man to perform all his duties in the trierarchy (21.80).

[23] See 27.67.

and of us, and of my deceased father. Preserve me, pity me, since they have taken no pity, though they are relatives. It's to you that I have turned for refuge. I beg you, I entreat you by your children, by your wives, by the good things you have: may you have full enjoyment of them if you don't neglect me, and don't cause my mother to be deprived of her remaining hopes in life and suffer a fate unworthy of her. [21] At present she thinks that, after I have obtained justice in your court, I will shelter her and give away my sister in marriage; but if you give a different verdict—as I trust you won't—what do you suppose will be her spirit when she sees me not only deprived of my patrimony but disfranchised as well, and has no hope that my sister will obtain anything of what she should, because of our future poverty? [22] I don't deserve to be denied justice in your court, men of the jury, nor does Aphobus deserve to keep so much money unjustly. Though you have not yet had a chance to test my loyalty to you, you should expect me not to be inferior to my father. But you have tested Aphobus, and you know very well that, after inheriting substantial property, he has not only done you no honorable service, but has been shown to have been misappropriating other people's money.

[23] So, considering those facts and remembering the rest, cast your votes on the side of justice. You have sufficient proof from witnesses, from arguments, from probabilities, and from the statements of these men who, acknowledging that they received my assets in full, assert that they have expended them though they have not, but have kept everything themselves. [24] Bearing all this in mind, you ought to show some consideration for me; for you know that, if I recover my possessions through you, I am likely to perform liturgies willingly out of a feeling of gratitude that you justly gave me back my property, whereas Aphobus, if you give him control of my possessions, will do no such thing. Don't imagine that he'll be willing to perform liturgies for you on the basis of assets which he has denied receiving. On the contrary, he'll keep them hidden, to make it appear that he was rightly acquitted.

29. AGAINST APHOBUS FOR PHANUS

INTRODUCTION

After Aphobus was condemned to pay Demosthenes the huge sum of 10 talents, he tried to avoid the payment by bringing a case for false witness (*dikē pseudomartyriōn*) against one of Demosthenes' witnesses. This witness, named Phanus, had given testimony concerning Milyas, the foreman of the workshop of slaves manufacturing knives which formed part of Demosthenes' estate. One of Demosthenes' accusations against Aphobus had been that he failed to report and hand over two years' profit from the manufacture of knives, and Aphobus had said that Milyas was the man who would know what had happened to it (cf. 27.18–22). But the testimony of a slave was not admitted in an Athenian court; only if a slave was subjected to interrogation under torture (*basanos*) was a report of his answers considered acceptable, and that could be done only if the slave's owner agreed to hand him over to the opposing litigant for that purpose.[1] Aphobus had accordingly demanded that Demosthenes should hand over Milyas for interrogation under torture; but Demosthenes had refused to do so on the ground that Milyas was no longer a slave, having been given his freedom by Demosthenes senior shortly before his death. When Aphobus denied that, Demosthenes called three witnesses, Phanus, Philippus, and Aphobus' own brother Aesius, to testify not only that Milyas was a free man but that Aphobus himself had admitted as

---

[1] The standard work on this subject, in German, is Thür 1977. For more recent discussion in English, see Gagarin 1996; Mirhady 1996, 2000b.

much on an earlier occasion,[2] so that his demand to interrogate Milyas under torture was hypocritical. That testimony was presented at the trial of Aphobus.[3] Hence Aphobus' complaint that Phanus' testimony was false and caused him to lose the case.[4]

The text we have is Demosthenes' supporting speech for Phanus, defending him against that accusation. It would have been preceded at the trial by Aphobus' speech of accusation and also by Phanus' own speech in his defense (which could have been quite short). Consequently Demosthenes does not find it necessary to explain all the facts, many of which he assumes will already be clear to the jury from Aphobus' and Phanus' speeches. This makes it harder for us, lacking those other speeches, to understand the details of the case. But it seems clear that no decisive evidence was available to prove whether Milyas had really been set free by Demosthenes senior or not—which has the interesting implication that manumission of a slave in Athens was not necessarily an action carried out in a formal manner in front of witnesses and publicly recorded.[5] It is possible that Milyas, though undoubtedly a slave originally, had for so long been treated as a trusted member of the household that his precise legal status had been more or less forgotten. It is clear that Demosthenes had not wanted him to testify, but it is hardly possible to say whether that was because he feared that the testimony would be unfavorable or simply because he did not want an old and faithful servant to be subjected to torture.

It appears from the text that some time has already passed since the trial of Aphobus; the date may be 362/1 BC.[6] Yet a good deal of the speech goes over old ground again, insisting that Aphobus did defraud Demosthenes and was justly condemned to pay him 10 talents.

---

[2] That occasion seems to have been one of the sessions of the public arbitration for Demosthenes' prosecution of Demophon; see 29.20n.

[3] It may have been among the testimonies presented at the end of 27.22.

[4] Aphobus initiated a prosecution of Philippus too, but evidently the prosecution of Phanus was the one that went ahead first. Aesius, on the other hand, afterwards denied his testimony and was presumably not prosecuted (29.15).

[5] See Todd 1994: 125–129.

[6] A reference in 29.3 shows that by this time Demosthenes had initiated his prosecution of Onetor but not necessarily that the trial of Onetor had yet been held.

Surely Demosthenes was right to maintain that Aphobus' main purpose in prosecuting Phanus was not to punish Phanus but to avoid making that heavy payment to Demosthenes. He therefore argues that it would be unjust if the jury were now to give a verdict which would let Aphobus off; Aphobus is still guilty, regardless of whether the details of Phanus' testimony about Milyas were correct or not. Since Aphobus did not in fact get off, we can infer that Phanus was acquitted, or else that Aphobus realized that he had little chance of winning the case and so abandoned it before it came to trial.

Anyway the surviving text is acceptable as a copy of the draft which Demosthenes made in preparation for the trial. In modern times some scholars have argued that this text is not authentic, but is a forgery or pastiche composed in imitation of Demosthenes by some rhetorician of a later age. That view is now generally rejected, and since I have discussed it elsewhere,[7] I shall not go into details here, except for one point of particular interest. This concerns Demosthenes' uncle Demon. Demon was present at Demosthenes senior's deathbed (described in 28.15–16), and yet he was not appointed to be one of the guardians of the children and the property, though his son Demophon was. But in the speech for Phanus we find Demon referred to as Aphobus' fellow-guardian (29.56). Some scholars have seized on this reference as evidence that the writer of this text wrongly believed that there were four guardians, not three; Demosthenes could not have made this mistake and so, it has been argued, could not have been the author. But this argument is unsound, because it is clear from the last sentence of the text (29.60) that the writer knew there were only three guardians. Instead we should assume that, Demophon being only a young man (perhaps not yet adult when Demosthenes senior died), his father Demon acted for him or with him during the first few years, performing some of the functions of a guardian without being one formally. At the same time, the authenticity of the text is strongly indicated by the inclusion of a great amount of detailed information of a kind which is unlikely to have been known to a writer of a later period and yet does not look like merely fictional invention.

---

[7] MacDowell 1989. See also Calhoun 1934; Thür 1972.

29. AGAINST APHOBUS FOR PHANUS,
ACCUSED OF FALSE WITNESS

[1] If I were not aware, men of the jury, that before, when I faced Aphobus in a trial and he told far bigger and more dreadful lies than these, I refuted him easily because of the patency of his offenses, I should be awfully concerned that today I might be unable to show how he misleads you in every particular of them. As it is, the gods willing, if you give me a fair and impartial hearing, I have high hopes that you will understand the shamelessness of this man as well as the earlier jury did. If that needed any elaborate speech, I should be hesitant, feeling that my age is insufficient; but in fact I have simply to relate and explain his treatment of me, and from this I think it will be easy for you all to decide which of us two is the villain.

[2] I know he has brought this case not because he is confident that he will prove that false evidence has been given against him, but in the belief that the amount of the penalty assessed in the case he lost would evoke resentment towards me and sympathy for him. That's the reason why he now defends himself concerning the past case, in which he had no just defense at the time. For myself, men of the jury, if I had obtained the payment which he incurred, or if I had refused to reach a moderate settlement, even so I shouldn't have been unjustified in exacting from him the sums decided in your court, but still it might have been said that it was too cruel and harsh of me to turn a man who is my relative out of all his property.[8] [3] But in fact it's just the opposite. He, with his fellow-guardians, has deprived me of all my patrimony, and even after being clearly proved guilty in your court he thinks he needn't do anything reasonable, but by dividing up the property and handing the building over to Aesius and the farm to Onetor[9] he has

---

[8] This implies that all the property that Aphobus possessed was worth no more than 10 talents, the sum which he had been condemned to pay Demosthenes.

[9] "Aesius" is an emendation first proposed by H. Wolf; the manuscripts have "Aphobus." Aesius was Aphobus' brother; Onetor was Aphobus' brother-in-law. The building (*synoikia,* a tenement building inhabited by more than one family) and the farm belonged to Aphobus; they were not part of Demosthenes' estate,

involved me in legal proceedings against them; and after taking the furniture out of his house and removing the slaves and destroying the cistern and tearing down the doors and doing everything but set fire to the house itself, he has moved to Megara and paid a metic's fee[10] there. So it would be far more justifiable for you to be hostile to him on account of this conduct than to consider me guilty of any unfairness.

[4] It seems best for me to describe to you later the man's avarice and wickedness—you've already heard a kind of summary just now —but I'll attempt now to explain to you the truth of the testimony given, about which you will be casting your votes. I make one request of you, men of the jury, a just one: to listen to us both equally. That is in your own interest too; for the more exactly you understand the facts, the more just and the more in accordance with your oath your voting about them will be. [5] I shall show that Aphobus not only acknowledged that Milyas was free but made that clear by his conduct and in addition that he avoided investigating the matter by interrogation under torture, the most reliable kind of proof, and refused to uncover the truth by those means, but acted dishonestly and provided false witnesses and concealed by his own speech the truth of the facts; and I shall give such strong and plain proofs that you will all know clearly that I am telling the truth and nothing that Aphobus has said is sound. I'll begin from the point which will make it easiest for you to understand and quickest for me to explain.

[6] I, men of the jury, brought guardianship cases against Demophon[11] and Therippides and this man because I was deprived of all my property. My case against this man was tried first, and I showed clearly to the jury, as I shall show to you, that this man, along with the others, deprived me of all the money that was left me.[12] I did not do it by

---

but Demosthenes claims that they ought to have been handed over to him in part-payment of the 10 talents owed him by Aphobus. The dispute between Demosthenes and Onetor is the subject of Orations 30 and 31.

[10] A fee entitling him to reside permanently as a non-citizen.

[11] Some manuscripts here say "Demon and Demophon." On Demon's position in relation to the guardians, see p. 50.

[12] "All" is not strictly correct, since the guardians did hand over a certain amount of money; cf. 27.6.

using false testimony against him, [7] and there is a very strong indication of that: although there were innumerable testimonies, all read out at the trial—some witnesses testifying that they gave him some item of mine, some that they were present when he received it, some that they bought it from him and paid him the price—he did not make an accusation of false witness against a single one of those, nor did he venture to prosecute any except this one alone, in which he cannot say that a single drachma was mentioned. [8] Yet, in assessing the money of which I had been deprived, it wasn't from this testimony that I reached such a large total in my calculations, for there's no money in it; I reckoned every individual item from the other testimonies, against which he made no accusation. That was why those who heard me at the time not only convicted him but fixed the damages at the amount I had written down. So why did he leave aside the other testimonies and make an accusation against this one? I'll explain that too. [9] In the case of all the testimonies which attested that he had kept money, he knew very well that the more they were each discussed in detail, the more clearly he would be proved to have it. That was what would happen in the trial for false witness; an accusation which I made along with the others at the trial, in a small part of my total allocation of water,[13] I would now be expounding on its own for the whole of it. [10] But if he made an accusation about an answer,[14] he thought that it would then be in his power to deny what he had previously admitted. That's why he is prosecuting this testimony. So I want to show you all clearly that this testimony is true, not from probabilities or from arguments devised for the present occasion but from what I believe will appear to you all to be just. Listen and consider.

[11] When I became aware, men of the jury, that the dispute I faced was about the testimony written in the document,[15] and I knew that you were going to vote on that, I thought that the first thing I should

---

[13] The speeches were timed by the water-clock; cf. 27.12.

[14] This compressed expression means challenging the testimony (of Phanus) that a certain answer to a question had been given (by Aphobus). If the testimony was then rejected by the jury in the trial for false witness, Aphobus would be able to claim that he had never given that answer.

[15] The testimony given by Phanus, which was put in writing for the trial of Aphobus and is now included in Aphobus' written charge against Phanus.

do was to refute Aphobus by a challenge. And what did I do? I offered to hand over to him for interrogation under torture a literate slave who was present at the time when Aphobus made this admission and wrote down his testimony. He wasn't told by me to cheat, or to write parts and omit parts of what Aphobus said on the matter, but was there simply to record the whole truth of his statement. [12] What better way to proceed than to prove I was lying by putting the slave on the rack? But Aphobus knew, better than anyone, that the testimony was true. That's why he declined the interrogation. These facts are known not just to one or two people; the challenge was not made in an underhand manner but in the middle of the Agora with many onlookers. [*To the clerk*] Please call the witnesses of this.

[WITNESSES]

[13] This man is such a sophist, and so ready to pretend not to know what is right, that, although he's prosecuting for false witness and that's what you're going to vote on under oath, he declined the interrogation under torture concerning the testimony, which is what he should have spoken about especially, and he says that he made requests for evidence concerning other matters, which is a lie. [14] But isn't it monstrous to assert that he was disgracefully treated because his request for a man who is not a slave—as I shall show you clearly—was rejected, and yet not to think that the witnesses are being treated disgracefully because, when I offer a man who is admittedly a slave to give evidence about their testimony, Aphobus refuses to accept him? It's surely not open to him to say that interrogation under torture is reliable on some questions of his own choosing but not reliable on others.[16]

[15] Besides, men of the jury, the first man to give this testimony[17]

---

[16] Aphobus wanted to interrogate under torture a man who, according to Demosthenes, was not a slave (Milyas), and yet refused to interrogate a man who was a slave (the literate slave mentioned in 29.11). The latter was the one who had heard Aphobus concede that Milyas had been freed and who thus knew that that part of Phanus' testimony was true.

[17] The testimony that Milyas was not a slave and that Aphobus had acknowledged that. This testimony was given by Aesius, Phanus, and Philippus at the public arbitration for the prosecution of Aphobus, and was read out at the court trial of that case.

was Aphobus' brother Aesius—who now denies it because he's supporting Aphobus in this trial, but at that time gave this testimony along with the others because he didn't want to perjure himself or immediately incur a penalty.[18] Surely, if I'd been devising false testimony, I wouldn't have included him among my witnesses, seeing that he was closer to Aphobus than anyone, and knowing that he would be supporting him in the case and besides was my legal opponent; it doesn't make sense to enlist one's own opponent and Aphobus' brother as a witness to an untrue testimony. [16] There are plenty of witnesses of this, and there are also arguments no less convincing than the witnesses. In the first place, if Aesius really hadn't given this testimony, he would not have denied it now but straightaway in the court as the testimony was read, when the denial would have been more use to him than it is now. In the second place, he would not have kept quiet, but would have brought a case for damage[19] against me if I'd wrongly made him liable to prosecution for false witness against his brother—a prosecution which puts men at risk both of a financial penalty and of disfranchisement. [17] And again, if he'd wanted to prove the point, he would have made me a request for the slave who wrote down the testimonies so that, if I refused to hand him over, it would have become apparent that what I was saying was wrong. But as it is, far from doing any of those things, he refused to accept the slave even when I offered him, once Aphobus denied the facts. It's clear that both of them alike are avoiding holding interrogations on this question.

[18] To prove that what I say is true, and that after Aesius had given his testimony among the witnesses he didn't deny the facts in the presence of the court, although he was standing beside Aphobus as the testimony was read, and that when I offered them the slave for interrogation about all this he refused to accept him, I will provide witnesses for you on each point. [*To the clerk*] Please call them here.

---

[18] A litigant could produce a written statement of evidence and insist that a witness either confirm it or take an oath to the contrary; if he refused, he could be punished by a fine of 1,000 drachmas.

[19] "Damage" (*blabē*) here means simply financial loss, in this case a payment of compensation to the person convicted on false evidence. A man found guilty of false witness on three occasions suffered disfranchisement (*atimia*).

[WITNESSES]

[19] Now, men of the jury, I want to describe what I think will be the strongest indication that I shall give you that Aphobus gave that answer, stronger than all I have said. When he made me a request for the man, after admitting the facts which have been attested, I wanted even at the time to expose his trickery, and so what did I do? [20] I summoned him to testify against Demon, who was his uncle and a partner in his misdeeds.[20] I compiled and told him to attest to the same evidence as is now the object of his prosecution for false witness. At first he brazenly refused, but when the arbitrator[21] ordered him either to attest to it or to take the oath to the contrary,[22] he did attest with great reluctance. Yet, if the man was a slave and Aphobus had not already acknowledged that he was free, what reason had he to attest instead of taking the oath to the contrary and disposing of the matter? [21] On these facts too I was willing to hand over the slave who wrote down the testimony, who would recognize his own writing and remembered clearly that Aphobus gave this testimony. I was willing to do that, not because I lacked witnesses who were present, for I had some, but so that they should not be accused of false witness by him but should have confirmation from the interrogation. How can it be fair to convict the witnesses on that account? Of all the men who have ever faced trial in your court, they are the only ones who can point to their prosecutor himself as a witness on their side of the case! [*To the clerk*] To prove that what I say is true, take the challenge and the testimony.

---

[20] When and why was Demosthenes accusing Demon? Probably this is a reference to the prosecution of Demophon, with whom Demon was associated in the guardianship (see p. 50). No doubt the arbitrations for Demosthenes' prosecutions of Aphobus and of Demophon were proceeding concurrently on different days, for it was normal for a public arbitration to take several meetings. We can suppose that one session of the arbitration for the case against Demophon and Demon happened to take place on a day in between two sessions of the arbitration for the case against Aphobus.

[21] Named as Notharchus in 29.31.

[22] See 29.15n.

[CHALLENGE, TESTIMONY]

[22] Although he avoided such fair tests and gives such clear signs that his accusation is malicious, he expects you to believe his own witnesses, but criticizes mine and says their testimony is not true. I want to discuss this on a basis of what is probable. I know you would all agree that men who give false testimony would be willing to do that sort of thing either for payment because of poverty or because of friendship or because of hostility to the opposing litigants. [23] Now, they[23] would not have testified for me for any of those reasons. Not for friendship: how could they, when they don't move in the same circles and some of them are not of the same age—not merely as myself, but even as one another? Nor for hostility to Aphobus, that's obvious too: one of them is his brother and supporter in the case, Phanus is his close friend and a member of his tribe,[24] and Philippus is neither his friend nor his enemy; so one can't justly attribute that motive to them either. [24] Nor could one say it was because of poverty: they all possess enough property to perform liturgies for you willingly and carry out what they are instructed to do. Apart from that, they are not unknown to you and don't have bad reputations but are respectable people. Yet, if they're neither poor nor enemies of Aphobus nor friends of mine, why should they come under any suspicion of giving false testimony? I'm sure I don't know.

[25] Aphobus realizes this, and he knows better than anyone that their testimony is true. Nevertheless he brings this malicious prosecution, and says not only that he didn't make that statement—and how could it be proved more conclusively that he did?—but also that the man[25] is a slave in fact. I want to prove to you in a few words that that's also a lie. On this matter too, men of the jury, I offered to hand over to him for interrogation under torture the slave-women[26] who remember that at the time of my father's death the man was set free. [26] In addition, my mother was willing to set beside her myself and

---

[23] Phanus, Philippus, and Aesius.

[24] Aphobus' tribe (*phylē*) seems to have been Acamantis.

[25] Milyas.

[26] Women working in Demosthenes' house.

my sister, her only children, for whom she passed her life in widow-hood, and give a pledge by us that the man was set free by my father when he was dying and was regarded in our family as free.[27] None of you should suppose that she would ever have been willing to swear this by us unless she was certain that what she would be swearing was true. [*To the clerk*] To prove that what I say is true and we were willing to take that step, call the witnesses of this.

[WITNESSES]

[27] Those were the strong proofs which we were able to propose, and we were willing to resort to the most stringent tests concerning the testimony. But Aphobus declined all of them, and thinks that by bringing slanders and accusations against me concerning the trial which has already been held he'll persuade you to convict the wit-ness—a scheme which is surely as unjust and selfish as it could be. [28] He himself has procured false witnesses on this subject, with his brother-in-law Onetor and Timocrates as fellow-producers of the cho-rus.[28] I didn't know that beforehand; I thought the trial would just be about the actual testimony, and so I haven't procured any witnesses to-day about the money which was under guardianship. Nevertheless, al-though he has used this sophistry, I think that just by relating the facts I shall easily show you that Aphobus fully deserved to lose the case, [29] not because I prevented the interrogation of Milyas, nor because he acknowledged that Milyas was a free man and these witnesses tes-tified to it, but because he was proved to have taken a large amount of my property and failed to lease the estate, although the laws autho-rized that and my father wrote it in his will, as I shall show you clearly. Everyone could see those things—the laws and the quantity of money that these men had plundered—whereas no one knew about Milyas, not even who he was. The charges will show you that that is the case.

[30] When I brought the case against Aphobus for his guardian-

---

[27] Such a pledge was equivalent to an oath: the mother would pray to the gods to send misfortune upon her children if she was not telling the truth. It was not considered proper for a woman to give testimony in a public court herself, but male witnesses could testify that she had given a pledge.

[28] On Onetor and Timocrates, see Oration 30.

ship, men of the jury, I did not compile just the total value, as one would if one were getting up a malicious prosecution, but I wrote down each item, where he got it and how much was the amount and from whom, and at no point did I add that Milyas knew any of these things. [31] So this is the beginning of the charge: "Demosthenes makes the following charges against Aphobus. Aphobus has money of mine which he held as a guardian: 80 minas, which he received as a dowry for my mother in accordance with my father's will." That's the first of the sums of which I say I have been deprived. And what testimony was given by the witnesses? "They testify that they were present before the arbitrator Notharchus when Aphobus acknowledged that Milyas was a free man, having been set free by Demosthenes' father." [32] Now, just consider for yourselves whether you think there could be any orator or sophist or magician so marvellously clever at speaking that from that testimony he could convince anyone at all that Aphobus had his mother's dowry. What would he say, I ask you by Zeus? "He acknowledged that Milyas was a free man"? And why does that make him any more in possession of the dowry? That fact surely would not make him appear so. [33] So how was it shown? First, Therippides, who was his fellow-guardian, testified that he had given it to him.[29] Second, his uncle Demon and others who were present testified that Aphobus agreed to give my mother maintenance because he had her dowry. He didn't make any accusation against those witnesses, evidently because he knew their testimony was true. Besides, my mother was willing to set myself and my sister beside her and give a pledge by us that Aphobus had received her dowry in accordance with my father's will. [34] Are we to say that he has these 80 minas, or not? And that he was convicted because of these witnesses, or because of those? I think it was because of the truth. After enjoying the profits of that money for ten years, and being so brazen as not to repay it even when convicted, he says that he's been badly treated and was convicted because of these witnesses. Yet none of these testified that he had the dowry.

[35] Now let me tell you about the loan and the bed-makers and the

---

[29] In 27.13 we read that Therippides gave Aphobus only a part of the dowry, raised by the sale of slaves.

iron and the ivory left to me and my sister's dowry, which Aphobus allowed to be misappropriated[30] in order to keep for himself as much of my money as he wanted; consider how he has been justly convicted, and there was no need to interrogate Milyas about those. [36] [*To Aphobus*] With regard to what you allowed to be misappropriated, there's a law which explicitly states that you owe it just as if you had kept it yourself; so what relevance does interrogation under torture have to this law? With regard to the loan, you all collaborated with Xuthus,[31] shared out the money, and canceled the written agreements, and after arranging it all to suit yourselves and destroying the documents, as Demon testified against you, you bluster and try to hoodwink the jury. [37] With regard to the bed-makers, if you received cash for them, made a large personal profit by lending on the security of my property—though it was your duty to prevent others from doing that—and then have made away with them,[32] what do these witnesses have to do with you? They did not testify that you admitted lending on the security of my property and taking over the slaves; you wrote that in the accounts yourself, and it was attested against you by the witnesses.[33] [38] [*To the jury*] Then with regard to the ivory and the iron, I can say that all the servants know that Aphobus was selling them; I offered before, and I offer again now, to hand over to him any of them he wishes to take for interrogation under torture. If he says I refused to hand over the man who knew about it and offered to give up only those who didn't know, that will make it all the more obvious that he should have accepted them; for if the men I offered to give up as being ones who knew the facts denied that he had any of those materials, he would surely have been exonerated. [39] But that's not the way it is; it would have been clearly proved that he was selling them and had kept the money. That's why he ignored the men who were agreed to be slaves and demanded for interrogation the free man whom it wasn't right to hand over. He didn't wish to get proof of the point, but wanted it to be thought that, if he wasn't given the man, there was

---

[30] Aphobus allowed Demophon to keep the dowry of Demosthenes' sister without marrying her.

[31] The borrower; cf. 27.11.

[32] On these maneuvers, see 27.24–28.

[33] The witnesses who testified at the end of 27.26.

something in what he said. Now with regard to all these matters—first the dowry, then the money he allowed to be misappropriated, and then the other things—the clerk will read the laws and the testimonies, to give you the facts.

[LAWS, TESTIMONIES]

[40] It's not only from those that you can tell he hasn't suffered any terrible consequence from my refusal to give the man up for interrogation; you can also tell by consideration of the actual facts. Let's imagine that Milyas is being tortured on the wheel, and think what Aphobus would most desire him to say. Wouldn't it be that he did not know Aphobus had any of the money? Well, suppose he says that. Does that mean he doesn't have it? Far from it; for I produced as witnesses the men who were present and know the facts.[34] It's an argument and a proof, not if there is someone who doesn't know that Aphobus has something (there'd be lots of those), but if someone does know. [41] [To Aphobus] So, when all those witnesses testified against you, against which one did you make an accusation of false witness? Point him out. You can't point him out. But surely you're proving clearly that you're a liar when you assert that you've been badly treated and unjustly convicted because the man wasn't handed over to you, and yet you failed to prosecute for false witness the men who testified that you took and kept the property, about which you demanded Milyas for interrogation claiming that it had not been left me. They are the men whom it was much more appropriate to prosecute, if you'd been wronged. But you haven't been wronged; you're just making a malicious accusation.

[42] There are many ways in which one can see your villainy, but particularly if one hears about the will. Although my father, men of the jury, specified in his will all the property which he left, and that they should lease the estate, Aphobus did not produce the will, so that I would not find out from it the amount of the property, but he acknowledged the items which it was hardest to deny because they were conspicuous. [43] These are the things which he says were written in the will: Demophon was to receive 2 talents immediately and my sis-

---

[34] The oldest manuscript adds "and paid it," but those words are omitted in the other manuscripts.

ter when she was old enough, which would be in the tenth year after-wards;[35] Aphobus, 80 minas and my mother and the house for his residence; Therippides was to have the use of 70 minas until I became adult. Everything that was left me apart from that, and the leasing of the estate, he suppressed from the will, thinking that it was not to his advantage to have these items revealed to you in court. [44] Since Aphobus himself had acknowledged that my father at his death gave so much money to each of them, the jury in that case took these acknowledgments as an indication of the size of his property. If he gave as dowries and gifts 4 talents 3,000 drachmas out of what he possessed, it was obvious that the property he was leaving to me, from which he took those sums, was not a small one but more than double that amount.[36] [45] It would not have seemed likely that he wanted to make me, his son, poor, while desiring to make these men, who were rich, still richer; rather, that it was because of the large amount of what was being left to me that he gave Therippides the 70 minas and Demo-phon the 2 talents to use, although he wasn't going to marry my sister yet. It was clear that Aphobus had never handed that money over, nor even a little less than that. Some, he said, he'd spent; some he hadn't received; some he didn't know about; some was kept by So-and-so; some was in the house; some—he could say anything rather than when he handed it over.

[46] With regard to the money not being left in the house, I want to show you clearly that he's lying. He slipped this story in when it became evident that the property was large and he could not show that he had paid it back; his aim was to make it seem likely that I was trying, quite inappropriately, to recover what was actually in my premises. [47] If[37] my father had distrusted these men, obviously he would not have entrusted the rest of his property to them, and if he left that money in hiding, he wouldn't have told them; so how do they know about it? But if he did trust them, he surely wouldn't have put most of his money in their hands and not given them charge of the rest.

---

[35] She was five when her father died (27.4); so this passage shows that the fif-teenth year of age was considered the earliest suitable time for a woman's marriage.

[36] Demosthenes here repeats some wording from 27.44–45.

[37] The wording of 29.47–49 is nearly the same as 27.55–57.

Nor would he have given this money to my mother to look after while betrothing her in marriage herself to Aphobus, who was one of the guardians: it doesn't make sense to try to protect the money by means of my mother while putting one of the men he distrusted in charge of both her and the money. [48] Besides, if any of this were true, do you think Aphobus would not have married her, when she was given to him by my father? He already had her dowry of 80 minas as her future husband, but then he married the daughter of Philonides of Melite out of avarice, in order to get another 80 minas from him in addition to what he had from me. If there had been 4 talents in the house in my mother's possession, as he alleges, don't you think he would have rushed to get control of it along with her? [49] He and his fellow-guardians seized so disgracefully the visible property which many of you too were aware my father had left: would he have refrained from taking, when he could, money of which you were not likely to have any knowledge? Who could believe that? It can't be so, men of the jury, it can't be. All the money which my father left was buried on the day when it fell into the hands of these men; and Aphobus, being unable to say when he repaid any of it, tells this story to make me seem to be well off and so get no sympathy from you.

[50] There are many other accusations I could make against this man, but I can't speak about offenses against myself when it's the witness's citizen-rights that are at risk.[38] But I want to read you a challenge; for you'll understand from it, when you hear it, that the witness's statements are true, and that, whereas Aphobus now says he was asking for Milyas to be handed over for interrogation about everything, at first he asked for him with regard to 30 minas only, and moreover he's not suffering any loss as a result of the testimony. [51] I wanted to refute him on every point and was trying to make his trickery and dishonesty plain to you, and so I asked him what was the total amount of the property with regard to which he had asked for Milyas, claiming that he had knowledge of it. He said, "All of it," which was a lie. "Well," I said, "concerning this, I will hand over to you the man who has the copy of the challenge you made me. [52] Then, when I have sworn first that you acknowledged that the man was free

---

[38] See 29.16n.

and you testified to that effect against Demon, if you swear by your daughter[39] the contrary of that, I will then give up to you the whole of the amount with regard to which you are shown, by interrogation of the slave under torture, to have been asking for the man at the beginning; the payment which you were condemned to make shall be reduced by the amount with regard to which you asked for Milyas, so that you won't suffer a loss in consequence of the witnesses." [53] I made this challenge, and many people were there to hear it, but he refused to do that. But if he has avoided giving this judgment in his own favor, how can it be right for you, who are under oath, to believe him and convict the witnesses? Shouldn't you rather consider him the most shameless man in the world? [*To the clerk*] To prove that what I say is true, call the witnesses of this.

[WITNESSES]

[54] I was not the only person ready to do this; the witnesses' view was the same as mine. They set their children beside them and offered to give a pledge by them to confirm the testimony they gave. But Aphobus refused to administer the oath either to them or to me. He has based his case on invented stories and witnesses who habitually give untrue testimony, and he hopes that he'll easily deceive you. [*To the clerk*] Take this testimony also for them.

[TESTIMONY]

[55] So how could anyone prove more clearly that we are being accused maliciously, that the testimony given against him is true, and that he was justly convicted, than by demonstrating in this way that Aphobus refused to interrogate about the actual testimony the slave who wrote it down, that his brother Aesius gave the testimony which he says is false, [56] that he himself gave for me against Demon, who is his uncle and fellow-guardian,[40] the same testimony as the witnesses whom he's prosecuting, that he refused to interrogate the slave-women on the subject of the man's freedom, that my mother offered to give a

---

[39] Aphobus was to invoke misfortune upon his daughter if he was not telling the truth. Presumably his daughter was his only child.

[40] On Demon's position, see p. 000.

pledge by us concerning this, that he refused to accept for interrogation any of the other servants who knew about everything better than Milyas did, that he did not make an accusation of false witness against any of the witnesses who testified that he had kept money, [57] that he did not produce the will or lease the estate as authorized by the laws, and that he thought fit not to give a pledge, after the witnesses and I had sworn, so as to be let off payment of the amount with regard to which he asked for Milyas to be handed over? I declare by the gods, I could not prove the case more thoroughly in any other way. It's so obvious that he is lying about the witnesses, and has suffered no loss from what has been done, and has been justly convicted—and yet he behaves in this shameless manner!

[58] If he had made these claims without having been previously condemned both by his own friends and by the arbitrator,[41] it would be less surprising. But in fact he persuaded me to entrust the case to Archeneos, Dracontides, and Phanus here, whom he is now prosecuting for false witness.[42] He dismissed them when they told him that, if they gave their decision under oath, they would find him guilty for his guardianship; but when he went to the arbitrator appointed by lot[43] and was unable to refute the charges, the arbitration was decided against him. [59] The jury, to which he appealed, heard the case, gave the same verdict as his friends and the arbitrator, and condemned him to pay 10 talents; and, by Zeus, that was not because he had acknowledged that Milyas was a free man, which was of no significance, but because, when property worth 15 talents had been left me, he did not lease the estate but, managing it for ten years with his fellow-guardians, he arranged on my behalf, as I was a child, to make contributions of 5 minas to the symmory, as much as Timotheus son of Conon and men with the highest assessments contributed,[44]

---

[41] The public arbitrator; cf. 27.49–52.

[42] This abortive attempt to obtain a private arbitration in the original dispute between Demosthenes and Aphobus is mentioned briefly in 27.1 and 30.2. On private arbitration, see the introduction to Oration 33. Archeneos and Dracontides are not mentioned elsewhere.

[43] The public arbitrator.

[44] See 27.7.

[60] and, after such a long time as guardian of the property for which he thought it right to contribute so much *eisphora,* what he passed on to me on his own account was worth less than 20 minas, and along with the others, he deprived me of the capital and the profits entirely. So the jurors, reckoning the interest on the whole property not at the rate at which estates are leased but at the lowest rate, found that altogether they were misappropriating more than 30 talents; therefore, they fixed the sum payable by this man at 10 talents.

30. AGAINST ONETOR I

◊◊

INTRODUCTION

The dispute between Demosthenes and Onetor was an outgrowth of the dispute between Demosthenes and Aphobus, outlined in the Introduction to this volume (pp. 9–11). Demosthenes was trying to recover the sum of 10 talents awarded to him by the court at the trial of Aphobus, and so he attempted to take possession of Aphobus' farm; but Onetor, Aphobus' brother-in-law, kept him out of it, claiming that it now belonged to him. Demosthenes therefore is bringing against Onetor a case of ejectment (*dikē exoulēs*). If he wins it, Onetor will have to leave the farm, and Demosthenes will have authority to seize it by force if necessary; Onetor will also have to pay to the state treasury a fine equal to the value of the farm. The date is 362/1 or early in 361/0 BC.[1]

The events leading up to this dispute were as follows. Onetor's sister, whose name is not known, had first been married to a man named Timocrates. Timocrates was an affluent person (his property is said in 30.10 to have been worth more than 10 talents), but it is not certain that he is to be identified with any of the other men of that name who are known; it was a common name. Onetor himself was even more affluent (with property said to have been worth more than 30 talents). He was the son of Philonides of Melite, a rich man who was satirized

---

[1] Aphobus' divorce from Onetor's sister was registered in Posideon, the sixth month of 364/3 (30.15), and she was not then married to anyone else "in three years" (30.33). That probably means within the three calendar years 364/3, 363/2, and 362/1, indicating merely that the year 362/1 had by now begun; it could, however, mean the period of three full years to Posideon 361/0.

in comedy of the previous generation[2] but who had died by the 360s, leaving Onetor as head of the family. Onetor, who had been a pupil of Isocrates,[3] had somehow formed a friendship with Aphobus and wanted to give him his sister in marriage. Timocrates apparently had no objection,[4] and her second wedding took place in the summer of 366, just before Demosthenes came of age.[5]

Timocrates should then have given her dowry back to Onetor, to be passed on to Aphobus. However, the three men agreed that the dowry, which was the substantial sum of 1 talent, should not be handed over immediately but retained by Timocrates, who would meanwhile pay Aphobus interest on it at a moderate rate. Demosthenes in his speech rightly focuses attention on this odd arrangement: surely Timocrates and Onetor were well enough off to have been able to pay the dowry immediately. Demosthenes' explanation is that they had already foreseen that Aphobus might be condemned to surrender most or all of his property to Demosthenes, and they were guarding against the risk of losing the dowry.

When a woman was given in marriage with a dowry, it was common to mark off (with *horoi*, marker-stones) some part of her husband's property, usually some land, at least equal in value to the dowry, so that, if the marriage ended and she returned to her original family but the husband failed to return the dowry, her family could claim that item of property instead.[6] When Demosthenes tried to take possession of Aphobus' farm, Onetor pointed out stones that marked the land as property due to be taken by Onetor because his sister's dowry had not been returned to him by Aphobus when they were divorced. But had they really been divorced? Onetor asserted that she had "departed" from Aphobus, and the divorce had been duly registered with

---

[2] Aristoph., *Wealth* 179, 303.

[3] Isoc. 15.93.

[4] According to Libanius' *hypothesis* to Oration 30, Timocrates was going to marry an heiress, but no earlier evidence confirms that.

[5] See the genealogy on p. 8.

[6] The legal problems of real security in Athens, including the functions of *horoi* and the valuation and setting apart (*apotimēma*) of property for this purpose, have been much discussed. Earlier work has now been superseded by Harris 1988 and 1993.

the Archon. But did that registration record a true fact? Anyway, surely
Aphobus did not have to return the dowry, because he had never received it in the first place? Oh yes, he had: Onetor, Timocrates, and
Aphobus himself all affirmed that the dowry was paid. Demosthenes
did not believe this story, and he argues in his speech that it had been
concocted as a device for keeping Aphobus' farm out of his hands.

30. AGAINST ONETOR FOR EJECTMENT I

[1] I would very much have liked, men of the jury, to avoid both
my previous dispute with Aphobus and my present one with this man
Onetor, his brother-in-law, but although I made both of them many
fair offers, I could not obtain any reasonable settlement, but have found
Onetor much more unaccommodating than Aphobus and more deserving of punishment. [2] In the case of Aphobus, although I thought
he should accept our friends' verdict[7] about his differences with me
and not resort to your trial,[8] I was unable to persuade him. But when
I urged Onetor to be the judge in his own case, to avoid the risks of
your court, he treated me with such contempt that he not only did not
allow me to speak to him but he expelled me in a most insulting manner from the land which Aphobus possessed at the time when he lost
the case against me. [3] So, since he is assisting his brother-in-law in
depriving me of my property and has come before you relying on his
own scheming, it remains for me to attempt to obtain justice from
him before you. I know, men of the jury, that I have to contend against
verbal scheming and witnesses who will give untrue testimony. Nevertheless, I think I shall so far surpass him by the greater justice of my
case [4] that, even if any of you previously supposed that he was not
dishonest, you'll certainly realize from his conduct towards me that in
the past too you failed to notice that he was an utterly wicked criminal. I shall show that not only did he never pay the dowry, for return
of which he now says the land was valued as security, but he plotted
from the beginning to obtain my possessions; and, in addition, that

---

[7] The private arbitration mentioned in 29.58.

[8] Here, as often when addressing a jury, Demosthenes calls the jury in another
case "you," even though it was not composed of the same individuals.

the woman on whose behalf he excluded me from this land has not left her husband, [5] and that he is shielding Aphobus and submitting to this litigation in the hope of depriving me of my possessions. I shall show all this by such strong arguments and clear proofs that you will all be certain that it is just and appropriate for him to face this prosecution by me. I'll try to explain it all to you, beginning from the point which will make it easiest for you to understand it.[9]

[6] I was badly treated by my guardians, men of the jury, as was observed by many other Athenians as well as by Onetor. It was obvious that I was being wronged from the start: there were so many proceedings and discussions about my affairs, both before the Archon and before others.[10] The quantity of property left me was plain, and the fact that the estate was not leased[11] by those in charge of it, so that they might have the use of the money themselves, was not hard to see. So everyone who knew what was going on expected me to obtain compensation from them as soon as I was certified as an adult.[12] [7] Timocrates and Onetor among others held this opinion all along. There is the strongest possible indication of that: Onetor wanted to give his sister in marriage to Aphobus, seeing that he had got control of my substantial property in addition to his own patrimony; but he did not have the confidence to hand over the dowry, apparently regarding the property of guardians as a security liable to be surrendered to their wards. Still, he gave him his sister, and Timocrates, the woman's previous husband, agreed to owe him the dowry at interest of 5 obols.[13] [8] When Aphobus lost the guardianship case to me and refused to fulfill his obligations, Onetor did not even attempt to mediate a settlement between us. Although he had not paid the dowry but had it under his own control, he claimed that his sister had left her husband and that he was unable to recover what he had given, and alleging that

---

[9] This sentence is repeated from the end of 27.3.

[10] The Archon had a general responsibility to see that satisfactory arrangements were made for the care of orphans (children left with no father, not necessarily with no mother). The "others" were probably relatives and friends, rather than other officials.

[11] See 27.58–59.

[12] See 27.5n.

[13] A lower rate of interest than was usual: 5 obols per mina per month = 10 percent per annum; cf. 27.17.

he had accepted the land as security, he went so far as to expel me from it—he had such contempt for me and you and the established laws. [9] Those facts are the reasons why he is being prosecuted and the issues about which you will cast your votes, men of the jury. As witnesses, I shall produce first Timocrates himself, to testify that he agreed he would owe the dowry and paid the interest on the dowry in accordance with their agreement, and also that Aphobus himself acknowledged receiving the interest from Timocrates. [*To the clerk*] Please take the testimonies.

[TESTIMONIES]

[10] So it is agreed that at the start the dowry was not paid and Aphobus didn't get possession of it. And it's an obvious presumption that it was for the reasons I have stated that they chose to owe the dowry rather than add it to Aphobus' property, which was likely to be at risk in this way. One can't say it was because of poverty that they didn't pay it immediately; for Timocrates has property worth more than 10 talents, and Onetor more than 30, so that that couldn't be the reason for not paying straightaway. [11] Nor was it the case that they had property but no ready cash and the woman was widowed, and that it was for that reason that they hurried on the marriage without paying the dowry at the same time; for these men lend substantial amounts of cash to other people, and the woman was a wife, not a widow, when they gave her away in marriage from Timocrates' house, so that one can't accept that from them as a reasonable excuse either. [12] And besides, men of the jury, I'm sure you would all agree with the view that anyone making an arrangement of this sort would prefer to owe money to someone else, rather than fail to pay a brother-in-law the dowry. For if he doesn't settle that, he becomes a debtor, and it is uncertain whether he will pay what is due or not; but if along with the woman he hands over what belongs to her, he becomes a relative and a brother-in-law. [13] He falls under no suspicion, because he has fulfilled all his obligations. So, since that was the situation, and they were not compelled to delay payment for any of the reasons I have mentioned, and would not have wished to do so, it's impossible to give any other pretext for their failure to hand it over, and it must have been for the reason I stated that they did not have the confidence to pay the dowry. [14] So I can prove that point indisputably in that way, and I think I shall easily demonstrate from the actual facts that they did not pay it

later either; this will make it clear to you that even if it wasn't for those reasons but with the intention of paying it soon that they retained the money, they never would have paid it or let it out of their hands; the situation imposed such constraints on them. [15] There were two years between the woman's marriage and the time of her alleged departure from her husband:[14] the wedding was in the Archonship of Polyzelus in the month of Scirophorion,[15] and her departure was registered in Posideon of the year of Timocrates.[16] Having been passed as an adult[17] immediately after the wedding, I began bringing charges and demanding accounts, and because I was being robbed of everything, I began initiating the prosecutions in the same Archonship.[18] [16] That timing makes it possible that he owed the dowry in accordance with their agreement, but it is not credible that he paid it. For since his original reason for choosing to owe it and pay interest was to avoid risking the dowry along with the rest of the property, how can it be that he paid it when the man was already facing prosecution? Even if he'd trusted him earlier, by then he would have wanted to get it back! It surely can't be so, men of the jury. [17] To prove that the woman's wedding was at the time I say, and we had already become litigants against each other in the intervening period, and it was after I initiated the prosecution that these men registered with the Archon her departure from her husband, [*To the clerk*] please take these testimonies on each point.

[TESTIMONY]

After that Archon there were Cephisodorus and Chion.[19] In their years I was certified as an adult and began bringing charges, and I ini-

---

[14] This refers to her marriage to Aphobus, not to Timocrates.

[15] Approximately June 366.

[16] Approximately December 364. Presumably the Archon was a different man from the woman's previous husband; Timocrates was a common name.

[17] See 27.5n. It is probable that the *dokimasia* took place at the beginning of the new year in the summer.

[18] This means the Archonship of Timocrates (364/3), not that of Demosthenes' *dokimasia*, as 30.17 shows. During the intervening two years, we may assume, Demosthenes was making his investigations and accusations informally, and also was performing his military service as an ephebe.

[19] Cephisodorus was the Archon in 366/5, Chion in 365/4.

tiated the prosecution in the year of Timocrates. [*To the clerk*] Take this testimony.

[TESTIMONY]

[18] Read this testimony too.

[TESTIMONY]

It's clear from what has been testified that they did not pay the dowry, but had the audacity to act in this way in order to preserve the property for Aphobus. When they say that within such a short time they owed the money and they paid it and the woman left her husband and they didn't recover it and they took the land as security, isn't it obvious that they're attempting to disguise the matter and deprive me of what you awarded me?

[19] Also from the answers given by Onetor himself and Timocrates and Aphobus it's impossible that the dowry has been paid, as I shall now try to explain to you. I asked each of them, men of the jury, in the presence of many witnesses, Onetor and Timocrates whether there were any witnesses present when they paid the dowry, and Aphobus himself whether any were there when he received it. [20] Each one of them gave me the answer that no witness was present but Aphobus collected from them in installments as much as he asked for. But the dowry was a talent, and can any of you believe that Onetor and Timocrates handed over such a large sum to Aphobus without witnesses? He's a man whom one wouldn't readily trust when paying money, not just in that manner, but even with many witnesses—to ensure that, if any dispute arose, one would be able to recover it easily in your court. [21] No one carrying out such a transaction, not merely with a man like Aphobus but with anyone else, would have acted without witnesses. For acts of this kind we hold wedding ceremonies and invite our closest relatives, because we are dealing with no trivial matter but the lives of our sisters and daughters, for whom we take the greatest precautions. [22] So one would expect that Onetor too, if he had really paid Aphobus the dowry, would have settled his account with him in the presence of the same witnesses before whom he had agreed to owe the dowry and pay the interest. If he had acted in that manner, he would have disposed of the whole business, but by paying one-to-one he would have left those who were present at the original agreement

as witnesses that he still owed it. [23] As it is, they couldn't persuade members of their family, more honest than themselves, to testify that they'd paid the dowry, and if they produced witnesses who were not related to them, they thought you wouldn't believe them. Besides, if they alleged they'd given him the dowry in a single payment, they knew we would ask for the slaves who delivered it[20] to be handed over for interrogation, and if they hadn't made the payment and refused to hand them over, they would be refuted; whereas if they said they'd paid it by themselves one-to-one in that manner, they thought they wouldn't be refuted. [24] That's why they had to choose to lie in this manner. By such dishonest tricks they expected to appear to be straightforward people and thought they would easily take you in, although where their interests were concerned they wouldn't carry out even a small transaction straightforwardly, but as strictly as possible. [*To the clerk*] Take for the jury the testimonies of the men before whom they gave their answers, and read them.

[TESTIMONIES]

[25] Well now, men of the jury, I shall also demonstrate to you that, although the woman is said to have left Aphobus, in fact she is living with him; for if you hear the details of this, I think you're more likely to distrust these men and give me the support I deserve for the wrongs done me. For some points I shall provide witnesses, and for others, strong arguments and adequate proofs. [26] After this woman's departure from her husband was registered with the Archon, men of the jury, and Onetor asserted that he had taken the land as security in place of the dowry, I saw that Aphobus was carrying on just as before, farming the ground and living with the woman, and I knew very well that all this was a story and a distortion of the facts. [27] Wishing to make this plain to you all, I proposed that Onetor should refute me in front of witnesses if he denied that it was so, and I offered to hand over for interrogation under torture a slave who had full knowledge of everything; he was one of Aphobus' slaves whom I had got because his

---

[20] A talent of silver (6,000 drachmas) would be a substantial weight, which Onetor and Timocrates would be unlikely to carry themselves.

payments to me were overdue.[21] When I made this proposal, Onetor declined the interrogation of the slave concerning the fact that his sister was living with Aphobus; but he couldn't deny that Aphobus was farming the ground, because it was obvious, and he acknowledged it.

[28] It was easy to tell that Aphobus was still living with the woman and in possession of the land before the trial was held, not only from this but also from what he did with them after losing the case. On the assumption that he had not given them as security but they would now belong to me in accordance with the judgment, he went off with the items which it was possible to carry away, the produce and all the agricultural equipment except the storage jars;[22] what it was impossible to remove he of necessity left behind, making it possible for Onetor now to claim the actual ground. [29] But it's strange for one man to say he's taken the land as security while the other, who has given it as security, is seen to be farming it; and to assert that his sister has left her husband but blatantly avoid the proof of these very matters; and for the man who is not living with her, according to Onetor, to be carrying off the produce and everything belonging to the farm, while the other, who is acting for the departed woman, for whom he says he's taken the land as security, is manifestly not complaining about any of this but quietly accepting it. [30] Isn't it perfectly plain? Isn't it undeniable concealment? Anyone duly examining each point would surely say so. So to prove that he acknowledged that Aphobus was doing the farming before my case against him was tried, and that he refused to hold the interrogation under torture concerning the fact that his sister was not living with her husband, and that after the trial the farm was stripped of its equipment except what was in the ground, [*To the clerk*] take these testimonies and read them.

[TESTIMONIES]

[31] There are all these arguments in my support, and, not least, Onetor himself showed that he did not regard the departure from her

---

[21] That is, the slave was one of the items of Aphobus' property which Demosthenes had taken to make up the sum Aphobus had been condemned to pay him.

[22] From 30.30 it appears that the jars were in or under the ground and so were difficult to move.

husband as genuine. He should have been indignant if, after paying the dowry, as he claims, he got back some disputed land instead of cash; but in fact he supported Aphobus in the trial against me, not as an adversary or a victim but as his closest relative. Along with him, he did his best to deprive me of my patrimony, although I'd never done him any harm at all; whereas for Aphobus, whom he should have considered to be an opponent if any of what they're now saying were true, he attempted to secure my property to add to what he had. [32] He not only did that at the trial, but even after the verdict had been given, he went up in front of the court and asked and begged the jury on behalf of Aphobus and entreated them with tears in his eyes to fix the amount payable at a talent,[23] for which he himself was prepared to be guarantor. That is confirmed from many sources, because it is known to those who were jurors at that trial and to many of the spectators; nevertheless, I'll also produce witnesses for you. [*To the clerk*] Please take this testimony.

[TESTIMONY]

[33] Besides, men of the jury, there is a strong indication which makes it easy to tell that she was really living with him and to this day has never left him. This woman, before going to Aphobus, was not without a husband for a single day. Timocrates was alive when she left his house and went to live with Aphobus, and now it's clear that in three years[24] she hasn't been living with anyone else. On that occasion she went from husband to husband to avoid being unmarried, and can anyone believe that this time, if she had really left Aphobus, she would put up with being unmarried when she could be married to someone else, since her brother possesses so much property and she is so young? [34] It's not credible that that's true, men of the jury; it's a story. The woman is openly living with her husband and doesn't disguise the

---

[23] After the jury gave its verdict against Aphobus, it had to decide the amount of the compensation which Aphobus should pay to Demosthenes. This sentence shows that Aphobus proposed that it should be 1 talent. However, the jury accepted Demosthenes' proposal of 10 talents.

[24] On the interpretation of this date, see p. 67, n.1.

fact.[25] I'll produce for you the testimony of Pasiphon,[26] who attended her when she was sick and saw Aphobus sitting beside her within this year, after this case had already been initiated against Onetor. [*To the clerk*] Please take Pasiphon's testimony.

[TESTIMONY]

[35] Since I was aware, men of the jury, that immediately after the trial Onetor had taken in the items from Aphobus' house and had both his and my possessions entirely under his control, and I knew very well that the woman was living with him, I asked him to hand over three female slaves, who knew that the woman was living with him and that the things were in their house, so that these facts might be the subject not just of assertions but of interrogations under torture. [36] But when I made this challenge and everyone present declared that what I said was fair, he refused to resort to this test, and—as if any other clearer proofs existed about such matters than interrogations and testimonies—he neither produced witnesses that he had paid the dowry nor handed over for interrogation the women who knew about his sister not[27] living with her husband, but because I made this request he refused, in a very insolent and abusive manner, to let me speak with him. Could any man be more brazen, or more ready to pretend ignorance of what is right? [*To the clerk*] Take the actual challenge and read it.

[CHALLENGE]

[37] Now,[28] you all consider interrogation under torture to be the most reliable of all methods of proof in both private and public affairs,

---

[25] Aphobus had left his own house to be taken over by Demosthenes, and had formally taken up residence in Megara (29.3). But presumably, he made frequent visits to Attica during which he stayed at Onetor's house, where Onetor's sister was now residing.

[26] Evidently a doctor.

[27] Some manuscripts omit "not," perhaps rightly.

[28] This passage (the whole of 30.37) is a close imitation of a passage of Isaeus (8.12).

and whenever slaves and free men are present and the facts need to be ascertained, you don't make use of the free men's testimonies, but you seek to discover the truth by interrogating the slaves. That's quite reasonable, men of the jury: some of those who have testified before now have been found to have given untrue testimony, but it has never been proved that any of those interrogated under torture have made untrue statements in consequence of the interrogation. [38] But Onetor has avoided such fair tests, and has ignored such strong and clear proofs. Instead, he produces Aphobus and Timocrates as witnesses, the latter to testify that he paid the dowry and the former that he received it, and he will ask you to believe him when he pretends that his transaction with them was carried out without witnesses; that's how simple-minded he's decided you are. [39] So their assertions will be neither true nor anything like the truth, as has I think been adequately proved both by their original acknowledgment that they had not paid the dowry, and by their subsequent allegation that they paid it without witnesses, and by there not being enough time for them to have paid the money when the property was already in dispute, and by everything else.

31. AGAINST ONETOR II

INTRODUCTION

For his prosecution of Onetor, as for his prosecution of Aphobus (see p. 16), Demosthenes has thought it worthwhile to draft some material for use in his second speech. But this draft is even more incomplete than the draft of the second speech against Aphobus. It begins with an announcement that Demosthenes will first present to the jury another indication, not included in the first speech, that Onetor and Timocrates never paid the dowry to Aphobus, and will afterwards "refute the lies this man has told you." In fact, the text that we have contains no such refutation, and this is a clear sign that it is a script written before the trial. Demosthenes evidently prepared his second speech as best he could by writing an opening passage which he was sure of being able to use, and he relied on extemporization for answering whatever points Onetor might make in his first speech.

The fresh point made about the dowry is that Onetor was inconsistent in his statements about it. At first he said that the amount was 8,000 drachmas (= 80 minas), and he placed markers (*horoi*)[1] on Aphobus' house for 2,000 drachmas and on the farm for 6,000 drachmas (= 1 talent). That was before the trial of Aphobus. But when Aphobus was convicted, Onetor realized that they could not hope to get free of the business without letting Demosthenes take over at least one substantial item of Aphobus' property. He therefore removed the markers from the house and said the dowry he had paid was only 6,000 drachmas. Since he appeared not to know how much he had paid, Demosthenes infers that he had paid nothing.

---

[1] On the use of *horoi* to mark property as security for a dowry, see p. 68.

Two rather weak arguments follow, about the likelihood that Onetor would have sworn a false oath (though in fact he did not), and about his friendly relationship with Aphobus. Some arguments from the first speech are repeated, and then the draft breaks off.

31. AGAINST ONETOR FOR EJECTMENT II

[1] I omitted in my previous speech an indication, no less important than any of those I included, that these men did not pay the dowry to Aphobus; so I'll explain that to you first, and afterwards attempt to refute the lies this man has told you. At the time when this man first planned to claim Aphobus' property, men of the jury, he didn't say that the amount of the dowry he had paid was a talent, as he says now, but that it was 80 minas, and he placed markers on the house for 2,000 drachmas and on the land for a talent, wanting to safeguard the former as well as the latter for him. [2] But after the trial of my case against Aphobus, seeing what your attitude is towards criminals who are too impudent, he came to his senses: he realized that I would appear to have been seriously mistreated if, after being deprived of so much money, I wasn't able to get anything at all of the property of Aphobus, who had kept mine, and Onetor was openly preventing me from doing that. [3] So what does he do? He takes the markers away from the house and says that the dowry was only a talent, for which the land was valued as security. Yet plainly, if the markers he placed on the house were right and truly correct, the ones he placed on the land were also right; but if the former ones were false because he had criminal intentions from the start, it's likely that the latter ones were untrue too. [4] So you must consider this point not from my account but from the man's own behavior. No one at all compelled him, but he removed the markers himself, making it clear by his action that he was lying. To prove that what I say is true, that he asserts even now that the land was security for a talent, and that he placed additional markers on the house for 2,000 drachmas and removed them again after the trial was held, I'll produce the men who know the facts as witnesses for you. [*To the clerk*] Please take the testimony.

[TESTIMONY]

[5] So it's clear that, when he put markers on the house for 2,000 drachmas and on the land for a talent, he was intending to make a claim

on the basis that he had paid 80 minas. Could you have any stronger indication that nothing of what he says now is true than if it's shown that his assertions are not consistent with what he originally said on the same subject? I don't think you could find anything stronger.

[6] Just consider the impudence of the man, who had the audacity to say before you that he was not depriving me of the amount by which the value of the land exceeds a talent,[2] even though he assessed its value as being no higher. [*To Onetor*] What reason had you to put additional markers on the house, at the time when you alleged that 80 minas was owed you, if the land was worth more? Why didn't you put markers on it for the 2,000 drachmas too? [7] Or is it the case that, whenever you think that you're safeguarding all of Aphobus' property, the land will be worth only a talent, and you'll hold the house to count for 2,000 drachmas in addition, and the dowry will then be 80 minas, and you'll demand to keep both the land and the house; but whenever it's not to your advantage, on the other hand, the house will be worth a talent, because it's now in my possession, and the extra value of the land will be not less than 2 talents, so that it may appear that I am defrauding Aphobus, not being robbed myself? [8] Do you see how, though you pretend to have paid the dowry, it's obvious that you haven't paid it in any way whatever? For business which is truly and honestly done simply remains just as it was done originally, but you are proved to have done the opposite in assisting Aphobus against me.

[9] [*To the jury*] Now, it's worthwhile also to see from the following facts what sort of an oath he would have sworn, if he'd been required to. He said the dowry was 80 minas: if he'd been permitted to recover it at that time on condition that he swore that that was true, what would he have done? Isn't it obvious that he'd have sworn? How can he deny that he'd have sworn then, since he offers to do so now? So he proves against himself that he'd have committed perjury; for now he says that the sum he gave was not 80 minas but a talent. Why is it any more reasonable to believe that his earlier assertion was perjurious than his present one? What is the right view to take of this man, who so readily convicts himself of perjury?

---

[2] That is, Onetor said that, although the farm was worth more than a talent, he would hand it over to Demosthenes if Demosthenes paid the sum of a talent which Onetor claimed Aphobus owed him.

[10] "Oh, but perhaps not all his actions were of that sort, and it's not clear that he was scheming on every occasion." But he openly advocated an assessment of a talent on Aphobus' behalf,[3] and besides offered to guarantee its payment to me himself. Yet notice that that's an indication not only that the woman is living with Aphobus as his wife and Onetor is on close terms with him, but also that he did not pay the dowry. [11] For what man is so foolish that, after handing over so much money and then receiving as security only a piece of land of disputed ownership, he would add to his previous losses by giving additional support to the offender—as if he could be trusted to do the right thing!—in the form of a guarantee for the sum he was condemned to pay? No one, I think. It's not even a rational action for a man who is unable to recover a talent owed to himself to say he'll pay it for someone else and to guarantee that. From these facts alone it's clear that he did not pay the dowry, but, being a close friend of Aphobus, he was willing to take those items as security in return for getting a large amount of my property, hoping to make his sister, along with Aphobus, an inheritor of what belonged to me. [12] And then he's now trying to mislead and delude you by saying that he set up the markers before Aphobus was found guilty. [*To Onetor*] Not before *you* found him so, if you're telling the truth now; for it's clear that you did it after concluding that he was in the wrong. [*To the jury*] And isn't it ridiculous for him to say this, as if you didn't know that all men who commit offenses of this sort think out what they are going to say, and no one who is found guilty ever remains silent or admits his guilt; but I suppose it's after he's proved to be lying that you can tell what sort of a man he is. [13] That, I think, is now happening to Onetor. [*To Onetor*] After all, tell us, how can it be right that if you place markers for 80 minas, the dowry is 80 minas, and if for more, more, and if for less, less? Or how can it be right, when your sister has never to this day been married to anyone else or separated from Aphobus, and when you have not paid the dowry, and when you refuse to have recourse to interrogation under torture or any other test on this sub-

---

[3] At the trial of Aphobus, Onetor argued that the amount of compensation to be paid by Aphobus should be a talent, in opposition to Demosthenes' proposal of 10 talents; cf. 30.32.

ject, that the land belongs to you just because you say you set up markers? No way, I think. One has to look at the truth, not at what a person has deliberately concocted for himself to make an impression, like
you. [14] Then the most dreadful thing of all: even if you absolutely
had paid the dowry—which you haven't—whose responsibility is
that? Isn't it yours, since you paid it using my property as security?
Didn't Aphobus get and keep my property, for which he has been convicted, ten whole years before becoming your brother-in-law? Or is it
right that you should obtain all that, while I who brought the case,
and was victimized because I was orphaned, and was robbed of the real
dowry,[4] and who more than anyone don't deserve to lose even the
epōbelia,[5] have to undergo such treatment without recovering anything at all, even though I was willing to leave the matter in your own
hands,[6] if only you'd been willing to do anything that you ought?

---

[4] The dowry of Demosthenes' mother.
[5] See 27.67n.
[6] Avoiding the need for a court hearing; cf. 30.2.

32. AGAINST ZENOTHEMIS

INTRODUCTION

The speech *Against Zenothemis* is written for delivery by a cousin of Demosthenes named Demon, who was probably a son of the Demomeles son of Demon mentioned in 27.11 (as shown in the genealogy on p. 8).[1] Probably the text was written by Demosthenes, though some scholars have suggested that it was written by Demon himself. Demon has been prosecuted by Zenothemis, a man from Massalia (modern Marseille in southern France), and now brings a counter-indictment[2] against Zenothemis, claiming that the prosecution is inadmissible. The date of the speech is not known, but is likely to be between 353 and 340 BC.

According to Demon, what happened was this. Hegestratus, who like Zenothemis was a Massaliot, was the skipper of a ship on a voyage from Athens to Syracuse in Sicily and back. For the return voyage from Syracuse to Athens, a merchant named Protus (whose nationality is unknown, but he was not Athenian) put on board a cargo of grain purchased in Syracuse with money which had been lent to him in Athens by Demon and his partners. (The partners are mentioned in 32.21, but evidently Demon was the principal.) Hegestratus and his friend Zenothemis then planned a fraud. Each of them borrowed money in Syracuse, pretending that the grain on the ship had been purchased by them and served as security for their creditors; but instead of using the money to buy goods, they sent it away to Massalia.

---

[1] On the relationship, see Davies 1971: 116–117.
[2] On the procedure of counter-indictment (*paragraphē*), see pp. 12–13.

When the ship was two or three days out of Syracuse on the way to Athens, they planned to sink it, so that according to the usual contractual terms they would not have to repay the loans and would keep the money. But the plan went wrong; Hegestratus was drowned, and the ship did not sink but got safely to the island of Cephallenia and thence, despite Zenothemis' protests, back to Athens.

The grain, having been unloaded, was claimed by Protus, who intended now to sell it in Athens. Zenothemis, however, claimed it too, saying that it was the security for money which he had lent to Hegestratus. He also took steps to prosecute Protus, alleging that Protus had got drunk during the voyage and had stolen some documents from him and opened them. But then the price of grain happened to fall. Protus realized that if he established his claim to the grain now, he would have to sell it for less than the amount he owed Demon, and so he decided to cut his losses and run. He accepted a payment from Zenothemis to leave Athens; thus he lost by default the case in which Zenothemis was prosecuting him, and left the cargo of grain to be kept by Zenothemis. But then Demon took over the grain, as being the security for his loan to Protus, which Protus had failed to repay.

The various claims to possession of the grain are referred to by the verb *exagein*, literally "lead away" or "eject" another person from possession. If a man thus ejected claimed that his right to ownership was already established, he could then prosecute the man who had ejected him by a case of ejectment (*dikē exoulēs*); if the defendant lost that case, he had not only to hand over the disputed property but also to pay a fine of an amount equal to the value of that property. That must be the type of case which Zenothemis has brought against Demon, claiming that his right to the grain is established by the contract designating it as the security for the loan which he made to Hegestratus. Zenothemis has brought this prosecution as a monthly case under the Athenian mercantile laws,[3] but Demon now brings a counter-indictment, asserting that prosecution under the mercantile laws cannot be allowed because there has never been any written contract between him and Zenothemis. This point may well have been emphasized in the last part of Demon's speech, which is now lost.

---

[3] On mercantile cases, see pp. 13–14.

Since we do not have the statements made by Demon's witnesses (at the end of sections 13 and 19), we do not know exactly which parts of his story they confirmed. Likewise we do not have Zenothemis' speech and so do not know exactly what his arguments were. But he must have denied that he had any prior knowledge of Hegestratus' attempt to sink the ship, and he must have insisted that the grain had been designated as the security for a loan he had made to Hegestratus. Probably he asserted that Protus stole and destroyed the written contract of Zenothemis' loan to Hegestratus and that this was why he was not able to produce that contract at the trial in Athens. It is possible that Zenothemis and Demon each honestly believed himself to be in the right, but the essential question was: did Hegestratus or Protus pay for the grain which was put on board the ship at Syracuse? If Hegestratus paid for it, it should belong to Zenothemis; if Protus paid for it, it should belong to Demon. But we do not know the answer to that question now, and perhaps it was not known then to anyone in Athens once Protus had absconded.

As for the counter-indictment, Demon's assertion that the prosecution under the mercantile laws should not be allowed, because there was no written agreement between him and Zenothemis, appears to be strictly correct. No doubt Zenothemis argued in reply that the grain was indeed the subject of a written agreement. But it was an agreement between him and Hegestratus, and we do not know whether the jury would have stretched the point and accepted that argument as justifying the prosecution of Demon under the mercantile laws. Even if the jury rejected it, it would still have been possible for Zenothemis to bring a case of ejectment against Demon by the regular slower procedure of the Athenian courts, but perhaps Demon hoped that Zenothemis would not want to linger in Athens any longer and would just abandon his claim in order to get home to Massalia. We have no information about the result.

32. COUNTER-INDICTMENT AGAINST ZENOTHEMIS

[1] Men of the jury, since I have brought a counter-indictment that the case is inadmissible, I want first to speak about the laws under which I brought it. The laws, men of the jury, authorize trials for skippers and merchants for contracts concerning cargoes to and from Ath-

ens and about which there are written agreements; any prosecution contrary to this is inadmissible. [2] Now, this man Zenothemis had no contract or written agreement with me, as he himself admits in the charge. He says that he made a loan to Hegestratus, a skipper, and after Hegestratus was lost at sea, we misappropriated the freight; that's the charge. In fact, from one and the same speech you will realize that the case is inadmissible and also perceive this fellow's whole wicked plot. [3] I ask you all, men of the jury, if you've ever given careful attention to any other business, to give it to this. What you'll hear is no ordinary example of a person's wicked audacity, if I can perhaps recount his activities to you. I think I can.

[4] This man Zenothemis was an assistant of Hegestratus the skipper, who was lost at sea, as Zenothemis himself has written in the charge—without adding how he was lost, but I shall explain that. With him he planned this terrible crime. He and Hegestratus borrowed money at Syracuse.[4] Hegestratus confirmed to the men lending to Zenothemis, if any of them asked, that Zenothemis had a large quantity of grain in the ship, and Zenothemis confirmed to those lending to Hegestratus that the ship's cargo was Hegestratus' own. Since the one was the skipper and the other a passenger, naturally what they said about each other was believed. [5] When they'd got the money, they sent it home to Massalia and put nothing on board the ship. The written agreements, as they all usually do, required repayment of the money upon the ship's safe arrival. So, in order to defraud the creditors, they decided to sink the ship. When they were two or three days' voyage from land, Hegestratus went down into the hold at night and began cutting a hole in the bottom of the vessel. Zenothemis stayed on deck with the other passengers, as if he knew nothing about it. As there was a noise, the people on board realized something wrong was happening in the hold, and they rushed down to help. [6] Hegestratus was caught and expected to be punished; so he ran away and, being chased, threw himself into the sea, but because it was dark, he missed the dinghy and was drowned. So that bad man died a bad death, as he deserved, himself suffering the fate that he planned to inflict on the others.

---

[4] The lenders (as becomes clear in 32.8) were other Massaliots who were going to board the ship as passengers.

[7] Zenothemis, his partner and accomplice, at first, while still on the ship at the scene of the crime, pretended he knew nothing about it and was as shocked as the rest; and he tried to persuade the bow-officer and the crew to get into the dinghy and abandon the ship as fast as possible, because there was no hope of saving it and it was going to sink immediately. His intention was that their plan should be fulfilled: the ship would be lost, and they[5] would get out of the contracts. [8] But he failed in this, because the man we had sent on the voyage[6] opposed it and promised the crew substantial rewards if they brought the ship safely into port. The ship was brought safely to Cephallenia,[7] thanks mainly to the gods and also to the crew's good work. So next, Zenothemis and the Massaliots, Hegestratus' fellow-citizens, tried to prevent the ship from sailing on to Athens, saying that he and the money came from Massalia, and the skipper and the creditors were Massaliots. [9] He failed in this too, and the officials at Cephallenia ruled that the ship should sail on to Athens, its home port. And now this man, who no one would have thought would have dared to come here after scheming and acting in that way, has been so extremely shameless and audacious, men of Athens, that he has not only come here but has also made a claim to our grain and initiated a suit against us!

[10] So what's the reason? What has encouraged the man to come and bring the prosecution? I'll tell you, men of the jury; I really don't like doing it, by Zeus and the gods! but I must. There are some gangs of scoundrels established in Piraeus; you'll recognize them yourselves if you see them. [11] At the time when Zenothemis was trying to prevent the ship from sailing on to Athens, we acquired one of their members as an agent, after consultation;[8] we were quite well acquainted

---

[5] If the plural is correct, it implies that Zenothemis had not yet realized that Hegestratus had been drowned.

[6] Presumably this means Protus, mentioned later in the speech as the merchant to whom Demon and his partners had lent money.

[7] An island off the west coast of Greece, rather more than halfway from Syracuse to Athens.

[8] The significance of the consultation is not clear. An alternative interpretation of the Greek words is that the man was a member of the Council, but the absence of the definite article makes that less likely to be correct.

with him but were not aware what he was. This was no less a misfortune for us, if I may say so, than getting mixed up with criminals in the first place. This man sent by us, whose name was Aristophon and who had also managed the business of Miccalion,[9] as we have now learned, has joined in the scheme himself and made an offer to Zenothemis, and he's the person who is arranging the whole thing, while this man here has gladly accepted it.[10] [12] For when he failed to get the ship destroyed, being unable to repay the loan to the creditors (how could he, since he didn't put it on board in the first place?), he laid claim to our goods, and said he'd made a loan to Hegestratus on the security of the grain which the man we had sent on the voyage had bought. The creditors who had been deceived in the first place, seeing that they have got nothing for their money except a bad debtor, and hoping to recoup their losses out of our goods if you are taken in by Zenothemis, are compelled, for their own benefit, to support our opponent in the case, whom they know to be lying.

[13] Such, in brief, is the matter on which you will cast your votes. Now I want first to provide you with the witnesses to what I say, and after that to explain the rest of the case. [*To the clerk*] Please read out the testimonies.

[TESTIMONIES]

[14] When the ship arrived here—in accordance with the decision of the Cephallenians, opposed by Zenothemis, that the ship should return to its home port—immediately afterwards the ship was held by those who had lent money on the security of the ship, and the grain was held by the purchaser; that was the man who owed us the money. But then along came Zenothemis with the agent sent by us, Aristophon, and claimed the grain, saying that he had lent to Hegestratus. [15] "What do you mean, man?" said Protus at once. (That was the

---

[9] Nothing is known about Miccalion and his business.

[10] It appears that Aristophon was sent by Demon and his partners to Cephallenia when they heard that the ship had been delayed there. The details of the offer made by Aristophon and accepted by Zenothemis are obscure, but Demon clearly means to say that it was Aristophon who induced Zenothemis to claim the grain from Demon. Probably he advised him on the procedure; Zenothemis may have been ignorant of Athenian law.

name of the importer of the grain, who owed us the money.) "Did you give money to Hegestratus, with whom you collaborated in deceiving other people so as to enable him to borrow, even though he repeatedly said to you that those who risked their money would lose it? When you heard that, would you have risked your own money?" He impudently said yes. "Well then," interrupted one of those who were there,[11] "if what you say is absolutely true, your partner and fellow-citizen, Hegestratus, it seems, deceived you, and he has condemned himself to death for it and perished." [16] "Yes," said another of those who were there, "and this man is Hegestratus' accomplice in everything; I'll prove it to you. Before trying to cut a hole in the ship, this man and Hegestratus made a written agreement with someone else on board.[12] But if you gave him the money on trust, why would you have been securing a confirmation for yourself before the crime? If, on the other hand, you distrusted him, why didn't you get the right documentation from him on land, like everyone else?"

[17] But why relate it all at length? We gained nothing at all by this talking; he just held on to the grain. Protus tried to eject[13] him from it, and so did Protus' partner, Phertatus, but he refused to be ejected and declared point-blank that he wouldn't be ejected by anyone unless I ejected him myself.[14] [18] After that, Protus challenged him, and we did also, to appear before the authorities of Syracuse: if it was found that Protus had purchased the grain, the taxes[15] had been deposited by him, and it was he who defrayed the costs, we proposed

---

[11] This probably means another man who had been on the ship, rather than merely a casual bystander in Athens.

[12] This seems to mean that Zenothemis and Hegestratus lent some money in Syracuse to a man who was going to be a passenger on the ship. When they were already at sea, they drew up a written contract to ensure that the borrower would still be liable to repay the loan even if the ship sank.

[13] This term (*exagein*) is used legally of making a formal claim to possession of an item, excluding another person from it.

[14] It is not explained why Zenothemis at this point expressed willingness to give up the grain to Demon, which he later refused to do. Possibly he thought that Hegestratus had borrowed money from Demon, giving Demon a claim on Hegestratus' grain as security, but later found that that was not the case.

[15] Export duties at Syracuse.

that Zenothemis be punished as a criminal; but if not, that he should recover his expenses and receive a talent in addition, and we would give up our claim to the grain. When Protus said this in his challenge, and we did also, nothing was gained by it. The alternatives were either to eject Zenothemis or to lose our property even after it had arrived safely. [19] Protus then earnestly urged us to eject Zenothemis and confirmed that he was willing to travel back to Sicily;[16] and he said that if, despite his offer, we let Zenothemis have the grain, that wasn't his responsibility.

To prove that what I say is true—that he said he wouldn't be ejected except by me, and that he didn't accept the challenge to travel back, and that he made the written agreement during the voyage—[*To the clerk*] read out the testimonies.

[TESTIMONIES]

[20] So, since he wouldn't agree either to be ejected by Protus or to travel back to Sicily for a trial, and it was obvious that he had advance knowledge of Hegestratus' crime, the only remaining possibility was for us, who had made the contract here in Athens and had taken over the grain from the man who had purchased it honestly in Sicily, to eject Zenothemis. [21] What else could we do? None of us—my partners and myself—yet supposed that you would ever determine that he owned the grain which he tried to persuade the crew to abandon, so that it might be lost when the ship sank. That's actually the clearest indication that none at all belongs to him. Who would have tried to persuade people to let his own grain go when they wanted to save it? Who wouldn't have accepted the challenge and traveled to Sicily, where it was possible to prove these matters clearly? [22] Indeed, we were not likely to suspect you of intending to vote that his suit about these goods could be admitted, when he'd tried in several ways to prevent them being admitted[17] to Athens—first when he tried to persuade the crew to abandon it, and then in Cephallenia when he tried to prevent the ship sailing to Athens. [23] But since the Cephallenians decided

---

[16] To attend a trial at Syracuse.

[17] There is a play on two senses of "admit": to allow legally and to import physically.

that the ship should sail here to save the goods for the Athenians, it would surely be disgraceful and shocking if you, who are Athenian yourselves, were to award your citizens' goods to those who wanted to jettison them, and if you were to vote that they may be admitted[18] for the very man who tried to prevent them from being imported to Athens at all. Zeus and the gods! Don't do that. [*To the clerk*] Please read out my counter-indictment.

[COUNTER-INDICTMENT]

Please read out the law.

[LAW]

[24] I think I've proved adequately that my counter-indictment, stating that the case is inadmissible, is in accordance with the laws. Now you shall hear about the trick played by the clever accomplice in all this, Aristophon. When they[19] saw that on the basis of the facts they simply had no just claim, they made an approach to Protus and urged him to put the matter in their hands. It seems they'd been trying to do this right from the start, as has now become clear to us, but hadn't been able to persuade him. [25] As long as Protus thought the grain would produce a profit when it reached Athens, he kept hold of it, and chose rather to make a profit himself[20] and repay what was due to us than to go into partnership with these men and let them share the proceeds, defrauding us. But when he had reached Athens and was occupied with this business, grain fell back in price and he immediately changed his mind. [26] At the same time—to tell you the whole truth, men of Athens—we, the lenders, had a disagreement with him and were annoyed with him, because the loss on the grain fell upon us,[21] and because we blamed Protus for bringing us a malicious accuser instead of goods. Consequently, being evidently a naturally dishonest person, he went over to their side, and consented to lose by

---

[18] Again there is a play on two senses of "admit."

[19] Zenothemis and Aristophon.

[20] Selling the grain for a sum larger than the sum he owed to Demon.

[21] When Protus failed to repay the loan, Demon could take possession of the grain which was the security for it, but that was now worth less than the sum Protus had been due to pay.

default the case which Zenothemis initiated against him before they reached agreement.[22] [27] For if he had let Protus off, that would at once have proved that his accusation of us was malicious;[23] but Protus wouldn't consent to lose the case while he was present in court, because, though it would be all very well if they kept to their agreement with him, if they did not he would want to reopen the case lost in his absence. But what does that matter? If Protus did what Zenothemis has written in the charge, I think he would have deserved not just to lose a case but to be put to death; for if in a dangerous storm he was drinking so much wine that he was acting like a madman, what punishment does he not deserve? Or if he was stealing documents and secretly opening them?

[28] Those are matters which you'll judge for yourselves. [*To Zenothemis*] But don't mix up that case with mine. If Protus has done you any wrong, either in what he said or in what he did, you seem to have got compensation;[24] none of us prevented it, and we're not pleading for him now. If you've accused him maliciously, we're not interfering. [29] "Oh, but the man's disappeared." Yes, thanks to you—so that he wouldn't confirm the evidence on our side, and you would now be able to say whatever you wish against him. If you had not arranged for the trial to be held in his absence, you'd have been summoning him to appear and demanding guaranties before the Polemarch;[25] and if he'd provided the guarantors for you, he'd have been compelled to remain in Athens, or you'd have had men to compensate

---

[22] It appears from 32.27 that Zenothemis accused Protus of causing him loss or damage by drunken misbehavior on board the ship and by stealing and opening some documents. It was the law that, if a litigant failed to attend the trial, the case was automatically decided against him. But if he subsequently showed that there was a good reason for his absence (such as illness), he could have the case reopened and a new trial held; that was not permitted if he had attended the original trial.

[23] If Zenothemis had dropped his accusation that his contract with Hegestratus had been destroyed by Protus, he would have been left with no explanation for his failure to produce that contract in his case against Demon.

[24] In the trial which Protus lost by default, the court must have awarded compensation to Zenothemis, but Protus has fled from Athens without paying it.

[25] The Polemarch, one of the nine Archons, had various legal responsibilities in connection with foreigners in Athens. If an alien was prosecuted, the prosecutor could apply to the Polemarch to demand guarantors, friends of the defendant

you, whereas if he hadn't provided them he would have gone to prison. [30] But as it is, you and he have gone into partnership: he thinks that you'll enable him to avoid paying us for the deficit which has occurred,[26] and you think that by accusing him you'll get possession of our property. To prove it, I shall summon him to appear as a witness, whereas you did not demand guaranties nor are you going to summon him as a witness now.[27]

[31] There's also another way in which they are hoping to deceive and mislead you, men of Athens. They will blame Demosthenes and say it's because I'm relying on him that I'm ejecting Zenothemis. They imagine that his being an orator and a well-known man makes their accusation plausible. Now, Demosthenes is a relative of mine (and I swear by all the gods that I'll tell you the truth about this), [32] but when I approached him and asked him to be here to support me in any way he could, he said, "Demon, I'll do whatever you tell me to; it would be disgraceful to refuse. However, you need to consider your position and mine. Since I began speaking on public affairs, I have never once intervened in any private case. Even in politics I've avoided such things . . ."[28]

---

who undertook to pay up if he failed to attend for trial. If he did not provide guarantors, he could be held in prison until the trial.

[26] If Protus had sold the grain at the low price now prevailing, he would have had to make up the difference between that sum and the sum he owed Demon.

[27] It is not clear exactly what legal procedure is meant here by "summon . . . as a witness" (*klēteuein*). In the present case, any such summons would have been an empty gesture, because everyone knew that Protus had left Athens.

[28] The surviving text breaks off in the middle of a sentence, presumably because the original manuscript or an early copy was damaged and the last part was lost. Demosthenes may have gone on to suggest that calling on a leading orator to oppose an insignificant foreigner might appear oppressive and prejudice the jury against Demon.

33. AGAINST APATURIUS

INTRODUCTION

The speech *Against Apaturius* is written for delivery by a man whose name is not mentioned; I therefore call him simply the speaker. He says that he used to travel as a merchant for many years (33.4–5). The speaker is therefore not Demosthenes himself, and since the style of the speech is plainer and more matter-of-fact than Demosthenes' speeches usually are, it is generally held that he did not write it. The date is not known, but it was no earlier than 341 BC, for the speaker mentions the failure of the bank of Heracleides some two years previously (33.9), and it is known from the speech *Against Olympiodorus* that that bank was still in operation in 343 (48.12, dated by the Archon's name in 48.26).

As in the speech *Against Zenothemis*, the ground for the counterindictment is that the speaker has been prosecuted by the procedure for mercantile cases although no written agreement exists between him and the prosecutor, Apaturius. However, that claim was not quite straightforward, because it appears that certain written agreements involving both of them had existed at an earlier time. In the first half of the speech we are told that more than two years previously Apaturius, a skipper from Byzantium, had got into financial difficulty, and the speaker arranged for him to borrow 40 minas. The sources of the money were Parmenon, an exile from Byzantium, for 10 minas and Heracleides' bank for the other 30; but the speaker took responsibility for the loans, taking over Apaturius' ship as security. Since Apaturius failed to repay the money, the ship was eventually sold, and the loans were repaid from the proceeds. The contracts for the loans were then canceled.

Meanwhile, a dispute had arisen between Apaturius and Parmenon. When the ship was still the security for the loans, Apaturius prepared to take it out on a voyage. Perhaps his understanding was that he was still permitted to make use of the ship even while it served as security; indeed he may have had no other source of income to support himself. But Parmenon and the speaker took the opposite view, that Apaturius was not entitled to make use of the ship; and when Apaturius tried to take the slaves who formed the ship's crew out of their quarters in Athens to board the ship, Parmenon forcibly prevented him. There was a fight; subsequently, Parmenon and Apaturius each prosecuted the other for assault, but then, instead of going to court, they agreed to submit their dispute to private arbitration.

Private arbitration (not to be confused with public arbitration, a quite different procedure) is more fully illustrated by the speech *Against Apaturius* than by any other surviving Athenian text.[1] It was an arrangement made by the disputants themselves, not involving any public authority. Before the arbitration began, there had to be an agreement saying who was to arbitrate (it could be either one man or more) and what the question was; then the verdict of the arbitrator, or of the majority if there was more than one, was legally binding. Parmenon and Apaturius made a written agreement, but the document was lost (or, as the speaker alleges, deliberately destroyed), and disputes arose about what it had said on two vital points.

A. The speaker claimed that the document had named three men as arbitrators: Phocritus (another Byzantine), Aristocles (an Athenian friend of Apaturius), and himself. Apaturius claimed that it had named Aristocles as the sole arbitrator; Phocritus and the speaker were merely to "conduct negotiations" (33.17) and had no authority to give a verdict.

B. The document had named two guarantors, friends of Parmenon and of Apaturius respectively, who were each to pay the amount of damages or compensation fixed by the arbitration if their man lost the case and failed to pay. But whereas the speaker claimed that Parmenon's guarantor was a man named Archippus, Apaturius claimed that Parmenon's guarantor was the speaker.

The document having been lost, Apaturius and Parmenon planned to draw up a new one, but before they had agreed what should be in

---

[1] For a recent discussion of private arbitration, see Hunter 1994: 55–62.

it another difficulty arose. News reached Parmenon that his home in Asia Minor had been destroyed in an earthquake, and his family had been killed. He promptly left Athens and, it seems, did not return. Aristocles then, assuming that he was the sole arbitrator (under *A* above), gave a verdict against Parmenon; it was legally correct to decide against a litigant who was absent without giving a good attested reason. He condemned Parmenon to pay 20 minas to Apaturius in compensation. But no more was heard of Parmenon, and so Apaturius claimed the money from the speaker as guarantor (under *B* above), and when the speaker did not pay it Apaturius prosecuted him for it. That was the prosecution which the speaker tried to block by the counter-indictment and by the existing speech.

The speaker has several arguments to support his contention that he does not owe money to Apaturius; but each of them is shaky.

A. He claims that Aristocles was not entitled to decide the arbitration as the sole arbitrator. But he cannot clearly prove this, because he cannot produce the document naming the arbitrators.

B. He claims that Aristocles, even if he was the sole arbitrator, ought not to have given his verdict in the absence of Parmenon, because Parmenon had a good reason for being away. But it is not clear whether an earthquake in Asia Minor would have been regarded by the Athenians as an adequate reason for a lengthy absence.

C. He claims that he was not Parmenon's guarantor. But on this point too he cannot produce the document as proof.

D. He argues that Apaturius would have begun proceedings against him sooner if he had genuinely believed him to be the guarantor. But that does not prove that he was not still legally liable.

Thus the speaker may not have been quite confident that he would win the case if Apaturius' prosecution of him went ahead, and it may have been for this reason that he has brought the counter-indictment to try to prevent the trial from taking place. He objects to the prosecution on the ground that Apaturius has used the procedure for mercantile cases even though there is no written agreement between him and the speaker.[2] Apaturius will naturally reply that there was a written agreement naming the speaker as guarantor, and it should therefore be enforced even though the actual document has unfortunately

---

[2] On counter-indictment and mercantile cases, see pp. 12–14.

been lost. But he too cannot produce the document to support his argument.

We might have expected the speaker to argue also that a document defining the terms of a private arbitration for a case of assault, even if it did name the speaker, was not a mercantile contract and so could not be the subject of a mercantile case. In fact he does not use this argument, and that seems to imply that an Athenian jury could be expected to draw the limits of mercantile cases fairly broadly. Presumably the arbitration agreement was regarded as an agreement concerning trade because it concerned a dispute arising from trade. So the speaker does not argue that the document should not be the subject of a mercantile case; he merely argues that it did not mention himself as guarantor. On this point we do not know whether the jury in the end believed the speaker or Apaturius.

33. COUNTER-INDICTMENT AGAINST APATURIUS

[1] For merchants and skippers, men of the jury, the law authorizes trials before the Thesmothetae[3] if they suffer any wrong in the port or when sailing from here to anywhere else or from anywhere else to here; and for offenders it has specified imprisonment as the sanction until they pay whatever penalty is imposed on them, to deter casual wrongdoing towards any of the merchants. [2] But those accused when no contracts have been made are permitted by the law to resort to counter-indictment, so that no one may suffer malicious accusation, but trials may be available only to those merchants and skippers who have genuinely suffered wrong. Many men before now, when prosecuted in mercantile cases, have entered counter-indictments in accordance with this law and on coming into your court have proved that the prosecutors were charging them wrongfully and using their mercantile business as an excuse for malicious accusation.

[3] The identity of this man's accomplice, who has devised this action against me, will become clear to you in the course of my speech;[4] but it's because Apaturius is accusing me falsely and prosecuting ille-

---

[3] The Thesmothetae were six of the nine Archons. Their main function was to arrange and preside over trials for many kinds of cases.

[4] It is actually not clear whether the speaker means Aristocles or Eryxias; cf. 33.18.

gally, and because I have been given release and discharge[5] from all the contracts made between him and me, and he and I have made no other contract for business either at sea or on land, that I have brought a counter-indictment that the case is not admissible, in accordance with these laws.

[LAWS]

[4] Those are the laws that Apaturius has broken by bringing the case against me and making false accusations, as I shall fully prove to you.

For a long time now, men of the jury, I have been engaged in business by sea. For a while I undertook ventures myself, and it's not yet seven years since I gave up seafaring and have been trying to carry on this shipping business with the moderate resources that I possess.[6] [5] Traveling about the world and spending my time around the port have made me acquainted with most of the men who sail the sea, and I'm especially familiar with these men from Byzantium because of the time I've spent there. That was my situation, as I say, when this man arrived here more than two years ago, and with him a fellow-citizen of his, Parmenon, of Byzantine origin but exiled from there. [6] This man and Parmenon approached me in the port and raised the subject of money. At the time, Apaturius owed 40 minas on the security of his ship. The creditors were pressing him with their demands and were going to seize the ship for the overdue debt. Since he had no resources, Parmenon agreed to give him 10 minas, and Apaturius begged me to contribute 30 minas. He blamed his creditors for blackening his name in the port out of desire for the ship; they hoped to get hold of the ship by making it impossible for him to repay the money. [7] I had no money available at the time, but, being friendly with Heracleides the banker,[7] I persuaded him to lend the money with me as guarantor. When the 30 minas had now been made available, Parmenon had some quarrel with Apaturius; but since he had agreed to provide him with 10 minas and had already given him 3 of them, he was compelled,

---

[5] A prosecution was not admissible if the prosecutor had already released his opponent from the obligations specified in their agreement. Cf. 36.25, 37.1.

[6] The speaker means that he is no longer a merchant but makes loans to merchants.

[7] Mentioned also in Dem. 48.12.

because of the money he'd handed over, to give him the rest as well.[8] [8] For that reason he didn't want to enter into the contract,[9] but asked me to ensure that his money would be as secure as possible. I then received the 7 minas from Parmenon and made a substitute arrangement with Apaturius for the 3 which Apaturius had got from Parmenon before;[10] and I made a purchase of the ship and the slaves[11] until such time as he repaid the 10 minas which he obtained through me and the 30 for which he had made me his guarantor to the banker. To prove that I am telling the truth, listen to the testimonies.

[TESTIMONIES]

[9] In that way this man Apaturius got rid of his creditors. Not long afterwards the bank failed, and Heracleides went into hiding for a while. So Apaturius made a plot to bring the slaves out from Athens and take the ship away from the harbor.[12] That was the cause of my first disagreement with him; for, when Parmenon realized that the slaves were being removed, he seized them and prevented Apaturius from taking the ship out; then he sent for me and told me what had happened. [10] When I heard about it, I thought that Apaturius was a very wicked man to have tried to do this, and I considered how I might myself be released from my guaranty to the bank and how the foreigner[13] might not lose the money he lent to him through me. Set-

---

[8] It is not clear whether it was a legal obligation for Parmenon to complete the loan because he had already made it in part, or merely a practical imperative because Apaturius would be unlikely to repay the 3 minas he had already received if Parmenon broke his promise to lend 7 more.

[9] Parmenon did not trust Apaturius to repay the loan, but he was willing to trust the speaker.

[10] An arrangement that Apaturius would repay the 3 minas, as well as the 7, to the speaker (who would then repay them to Parmenon).

[11] The ship's crew. The transaction was a purchase, in which Apaturius retained the option to repurchase by repaying the total of 40 minas. See the introduction to Oration 37 on "sale with right of redemption."

[12] The ship was at Piraeus, while the crew was accommodated in the town of Athens. Formally the ship and crew now belonged to the speaker, but perhaps Apaturius assumed that he could continue to use them even though he had not yet paid his debt.

[13] Parmenon.

ting guards on the ship, I explained to the bank's guarantors what I had done and delivered the security to them, advising them that the foreigner had 10 minas invested in the ship. After arranging this, I pledged the slaves also, so that if there was any deficiency the difference might be made up from the slaves.[14]

[11] So, when I caught this man doing wrong, I set matters right, for myself and for the foreigner. But Apaturius criticized me, as if he were the victim and not the criminal. He asked if I wasn't satisfied with being released from my own guaranty to the bank but was pledging the ship and the slaves as security for Parmenon's money too, and was siding with an exiled man against him.[15] [12] I replied that, when a man put his trust in me, I should be even less likely to neglect him if he had the misfortune to be exiled and then was cheated by Apaturius. After doing everything possible and quarreling with him outright, I raised the money with difficulty by selling the ship for 40 minas, the amount for which it was pledged.[16] When the 30 minas had been repaid to the bank and the 10 minas to Parmenon, in the presence of a large number of witnesses we canceled the written agreements by which the loans had been made and granted each other discharge and release from the transactions, so that he has no business with me nor I with him. To prove that I am telling the truth, listen to the testimonies.

[TESTIMONIES]

[13] Since then I have had no contract with him, large or small. But Parmenon prosecuted him, both for the blows which he received from him at the time when he seized the slaves that were being removed, and because through Apaturius' fault he was prevented from making his voyage to Sicily.[17] When the action had been initiated, Parmenon

---

[14] The ship served as security for the loan of 40 minas, of which 30 minas was due to be repaid to the bank and 10 to Parmenon. If the ship, when sold, raised less than 40 minas, the deficiency could be made up by sale of the crew.

[15] Evidently Apaturius had assumed that the ship and crew were security for the debt due to the bank only.

[16] We are not told whether in the end the crew was included in the sale or not.

[17] Before Apaturius' ship became subject to seizure, Parmenon had probably intended to transport some goods to Sicily in it.

proposed an oath for Apaturius to take about certain of the charges.[18] Apaturius agreed to it, depositing a sum of money which he would forfeit if he did not swear the oath. To prove that I am telling the truth, [*To the clerk*] please take the testimony.[19]

[TESTIMONY]

[14] Although he agreed to the oath, he knew that many men would be aware that he had committed perjury, and so he didn't show up to swear it, but in order that the oath might be overtaken by a trial, he issued a summons to Parmenon.[20] When both their cases had been initiated, they were persuaded by their supporters to go to arbitration,[21] and they referred the case on written terms to one arbitrator nominated by them both—Phocritus, a fellow-citizen of theirs—and each of them nominated one other: Apaturius named Aristocles of Oe,[22] and Parmenon named me. [15] In the terms they agreed that, if the three of us were unanimous, that decision was binding on them; otherwise they must abide by the decision of two. On agreeing to these terms, they provided guarantors to each other: Apaturius provided Aristocles, while Parmenon provided Archippus of Myrrhinus.[23] And at first they were going to deposit the terms with Phocritus, but then Phocritus told them to deposit them with someone else, and so they deposited them with Aristocles. To prove that I am telling the truth, listen to the testimonies.

[TESTIMONIES]

[16] That the terms were deposited with Aristocles, and the arbitration was referred to Phocritus and Aristocles and me, has been tes-

---

[18] The meaning is that, after the legal proceedings had been started but before the trial was held, Parmenon offered to drop some charges (we are not told which) if Apaturius swore an oath that his version of the facts was true.

[19] "Take" means "pick up and read out."

[20] This means that Apaturius initiated a counter-prosecution, accusing Parmenon of starting the fight over the slaves and preventing the voyage to Sicily.

[21] On private arbitration, see p. 96.

[22] Oe was an Athenian deme.

[23] The guarantors guaranteed payment of any compensation or damages awarded by the arbitrators against either litigant. Myrrhinus was another Athenian deme.

tified for you by those who know the facts. Now, I ask you, men of the jury, to listen to my account of what happened after that; this will make it clear to you that this man Apaturius' prosecution of me is malicious. When he saw that Phocritus and I were of the same opinion, and realized we were going to give our decision against him, he wanted to stop the arbitration, and he made an attempt to destroy the terms in collaboration with the man who held them. [17] He proceeded to claim that as far as he was concerned Aristocles was the arbitrator, and he said Phocritus and I had no authority to do anything except conduct negotiations. Parmenon was very indignant at this statement, and demanded that Aristocles should produce the terms; it was easy enough to prove, he said, if there was any fiddling about with the document, since it was in his own slave's handwriting. [18] Aristocles consented to produce the terms, but to this day he has still not produced them openly; on the agreed day he showed up at the temple of Hephaestus[24] and made the excuse that his slave, while waiting for him, had fallen asleep and lost the document. (The man who arranged that was Eryxias, the doctor from Piraeus,[25] who is a friend of Aristocles. In fact it's his fault that I'm involved in this trial, because he has a dispute with me.) To prove that Aristocles claimed that he'd lost it, listen to the testimonies.

[TESTIMONIES]

[19] So after that the arbitration was at a standstill, because the terms had disappeared and the arbitrators were arguing; and when they tried to write fresh terms, they quarreled about those, Apaturius wanting Aristocles only, and Parmenon all the three original arbitrators. And when fresh terms had not been made, and the original ones had disappeared, the man who had caused their disappearance was shameless enough to say he would declare the result of the arbitration by himself! But Parmenon summoned witnesses and told Aristocles not to declare the result against him without his fellow-arbitrators,

---

[24] It was usual to arrange for an arbitration to be conducted in a temple or other public building. The temple of Hephaestus was probably the one which still stands beside the Agora in Athens.

[25] It is possible, but not certain, that Eryxias was related to Eryximachus, the doctor who appears in Plato's *Symposium* and in Andoc. 1.35, and that the medical profession was hereditary in that family.

contrary to the terms. Listen to the testimony of the men in whose presence he told him that.

[TESTIMONY]

[20] After that a terrible disaster happened to Parmenon, men of the jury. Because of his exile from home, he was living in Ophrynium[26] when the earthquake in the Chersonese area occurred. His house collapsed, and his wife and children were killed. When he heard of the disaster, he at once left Athens by ship; but although he had warned Aristocles in the presence of witnesses not to declare the result against him without his fellow-arbitrators, once the man had left Athens because of the disaster, Aristocles did declare the result of the arbitration against him as a deserted case.[27] [21] Although Phocritus and I were named in the same terms as Aristocles, we refrained from arbitrating because Apaturius rejected us as his arbitrators; yet Aristocles, though not only challenged but expressly forbidden, nonetheless declared the verdict—a thing which neither any of you nor any other Athenian would venture to do.

[22] For the actions of Apaturius and the arbitrator concerning the disappearance of the terms and the verdict in the arbitration, the victim, if he ever gets back safely, will obtain compensation from them. But since Apaturius has now been so shameless as to prosecute me too, alleging that I undertook to pay whatever amount was awarded against Parmenon, and he asserts that I was named as a guarantor in the terms, I shall do what is appropriate to rebut such an accusation: first I shall provide witnesses for you to prove that Parmenon's guarantor was not myself but Archippus of Myrrhinus,[28] and then I shall try to make my defense by arguments also, men of the jury.

[23] In the first place, I think that the lapse of time is evidence that the charge against me is not true. It's over two years since the arbitra-

---

[26] A town in the Troad, on the Asiatic side of the Hellespont.

[27] In an arbitration, as in a trial, the verdict was given automatically against a litigant who was absent without good reason. Such a case was called "deserted" (erēmos). From 33.32 it appears that Aristocles' verdict was that Parmenon should pay Apaturius 20 minas.

[28] In the text of the speech as we have it, no witnesses are in fact provided for this point.

tion between this man and Parmenon took place and Aristocles gave his verdict. Yet allotments of trials for merchants are monthly from Boedromion to Munichion, so that they may obtain justice promptly and depart on their voyages.[29] If I was really Parmenon's guarantor, why, in the first place, didn't Apaturius demand payment from me as soon as the verdict was given? [24] It's not possible for him to argue that he was reluctant to quarrel with me because he was my friend. I had already quarreled with him when I made him repay Parmenon's 1,000 drachmas;[30] and at the time when he was trying to take the ship out of the harbor, plotting to run away and welsh on his debt to the bank, it was I who prevented him. So if I had been the guarantor for Parmenon, he would have been demanding payment from me immediately, not in the third year afterwards. [25] Oh, you may say, he was well off, so that he was in a position to leave his proceedings against me until later, and at that time he was busy with preparations for a voyage. On the contrary, he was so short of funds that he'd lost his property and sold his ship. And if there had in fact been anything to prevent him prosecuting immediately, why, when he was in Athens last year, did he not take any steps to prosecute or even make an allegation against me? If Parmenon had been condemned to pay him and I was the guarantor, he should have come to me with witnesses and requested payment of the guaranty last year, if not the year before; if I had paid him, he'd have obtained his money, and otherwise he should have prosecuted. [26] In cases of this sort, people always make requests before they prosecute. Yet there's no one who will testify to being present on any occasion, either last year or the year before, when

---

[29] Magistrates sat on various days to receive accusations and assign dates for trials; obtaining a date for trial was called "allotment" (*lēxis*), presumably because the dates were selected by lot. Mercantile cases (and some others; cf. 37.2 on cases concerning mines) were called "monthly" because accusations were accepted and trial-dates were assigned on one day every month (rather than because the proceedings were completed within a month, as used to be thought); cf. Cohen 1973: 23–59. Boedromion and Munichion were the months corresponding approximately to our September and April respectively; thus trials of mercantile cases were held during the winter, so as not to keep merchants in Athens during the summer sailing season.

[30] This sum was paid out of the proceeds from the sale of the ship; cf. 33.12.

this man prosecuted me or said a single word to me about the matter for which he's prosecuting me now. To prove that he was in Athens last year at the time when the trials were on,[31] [*To the clerk*] please take the testimony.

[TESTIMONY]

[27] Please take also the law which lays down that guaranties are for one year.[32] Not that I rely on the law to prove that I should not pay a penalty if I was the guarantor; what I'm saying is that the law, along with Apaturius himself, testifies that I was not the guarantor, for he would have prosecuted me for payment of the guaranty within the time specified in the law.

[LAW]

[28] Here is another indication for you that Apaturius is lying: if I had been the guarantor to him for Parmenon, there's no way that after quarreling with him for Parmenon's sake because I wanted to ensure that Parmenon would not lose the money he'd contributed for Apaturius through me, I would then have allowed myself to be left in the lurch by Parmenon as guarantor to Apaturius. What hope had I that Apaturius would let me off, when I myself had compelled him to pay what was due to Parmenon? And after I'd made him my enemy, by making him pay the guaranty to the bank, how did I expect I myself would be treated by him?

[29] There's another consideration worth bearing in mind, men of the jury. If I'd been the guarantor, I would never have denied it, because I had a much stronger argument: I could admit the guaranty and rely on the terms on which the arbitration was based. Testimony has been given to you that it was entrusted to three arbitrators. When the verdict had not been given by the three, what was the point of deny-

---

[31] Between Boedromion and Munichion; cf. 33.23.

[32] The speaker seems to concede that this law does not in itself exonerate him from liability. The meaning of the law must therefore have been that a guarantor was liable only for payments falling due within one year, not that legal proceedings against him must be taken within one year.

ing the guaranty? If the verdict was not in accordance with the terms, I would not have been liable for the guaranty. So if I had been the guarantor, men of the jury, I would not have resorted to denying it while ignoring the defense which actually was available to me.

[30] Besides, testimony has also been given to you that, after these men made away with the terms, Apaturius and Parmenon attempted to have new ones written, on the assumption that the ones they had previously agreed to were now void. But when they were taking steps to have new terms written concerning the verdict which would be given in the future, since the existing ones were lost, how was it possible, before new terms were written, for there to be either an arbitration or a guaranty? This was the very point of disagreement which stopped them writing a new document: one wanted to have a single arbitrator, and the other wanted three. When the original terms, according to which he says I was the guarantor, had disappeared, and new ones had not been written, how can it be right for him to prosecute me when he cannot produce any terms of agreement against me?

[31] Besides, testimony has also been given to you that Parmenon warned Aristocles not to give a verdict against him without his fellow-arbitrators. So when the same man has evidently made away with the document which should have been the basis for the arbitration and also claims to have decided the arbitration without his fellow-arbitrators in defiance of the warning, how can it be right for you to trust that fellow and ruin me? [32] Consider it this way, men of the jury. If this man Apaturius were prosecuting not me but Parmenon today, demanding the 20 minas on the basis of Aristocles' verdict, and Parmenon were present, making his defense to you and producing witnesses to prove firstly that he entrusted the case to Aristocles not as sole arbitrator but with two others, [33] and secondly that he warned him not to declare the result against him without his fellow-arbitrators, and that, after he lost his wife and children in the earthquake and departed home to face that dreadful disaster, the man who had made away with the terms decided the arbitration against him in his absence as a deserted case[33]— is there a single one of you who, if Parmenon had offered that defense,

---

[33] Cf. 33.20 with note.

would have judged that an arbitration decided in so illegal a manner was valid? [34] Not to mention that all the facts were disputed; but even if the terms had actually been produced, and it had been conceded that Aristocles was the sole arbitrator, and Parmenon had not warned him not to decide the arbitration against him, still, if the disaster had befallen the poor man before the result of the arbitration was declared, what opponent or arbitrator would have been so harsh as not to postpone it until the man's return to Athens? And if Parmenon, had he been present to speak, would clearly have had a stronger case than Aparturius on every point, how can it be right for you to convict me, who have no contract whatever with this fellow?

[35] So I have been right to bring this counter-indictment, while Aparturius' charges are false and his initiation of the case is illegal; I think that has been fully proved to you, men of the jury. The essential point is that Aparturius won't even try to assert that he has any terms of agreement with me. When he says, untruthfully, that I was named as guarantor in his terms of agreement with Parmenon, you should demand that he produce the terms. [36] Confront him with the fact that all men, when they make written contracts with one another, seal them and deposit them with people they trust for this very purpose, so that, if anything is disputed, it may be possible for them to refer to the document and so settle the point at issue. But when a man makes away with the accurate evidence and tries to deceive you by talk, how can it be right for you to believe him? [37] Oh, you may say, some witness will testify for him against me—the easiest thing in the world for criminals wanting to make false accusations. Then if I make objection against him,[34] what will he use to show that his testimony is true? The terms? Then there should be no delay; the man who has them should produce them now. If he says they're lost, what am I to use to refute false evidence given against me? If the document had been deposited with me, it would have been possible for Aparturius to accuse me of making away with the terms because of the guaranty. [38] But if it was with Aristocles, and the terms have been lost without Aparturius' connivance, why doesn't he prosecute the man who received them and

---

[34] Making a formal objection (*episkēptesthai*) was the first step towards prosecuting a witness for giving false evidence.

hasn't produced them, but instead charges me and produces as a witness against me the man who has made away with the terms? That's the man with whom he should be quarreling, if he were not his accomplice.

I have done my best to say what is right; so now you must give the right verdict according to law.

34. AGAINST PHORMION

INTRODUCTION

The speech *Against Phormion* concerns a dispute between two grain-merchants named Chrysippus and Phormion. Neither is otherwise known. (This Phormion is not to be identified with the one in Oration 36.) Several passages of the speech imply that they are not Athenian citizens; notice especially "we . . . have been coming to your port for a long time" (34.1), and "he [unlike Phormion, it is implied] was an Athenian citizen" (34.50). Both evidently are often in Athens, and it is possible that either or both have been registered as metics, but that is uncertain. The date of the speech is 327/6 BC (34.39). It is generally thought that Demosthenes is unlikely to have been still writing speeches for other people at that time, and many scholars have considered that the style of the speech is not characteristic of him, but it cannot be definitely proved that he did not write it.

Chrysippus recounts that in the previous year (328/7) he made a loan of 20 minas (2,000 drachmas) to Phormion. According to the contract, Phormion was to make a voyage to the kingdom of Bosporus (on the northern side of the Black Sea) and back to Athens on a ship skippered by Lampis. He was to provide a further 2,000 drachmas himself so as to put on board the ship goods worth 4,000 drachmas in all, take those goods to Bosporus and sell them there, use the proceeds to buy another cargo (doubtless, grain) in Bosporus and bring it to Athens for sale there, and from the profits repay 2,600 drachmas to Chrysippus. As was usual in such contracts, a clause provided that no repayment was to be made if the ship was lost on the voyage.

However, when Phormion reached Bosporus, he found that a war had broken out there, and he had difficulty in selling the goods he had brought from Athens. Lampis was ready to set out on the return journey; so Phormion told Lampis to go without him. Lampis set off, but not far into the voyage the ship sank. The cargo and some passengers were lost, but Lampis himself was saved and eventually got back to Athens on another ship. Chrysippus gathered from Lampis that Phormion had had no goods on board the ship when it sank, and he therefore looked to have his loan repaid when Phormion returned to Athens later. But then Phormion claimed that he had in fact repaid the loan already in Bosporus by giving the equivalent in gold coins (120 Cyzicene staters) to Lampis for conveyance to Chrysippus; this method of repaying the loan seems to have been permitted by the contract if Phormion decided not to return to Athens himself. If he had given the money to Lampis, of course it would probably have gone down with the ship.

Chrysippus did not believe this story, and he raised a legal action against Phormion by the usual procedure for mercantile cases to claim repayment of the loan. In the charge he asserted that Phormion had neither put a cargo on board Lampis' ship for the return journey nor repaid the debt in gold coins (34.17). Phormion tried to block the prosecution by bringing a counter-indictment (*paragraphē*). He claimed that the sinking of the ship canceled the contract between him and Chrysippus; therefore Chrysippus' prosecution was inadmissible, because mercantile cases could be brought only if there was a written agreement between the disputants.[1] However, before the case came to trial, Phormion asked Chrysippus to agree to a settlement by private arbitration.[2] In the course of this, Lampis changed his story and said that Phormion had indeed given the money to him; but the arbitrator, a man named Theodotus, even though, according to Chrysippus (34.21), he was actually a friend of Phormion's, refused to give a verdict in Phormion's favor, and merely said that the dispute should go to a court.

By now the next year (327/6) had begun. Chrysippus therefore

---

[1] On mercantile cases and counter-indictments, see pp. 12–14.
[2] On private arbitration, see p. 96.

started fresh proceedings against Phormion. His charge this time apparently differed in some way from his charge in the previous year,[3] but the nature of the difference is not clearly stated. It may be that this time he claimed that Phormion should pay a penalty for failure to fulfill the terms of the contract; a figure of 5,000 drachmas is given (34.33). Again Phormion tried to block the prosecution by a counter-indictment, and it is to the trial of this counter-indictment that the extant speech belongs.

We must assume that Phormion has already spoken. Our speech is a draft of Chrysippus' reply, arguing that he should be allowed to prosecute Phormion in a straight trial (*euthydikia*). On this point there can be little doubt that Chrysippus is correct. A written agreement between him and Phormion certainly existed; the question was whether its terms had been fulfilled or not, and that was a matter for a straight trial, not for a counter-indictment. So it is likely that Phormion's motive for bringing the counter-indictment was simply to avoid or delay a straight trial in which he thought he would lose. It is in order to establish this motive of Phormion's that Chrysippus recounts the entire course of their dispute, and this long and complicated narrative enables us to consider not just whether the prosecution was admissible but also whether Phormion did really owe Chrysippus the money.

It appears that the contract required Phormion to put goods on board Lampis' ship for the return journey from Bosporus to Athens, and he did not do so. Nevertheless, if he did put on board 120 Cyzicene staters in Lampis' keeping for conveyance to Chrysippus, that evidently would have been an acceptable way of discharging his debt; and if the gold coins then went down with the ship when it was wrecked, that could reasonably be regarded as being covered by the clause of the contract annulling the requirement to make repayment if the ship was lost. The real question, therefore, was whether Phormion had in fact given the gold to Lampis or had merely bribed Lampis to say that he had.

No one else apparently had been present on the occasion when the gold was allegedly handed over, and Lampis himself was not available

---

[3] This is implied by the specific request in 34.16 for the reading of last year's charge.

to give evidence at the trial. It has been suggested that this was because he was a slave; he and the crew of the ship were slaves of Dion, who was presumably the ship's owner, and slaves were not allowed to appear as witnesses in Athenian courts. Yet it was permitted to produce testimony which a slave had given previously under torture, and the speech contains no suggestion that Lampis' testimony might have been procured in that way. It is more likely that the reason why Lampis' testimony was not available was simply that he was no longer in Athens, having left on another voyage. So, on the question whether he had been given the gold, the only testimony that could be produced at the trial was the assertion of some supporters of Chrysippus that they heard Lampis say that he had not received it, and the assertion of some supporters of Phormion that they heard Lampis say that his previous statement was wrong ("he was out of his mind at the time," 34.20) and he had indeed received it.

Thus both sides equally (despite the attempt in 34.46 to distinguish them) relied on one or the other of Lampis' two contradictory statements. No other evidence was strictly relevant to the question whether Phormion had given the gold to Lampis. Most of the speech, therefore, is devoted to circumstantial arguments, intended to show that Phormion is an unscrupulous person and is unlikely to have paid the money: before the start of the voyage, he did not provide the required amount of his own money, but obtained further loans using Chrysippus' money as security; he failed to deliver letters entrusted to him; it is incredible that he really paid the amount of gold he says he paid, because that would have been more than he owed; he contrived to have a friend of his, Theodotus, appointed as a supposedly impartial arbitrator; and so on. Likewise, Lampis is depicted as a dishonest accomplice and habitual cheat: on one occasion he claimed a subsidy for transporting grain to Athens and then took the grain to Acanthus instead. Chrysippus, by contrast, was a strong supporter of Athens who had made generous donations of grain to the citizens in times of famine (34.38–39). In this way the speech is cleverly composed to give the impression that it is Phormion, not Chrysippus, who is more likely to be lying. Whether Phormion was indeed lying, we cannot say. He alone (and Lampis, who was no longer there) knew whether he was lying or not. Chrysippus merely thought it likely that Phormion was lying.

A notorious puzzle in this speech arises from the bewildering mixture of pronouns. Sometimes "I" lent the money (e.g., 34.6), and sometimes "we" lent it (e.g., 34.2); sometimes "Phormion" or "he" or "this man" borrowed it (e.g., 34.2), and sometimes "they" or "these men" borrowed it (e.g., 34.5). The variations between singular and plural should probably be explained by saying that, although Chrysippus and Phormion were the principals, each had one or more associates who contributed to the financial arrangements and were present at the trial as supporters. Probably Chrysippus' brother (mentioned in 34.39) was one of his supporters, and he alludes to his "friends" in the last sentence of the speech. Phormion's supporters are also mentioned explicitly (34.12).

More baffling is the fact that Chrysippus, though usually "I," sometimes becomes "this man" (34.20, 23, 26, 27, 29) and in one place "these men" (34.32). Most scholars, beginning with Libanius in the fourth century AD, have tried to explain this by supposing that the first part of the speech was delivered by Chrysippus and the later part by his partner. But that is not convincing. There is nothing in the course of the text to indicate that one speaker is finishing and another starting, and in the final sentence the singular pronoun is clear in "I've said all I could." Besides, in the later part of the speech, Chrysippus continues to be "I" from time to time (34.22, 31, 35, 41, etc.), and it is not credible that he and his partner changed places repeatedly. A simpler explanation is the one proposed by Lofberg; he argues that "this man" is just an alternative form of words for "myself."[4] But a preferable explanation is the one first suggested by Blass: when the speech was drafted, it was not certain whether it would be delivered by Chrysippus himself or by a supporter.[5]

We can imagine a possible scenario. Chrysippus was probably not an expert orator, but his substantial contributions to the Athenian food-supply in times of famine may have put him on friendly terms with leading politicians such as Demosthenes. Perhaps Demosthenes or another friend drafted a speech for Chrysippus to deliver, but at a late stage Chrysippus became nervous and asked his friend to deliver

---

[4] Lofberg 1932.
[5] Blass 1893: 580–581.

the speech instead as his advocate (*synēgoros*); his friend then called Chrysippus "this man" in any sentence which he inserted or altered after that, but did not trouble to correct all the pronouns throughout the text since he could easily do that while actually speaking. That scenario is speculative, and may be wrong. But something like it is probably the reason for the inconsistencies in the text as we have it.

34. AGAINST PHORMION CONCERNING A LOAN

[1] We are going to make a just request of you, men of the jury: to give us a favorable hearing as we speak in our turn.[6] You should realize that we are simply private individuals, who have been coming to your port for a long time and have made contracts with a large number of men but have never entered your court, either as accusers or accused by others. [2] And we would never have been raising the action[7] against Phormion now, you can be sure, men of Athens, if we supposed that the money[8] we lent him had been lost on the ship that was wrecked; we're not as brazen as that, and we know what it is to suffer a loss. But since we've been called cowards by many people, especially those who were in Bosporus[9] at the same time as Phormion and knew he hadn't lost the money along with the ship, we thought it was a terrible thing not to stand up for ourselves when we were his victims.

[3] About the counter-indictment there is little to say. Our opponents themselves don't deny that any contract at all was made in your port, but they say that no contract with them exists any longer, be-

---

[6] Phormion has spoken first, in accordance with the normal procedure for a counter-indictment.

[7] The original prosecution, which Phormion is trying to block by his counter-indictment.

[8] Throughout this speech the same Greek word, *chrēmata*, is used both for money and for goods purchased with it. I translate it "money" or "goods," whichever seems more appropriate in each context, but sometimes either is possible.

[9] Bosporus was the name of a kingdom occupying land in the Crimea and the Taman peninsula, on either side of the Cimmerian Bosporus strait (joining the Black Sea and the Sea of Azov; not to be confused with the Thracian Bosporus, joining the Black Sea and the Sea of Marmara). Its capital was Panticapaeum (modern Kerch).

cause they have not transgressed anything written in the agreement. [4] Now, the laws, in accordance with which you sit here as jurors, don't say this. They permit counter-indictments concerning contracts which have not been made at all, at Athens or for the Athenian port; but anyone who admits that a contract was made but maintains that he has fulfilled all its conditions is required to make his defense facing a straight trial,[10] not to accuse the prosecutor. All the same, I hope to prove from the actual facts that the case is admissible. [5] Consider, men of Athens, what is admitted by our opponents themselves, and what is disputed; that's the best way for you to examine it. They admit that they borrowed the money and made terms for the loan, but they allege that they repaid it in gold[11] to Lampis, Dion's servant, in Bosporus. Now we shall prove not only that he did not repay it, but that it was not even in his power to repay it. But I must briefly tell you the story from the beginning.

[6] I, men of Athens, lent this man Phormion 20 minas for a voyage to the Pontus[12] and back on security of as much again,[13] and I lodged a written agreement with Cittus the banker.[14] But although the written agreement required him to put on board the ship a cargo worth 4,000 drachmas, he did an absolutely outrageous thing: straightaway, before leaving Piraeus, without telling us, he obtained further loans of 4,500 drachmas from Theodorus the Phoenician and 1,000 drachmas from the skipper, Lampis. [7] Although he needed to purchase at Athens a cargo worth 115 minas[15] if he was going to fulfill what was writ-

---

[10] A straight trial (*euthydikia*) was a trial on the original charge; a counter-indictment was an attempt to block the trial.

[11] The gold coins (actually electrum, an alloy of gold and silver) were Cyzicene staters, which were often used in international trade; cf. 34.23.

[12] The Black Sea.

[13] This means that Phormion was to provide a further 20 minas from his own resources.

[14] Cittus, not mentioned elsewhere, could be a relative (perhaps grandson) of the Cittus who worked in Pasion's bank (Isoc. 17.11). There were two copies of the contract (34.32); probably Phormion held one, and Chrysippus, instead of holding the other himself, deposited it at the bank.

[15] This figure does not seem to match the figures given for the loans. There may be corruption in the text; Reiske suggested that the figure should be 150, double the total amount borrowed. Alternatively, Theodorus' and Lampis' con-

ten in the agreements for all the creditors, he purchased goods worth only 5,500 drachmas, including the provisions for the voyage; yet he owed 75 minas.[16] That was the beginning of his crime, men of Athens; he neither provided the security nor put the goods on board the ship, although the written agreement made it compulsory for him to do so. [*To the clerk*] Please take the written agreement.

[WRITTEN AGREEMENT]

Take also the two-percent collectors' record and testimonies.[17]

[RECORD, TESTIMONIES]

[8] So he went to Bosporus, taking letters from me, which I gave him to deliver to my slave, who was spending the winter there, and to a partner of mine. I wrote in the letter the amount of the money I had lent and the security, and I instructed them, as soon as the goods were unloaded, to examine them and keep track of them; but he didn't deliver the letters I gave him, to ensure that they wouldn't know what he was up to. He found that business was bad in Bosporus because of the war that had broken out between Paerisades and the Scythian,[18] and there was little demand for the cargo he brought. He was quite at a loss what to do, for the creditors who had lent for the single voyage[19] were also pressing him. [9] So when the skipper[20] told him to put on board the goods bought from my money, in accordance with the written agreement, he said—this man who now alleges that he repaid it in gold!—that he couldn't put the goods on board the ship, because his

---

tracts for the single voyage to Bosporus may have required securities at lower rates than Chrysippus' for the double voyage to Bosporus and back.

[16] What did Phormion do with the rest of the money, then? He may have used it to pay off earlier debts or for some other purpose.

[17] The collectors of export duties would have records of goods exported from Piraeus.

[18] Paerisades was the ruler of Bosporus from 344/3 to 309. He had friendly relations with the Athenians, who erected a statue of him in their Agora; cf. Din. 1.43. The Scythians occupied the area to the north (modern Ukraine), but details of the war mentioned here are not known.

[19] Theodorus and Lampis. Evidently Theodorus had also traveled to Bosporus with Phormion on Lampis' ship.

[20] Lampis, preparing to set off on the voyage back to Athens.

junk[21] was unsaleable. He told Lampis to put to sea, and said he would make the voyage on another ship when he'd disposed of the cargo. [*To the clerk*] Please read out this testimony.

[TESTIMONY]

[10] So after that, men of Athens, Phormion was left behind in Bosporus, while Lampis put to sea and was shipwrecked not far from the port. We are told the ship was already overloaded when he took a thousand hides on to the deck in addition, and that was the cause of the destruction of the ship.[22] He himself got away in the dinghy along with Dion's other slaves,[23] but he lost more than thirty[24] free persons, besides the rest.[25] There was much grief in Bosporus when they heard of the ship's destruction, and they all congratulated this man Phormion because he hadn't gone to sea with the ship or put anything on board. The same account was given by him as by everyone else. [*To the clerk*] Please read these testimonies.

[TESTIMONIES]

[11] Even Lampis, to whom he says he repaid it in gold (notice this point especially), when I approached him as soon as he returned to Athens after the shipwreck and asked him about this, said that Phormion neither put the goods on board the ship in accordance with the written agreement nor gave him the gold while they were in Bosporus. [*To the clerk*] Please read the testimony of those who were present.[26]

---

[21] Chrysippus' contemptuous word for the goods which Phormion had brought from Athens to Bosporus. He needed to sell those in order to buy other goods (probably grain) to take from Bosporus to Athens.

[22] Hides would be weighty, and when stowed on the deck would make the ship top-heavy.

[23] The ship's crew.

[24] The manuscripts all say either "three hundred" or "two hundred," but such high figures seem incredible, and the emendation "thirty" is generally accepted.

[25] Some manuscripts omit "free," but if it is rightly included, "the rest" then covers slave passengers as well as cargo.

[26] Chrysippus took some friends with him to hear what Lampis would say; cf. 34.20.

[TESTIMONY]

[12] So after this man Phormion got safely back to Athens on another ship, men of Athens, I approached him and asked for repayment
of the loan. At the beginning, men of Athens, he never told this story
which he tells now, but he kept agreeing that he would repay it; but
after consulting with the men who are now supporting him and speaking for him, he became a changed man and not the same. [13] When
I perceived that he was evading me, I approached Lampis and said
that Phormion wasn't acting rightly at all and wasn't repaying the loan,
and at the same time I asked him if he knew where Phormion was, so
that I might issue a summons to him. Lampis told me to go with him,
and we found Phormion at the perfume-sellers'.[27] I had summons-
witnesses with me, and I summoned him.[28] [14] Lampis, men of Athens, was there when I was issuing the summons, and at no point did
he venture to say that he had received the gold from Phormion; nor
did he say, as you'd expect, "Chrysippus, you're crazy! Why are you
summoning this man? He's made the repayment to me in gold." Not
only did Lampis not utter a word, but even Phormion himself didn't
think fit to say anything, although Lampis, to whom he now says he
made the repayment in gold, was standing there. [15] And yet you'd
expect him to say, men of Athens, "Why are you summoning me,
man? I've made the repayment in gold to this man standing here," and
at the same time to bring Lampis forward to confirm it. But in fact
neither of them took the opportunity to say anything at all. [*To the
clerk*] To show that I'm telling the truth, please take the testimony of
the summons-witnesses.

[TESTIMONY]

[16] Please take also the charge which I initiated against him last
year. It is evidence as good as any that at that time Phormion had not
yet alleged that he had made the repayment in gold to Lampis.

---

[27] The part of the Agora where the perfume-sellers had their stalls.

[28] A summons to appear before a magistrate was delivered orally, but two witnesses were required to make it valid.

[CHARGE]

When I wrote that charge, men of Athens, I based it simply on Lampis' statement. He asserted that Phormion neither put the goods on board nor gave him the gold. Don't imagine that I'm so deranged and completely crazy as to write a charge like that if Lampis had confirmed that he'd received the gold, since I was sure to be refuted by him.

[17] Consider this further point too, men of Athens. They themselves, when they submitted a counter-indictment last year, didn't venture to write in it that they had made the repayment to Lampis in gold. [*To the clerk*] Please take the actual counter-indictment.

[COUNTER-INDICTMENT]

You hear, men of Athens, that nowhere in the counter-indictment is it written that Phormion made the repayment in gold to Lampis, even though I had explicitly written in the charge, which you heard just now, that he neither put the goods on board the ship nor made the repayment in gold. So what other witness need you wait for, when they themselves have given you such strong testimony?

[18] When the case was about to come into court, they asked us to refer it to an arbitrator,[29] and we referred it to Theodotus, an equal-tax man,[30] in accordance with agreed terms. After that Lampis, thinking it was now safe for him to give any evidence he liked before an arbitrator,[31] went shares in my gold with this man Phormion, and gave testimony which was the opposite of what he'd said before. [19] Giving false evidence before an arbitrator, men of Athens, is not like giving it face to face with you. In your court severe anger and punishment await those who give false evidence, but before the arbitrator they give any evidence they like, without risk and without shame. I was indignant and protested, men of Athens, at Lampis' audacity, [20] and I

---

[29] On private arbitration, see the introduction to Oration 33.

[30] "Equal-tax man" (*isotelēs*) means that Theodotus was a metic (a non-citizen residing permanently in Attica) who had been given the privilege of paying only the same taxes as citizens, without the additional tax normally paid by metics.

[31] The words "before an arbitrator" are deleted by some editors, including Rennie in the Oxford Classical Text, as being a scholiast's gloss anticipating the same words in the next sentence.

provided for the arbitrator the same testimony as I am now providing for you,[32] the testimony of the men who approached him with us at the beginning, when he said that Phormion neither gave him the gold nor put the goods on board the ship. When Lampis was absolutely proved in this way to be a false witness and a scoundrel, he admitted that he had said that to this man,[33] but said he was out of his mind at the time! [To the clerk] Please read this testimony.

[TESTIMONY]

[21] Theodotus listened to us over and over again, men of Athens, and thought Lampis' testimony was false; so he did not dismiss the case but told us to go to court. He did not want to convict because of his connection with this man Phormion, as we learned subsequently;[34] but he was reluctant to dismiss the case for fear of committing perjury himself.[35]

[22] Think it out for yourselves, men of the jury, on the basis of the actual facts. Where was Phormion to get the gold to make the repayment? When he sailed out from Athens, he hadn't put the goods on board the ship, and he had no security,[36] but had used my money to obtain further loans. In Bosporus he found no demand for his cargo, and he had difficulty in paying off the creditors who had lent for the single voyage. [23] This man[37] lent him 2,000 drachmas for the double voyage, to be repaid 2,600 drachmas at Athens; but Phormion says that he repaid 120 Cyzicene staters to Lampis in Bosporus (notice this point especially), having borrowed it at land-rate interest.[38] Land-rate

---

[32] The testimony read out at 34.11.

[33] "This man" is Chrysippus; see p. 114.

[34] The nature of the connection which subsequently came to light is not explained, but it seems more likely to have been a business relationship than a family one.

[35] As arbitrator, Theodotus must have sworn an oath to give a true verdict.

[36] This rather vague phrase must mean only that he provided no security for Chrysippus. He did provide some security for Theodorus and Lampis—in the shape of Chrysippus' money or the goods purchased with it.

[37] Chrysippus.

[38] Land-rate interest (*engeioi tokoi*) was interest payable at a certain rate for each month or each year, in contrast to a maritime loan, which was repayable with a

interest was one-sixth,[39] and the Cyzicene stater was worth 28 Attic drachmas there.[40] [24] You need to understand how much money he says he has repaid. The 120 staters amounts to 3,360 drachmas, and the land-rate interest of one-sixth amounts to 560 drachmas; the total comes to such-and-such.[41] [25] Now, is there any person, men of the jury, or will there ever be, who instead of 2,600 drachmas would prefer to pay 3,360, plus interest of 560 drachmas on the loan? That's what Phormion says he paid to Lampis, 3,920 drachmas.[42] Although he was allowed to pay the cash at Athens after the return voyage, did he pay it in Bosporus, and 13 minas too much? [26] [*To Phormion*] Although you had difficulty in repaying the principal to the creditors who had lent for the single voyage, who were on the ship with you and were keeping their eye on you, did you repay to this man, who wasn't there, not only the principal and the interest but also the penalty specified in the written agreement, when you had no need to?[43] [27] And although you weren't worried about the men who were allowed by their written agreements to demand repayment of their loan in Bosporus, are you saying you were concerned about this man, whom you wronged right from the start by not putting the goods on board the ship at Athens in accordance with the written agreement? And although, now that you've reached the port where the contract was made, you have no hesitation in defrauding your creditor,[44] are you saying you did

---

fixed total amount of interest at the conclusion of a certain voyage. Cf. Cohen 1992: 58–60.

[39] 16⅔ percent per annum.

[40] "There" refers to the rate of exchange in Bosporus, not at Cyzicus. The rate of exchange must have varied from place to place and from time to time.

[41] It is strange that the total figure is given a few lines later but not here. Some editors rearrange the text to make the exposition clearer.

[42] More precisely, Phormion's claim is that he paid the equivalent of 3,360 drachmas to Lampis and will have to pay 560 drachmas to a creditor in Bosporus.

[43] The penalty for failure to put a cargo on board for the return voyage; cf. 34.33. Actually, the amount of this penalty (5,000 drachmas) was much higher than the sum Phormion claimed to have paid in Bosporus, but it was not payable unless he arrived back in Athens with no cargo.

[44] Phormion, of course, claims that he is *not* defrauding Chrysippus.

more than was due in Bosporus, where you were not liable to punishment? [28] All other men who take loans for a double voyage, when they are setting off from their ports, arrange to have plenty of witnesses to attest that the creditor's money is at risk from that time on,[45] but you rely on a single witness, the very man who is your accomplice; you did not call in our slave, who was in Bosporus, nor our partner, nor did you deliver to them the letters we entrusted to you, in which it was written that they should keep track of your activities.

[29] Well, men of the jury, what crime is there that a man like that wouldn't commit, a man who accepted letters and did not deliver them rightly and honestly? Isn't this man's offense plain to you from the very things he did? O Earth and gods! When he was repaying such a large amount in gold, more than the amount of the loan, he ought to have made it the talk of the port. He ought to have invited everyone to watch, especially this man's slave and partner. [30] Surely you all know that people borrow with few witnesses, but when they repay, they bring along plenty of witnesses, to let people see they are trustworthy with regard to their contracts. [*To Phormion*] And when you were repaying the loan, together with the double interest after using the cash for only the single voyage, plus 13 minas more, surely you ought to have taken along lots of witnesses! And if you'd done that, no seafarer would have been more admired than you. [31] But instead of making many men witnesses of it, you tried to avoid being seen by anyone, as if you were doing something wrong! If you'd been making the repayment to me, the lender, there'd have been no need of witnesses, because you'd have taken back the written agreement and been released from the contract; but as it was, though you were not making the repayment to me but to another man on my behalf, and not at Athens but in Bosporus, and though your written agreement was deposited at Athens and was made with me, and the man to whom you paid the gold was mortal and was about to make such a long voyage by sea, you made nobody your witness, neither a slave nor a free man. [32] "Yes," he says, "because the written agreement told me to repay

---

[45] Once the voyage had begun, the borrower would not be required to repay the loan if the ship was lost.

the gold to the skipper."[46] Yes, but it did not prevent you calling in witnesses or delivering the letters. These men[47] drew up two written agreements[48] for their contract with you, as if they strongly distrusted you; but you say you gave the gold to the skipper with nobody else present, although you knew that a written agreement placing you under obligation to this man was deposited at Athens!

[33] He says that the written agreement instructs him to repay the money when the ship has arrived safely. [*To Phormion*] Yes; it also instructs you to put on board the ship the goods bought or else pay 5,000 drachmas.[49] But you don't take up that point in the written agreement; after transgressing it right from the beginning and not putting the goods on board, you base your argument on one phrase in the agreement, even though you've nullified it yourself. For since you say you didn't put the goods on board the ship in Bosporus but paid the gold to the skipper, why are you still talking about the ship? You didn't share the risk, because you put nothing on board. [34] At first, men of the jury, he seized on that excuse,[50] pretending he'd put the goods on board the ship; but when it became clear that this would be proved in several ways to be a lie—from the record kept by the collectors of harbor dues in Bosporus, and by men who were staying in the port at the same time—he has then changed his story and, getting together with Lampis, says he paid the gold to him. [35] He found support in the instruction in the written agreement, and thought it would not be easy for us to establish what they did on their own between themselves. As for what Lampis said to me before being cor-

---

[46] This implies that the contract did in fact permit Phormion to repay Chrysippus' loan to Lampis in Bosporus, even though it was a loan for the double voyage. Perhaps the arrangement was that he would do this if he decided not to return to Athens.

[47] Chrysippus and his associates; see p. 114.

[48] Two copies of the contract, to guard against unauthorized alterations. One was deposited at a bank (see 34.6).

[49] If the figure is correct, the penalty prescribed is a huge one, intended perhaps to encourage strongly the importation of grain to Athens by penalizing the use of the borrowed money for any different purpose.

[50] The excuse that repayment was not required because the ship had been lost.

rupted by Phormion, he asserts that he was out of his mind when he said it; but after getting a share of my gold, he says he is not out of his mind any more and remembers everything accurately!

[36] If it were only me, men of the jury, whom Lampis was treating with contempt, there would be nothing remarkable in that; but in fact his offenses against all of you are much more serious. When Paerisades made a proclamation in Bosporus that anyone wishing to convey grain to Athens, to the Athenian port, could export the grain free of tax,[51] Lampis, who was in Bosporus at the time, took up the exportation of grain and the tax exemption in the name of Athens, loaded a large ship with grain, and conveyed it to Acanthus;[52] and there he—Phormion's associate—disposed of it, exploiting your funds.[53] [37] And he did this, men of the jury, although he lives at Athens and has a wife and children here, and the laws have prescribed the severest penalties for anyone living at Athens who conveys grain to any place other than the Athenian port; and he did it at a time when those of you who live in the town were having rations of meal measured out in the Odeum, and those in Piraeus were getting bread in the dockyard, an obol's worth at a time, and meal at the Long Stoa, receiving rations of one *hēmiekton*[54] and getting trampled underfoot! [*To the clerk*] To show that I'm telling the truth, please take the testimony and the law.

---

[51] See 34.8n. The waiving of customs duties on grain was a measure of support for Athens.

[52] A city in Chalcidice.

[53] The waiving of customs duties in Bosporus ought (according to the speaker) to have been passed on to ordinary Athenians in the form of lower prices, but instead Lampis used it to increase his own profit from transporting grain to Acanthus. The incident is not strictly relevant to the case against Phormion; Chrysippus mentions it as a way of blackening Phormion's character by showing the dishonesty of his accomplice, in contrast to Chrysippus' own patriotism (34.38–39). However, "your" is an emendation adopted by Rennie in the Oxford Classical Text; the manuscripts have "our," and if that reading is retained, the sentence can be interpreted as meaning that Lampis, in partnership with Phormion, used Chrysippus' money to purchase the grain which he exported to Acanthus.

[54] Approximately a gallon.

[TESTIMONY, LAW]

[38] So Phormion, with that man[55] as his partner and witness,[56] thinks he should defraud us of money, though we have continually conveyed grain to your port. Athens has now suffered three emergencies[57] in which you discovered which men were of use to the people, and in none of them have we been found wanting. When Alexander was advancing on Thebes, we donated a talent of silver to you. [39] When the price of grain rose on the earlier occasion and reached 16 drachmas, we imported more than 10,000 *medimni*[58] of wheat and distributed it to you at the established[59] price of 5 drachmas a *medimnus,* as you all know from receiving distributions in the Pompeium.[60] And last year my brother and I donated a talent to you for the purchase of grain for the people. [*To the clerk*] Please read the testimonies of these facts.

[TESTIMONIES]

[40] Now, if it's right to draw conclusions from these facts too, it's not plausible that, while donating so much money to gain your approval, we should accuse Phormion maliciously so as to throw away even our existing good reputation. So you would be right to support us, men of the jury. I've proved to you that at the beginning he did not put on board the ship cargo to the value of all he borrowed at Athens, and that from what he sold in Bosporus he had difficulty paying off the men who lent for the single voyage, [41] and also that he's not affluent or stupid enough to pay 39 minas instead of 2,600 drachmas,

---

[55] Lampis, mentioned in the testimony which has just been read out.

[56] Here "witness" means only that Phormion referred to Lampis' assertion. Lampis did not provide testimony in court; cf. 34.46.

[57] The three years in which Athens suffered severe shortages of grain were 335/4 (which was also the year in which Alexander the Great destroyed Thebes), 330/29, and 328/7. Cf. Isager and Hansen 1975: 200–202.

[58] One *medimnus* was approximately 12 gallons or 55 liters.

[59] In what way the price was established is not clear. Cf. Rosivach 2000: 53–54.

[60] A public building near the Dipylon and Sacred gates, with a courtyard used primarily for the preparation of the Panathenaic procession and sometimes, as here, for other purposes.

and, besides, that when he says he paid the gold to Lampis he took along neither my slave nor my partner, who was in Bosporus at the time. I am clearly supported by the testimony of Lampis himself, before he was corrupted by Phormion, that he had not received the gold. [42] If Phormion had provided proof point by point in that way, I don't know of any better defense he could have used. But on the admissibility of the case the law itself gives testimony: it authorizes mercantile cases for contracts made at Athens and for the Athenian port—not only those made at Athens but also all that are made for a voyage to Athens. [*To the clerk*] Please take the laws.

[LAWS]

[43] That my contract with Phormion was made at Athens, not even they themselves deny, but they are bringing a counter-indictment claiming that the case is not admissible. But what court are we to go to, men of the jury, if not to you, in the city where we made the contract? It would be outrageous that, if I suffered wrong concerning a voyage *to* Athens, I should be allowed to obtain justice in your court from Phormion, and yet when the contract was made *in* your port, these men refuse to stand trial in your court. [44] When we entrusted the arbitration to Theodotus, they conceded that my case against them was admissible; but now they say the opposite of what they themselves previously agreed—as if they should stand trial before Theodotus the equal-tax man[61] without any counter-indictment, and yet when we come to the Athenian court, the case is no longer admissible! [45] I wonder what he would have written in the counter-indictment if Theodotus had dismissed the case, when, now that Theodotus has decided we should go to court, he says the case is not admissible before you, to whom Theodotus decided we should go![62] It really would be

---

[61] See 34.18n. Here the reference is disparaging: Theodotus was not even a citizen, and yet Phormion submitted to his judgment as if he were a more authoritative judge than a full-blown Athenian jury.

[62] The argument is: Phormion has brought a counter-indictment because he wants you to set aside Theodotus' recommendation that the case should be tried; but if Theodotus had decided in favor of him, he would have been happy to accept that verdict and would not have brought a counter-indictment at all.

outrageous treatment of me if, when the laws authorize trials before the Thesmothetae[63] for contracts made at Athens, you were to dismiss the case after swearing to vote in accordance with the laws.

[46] That we lent the money is attested both by the terms of the agreement and by Phormion himself; that he has repaid it is attested by nobody except Lampis, his accomplice. Phormion's claim to have paid relies on Lampis alone; but I rely not only on Lampis himself but also on those who heard him say he had not received the gold. So Phormion can put my witnesses on trial,[64] if he says their testimony is untrue; but I have no way of dealing with his witnesses, who say they know that Lampis testified that he had received the gold. For if Lampis' testimony had been submitted here in court, they would perhaps have said it was right for me to give notice that I would prosecute him; but in fact I don't have that testimony, and yet Phormion thinks he ought to be let off, although he has provided no guarantee of the proposition for which he's urging you to vote.[65] [47] Surely it would be absurd if, when Phormion himself admits that he borrowed the money but alleges that he's repaid it, you were to reject what is admitted by himself and confirm by your vote what is disputed;[66] and if, when Lampis, on whom he relies for testimony, gives him testimony, although he said at the beginning that he had not received the gold, you were to decide that he had received it, though there are no witnesses of the fact; [48] and if you were not to base your conclusion on his true statements, but were to consider the lies he told later, after being corrupted, to be more trustworthy! Really, men of Athens,

---

[63] See 33.1n.

[64] By a prosecution for giving false evidence (*dikē pseudomartyriōn*).

[65] The argument is: Lampis is not in Athens and has given no testimony to the court; Phormion's witnesses are men who have testified that Lampis said he had received the money, and that testimony is no doubt true, even if Lampis was lying; the speaker therefore has no one whom he can prosecute for giving false evidence, so as to overturn the verdict in the present trial if it goes against him. However, a similar argument could have been used by Phormion, for the speaker too relies on witnesses who have merely given testimony about what Lampis said.

[66] In the counter-indictment Phormion claims that no agreement exists between the speaker and himself. That, the speaker argues, is equivalent to saying that the loan was never made.

it is much more justifiable to base your conclusion on his statements at the beginning than on his later fabrications; for the former were not planned but truthful, whereas the latter were lies told in his own interest.

[49] Remember, men of Athens, that even Lampis himself did not deny saying he had not received the gold. He admitted he'd said it but claimed he was out of his mind at the time. Then isn't it absurd if you're going to believe the part of his evidence which is on the side of the defrauder but disbelieve that which favors the defrauded? [50] Don't do that, men of the jury. It was you yourselves who imposed the death penalty on the man who was denounced in the Assembly for obtaining substantial further loans in the port without providing security for the lenders—even though he was an Athenian citizen and the son of a man who had been a general.[67] [51] You take the view that such men not only wrong those who encounter them but harm your port generally. That's quite reasonable: funds are made available to dealers not by borrowers but by lenders, and no ship or skipper or traveler can put to sea if the lenders' share is removed.[68] [52] So the laws contain many good provisions to assist them, and you must show that you support the laws in redressing wrongs and do not side with the criminals, so that you may get as much benefit as possible through your port. That will happen if you protect men who risk their own money, and don't allow them to be wronged by beasts like Phormion.

I've said all I could; I shall now call on another of my friends, if I may.

---

[67] This case is not otherwise known. Denunciation (*eisangelia*) in the Assembly was a method of initiating a prosecution for a serious offense against the state.

[68] "The lenders' share" can be taken to mean both the share which lenders contribute to the costs of a voyage and the share of the profits which they receive from it.

35. AGAINST LACRITUS

❖❖

INTRODUCTION

Lacritus originally came from Phaselis in Asia Minor, but at the time of this oration he was living in Athens, where he must have been registered as a metic (resident alien). He was a rhetorician; he had been a pupil of Isocrates and taught rhetoric himself (35.15, 35.41). Little else is known about him. One later text calls him an orator who had pupils;[1] another calls him a legislator for the Athenians, but it is hardly credible that a metic could have been a legislator in any sense, and that text is suspected of being corrupt.[2] His opponent, the speaker of the oration, was an Athenian named Androcles son of Xeinis of Sphettus. He is known from two inscriptions, and his brother Xenocles from a larger number, to have performed liturgies and other financial business; both brothers were probably affluent and prominent figures.[3] A man named Androcles was a target of jokes in two comedies, but it is doubtful whether that was the same person.[4]

The date of the speech is probably close to 351 BC. It cannot be earlier than 355, which is the earliest possible date of the enactment of the mercantile laws. On the other hand, trade from Athens to Mende and Scione (35.10) is unlikely to have continued after the Macedonians took control of neighboring Olynthus in 348. In any case, the date cannot be later than 338, because Isocrates, who is mentioned as living

---

[1] Plut. *Demosthenes* 28, quoting Hermippus of Smyrna (third century BC).

[2] Plut. *Moralia* 837d.

[3] For details, see Lambert 2001: 57–58.

[4] Menander, *Samia* 606, and there was a comedy by Sophilus entitled *Androcles,* now lost (Athenaeus 123e).

(35.40), died in that year. Many scholars think that the speech is not written in the style of Demosthenes, but there is otherwise no evidence that he is not the author.

One interesting feature of this oration is that the various documents preserved within the text appear to be all genuine, not composed by scholiasts in a later age to fill the gaps. A few of the men named in them as witnesses are also named in fourth-century Athenian inscriptions (see the footnotes for individual names), which confirms that they have not been invented. Besides, many of the details in the documents are not drawn from the speech itself but deal with complications which would have been unlikely to occur to a reader in later times. That is true especially of the agreement given in 35.10–13. This contract is of particular importance for the study of Athenian mercantile practice because, although maritime contracts are mentioned in several other orations, this is the only one of which we have the complete text.

Androcles says that he and a friend of his from Carystus in Euboea lent the sum of 3,000 drachmas to Artemon and Apollodorus, two young brothers who were merchants from Phaselis. Much of the negotiation was carried on by Lacritus, who was the elder brother of the two Phaselites. According to the agreement, which Lacritus drew up for them, the money was to be used to buy cargo for a voyage from Athens, via Mende or Scione in northern Greece, to Bosporus on the north side of the Pontus (the Black Sea) and back to Athens. The security was to be 3,000 jars of Mendaean wine, which evidently were to be taken on board at Mende or Scione and sold in Bosporus in order to buy a return cargo to Athens, probably grain; this (the wine or the grain) would be forfeited to the lenders if the borrowers failed to repay the loan.

But when in due course the two brothers returned to Athens, they neither repaid the loan nor unloaded any grain, wine, or other cargo which Androcles and his friend could take over in lieu of repayment. Lacritus asserted that the cargo had been lost in a shipwreck, and the remaining money had been lent to another Phaselite and was probably lost as well. Artemon and Apollodorus then left Athens again for Chios. Subsequently, Artemon died (we are not told how). Androcles therefore prosecuted Lacritus, as Artemon's heir, along with Apollodorus for recovery of his money by the procedure for mercantile cases.

Lacritus, however, has brought a counter-indictment (*paragraphē*), objecting that he should not be prosecuted by that procedure. The surviving oration is Androcles' reply to the counter-indictment, arguing that his prosecution should go forward to a straight trial (*euthydikia*). It is directed against Lacritus only; Apollodorus, although he too is being prosecuted by Androcles (as 35.34 shows), is not involved in the counter-indictment.[5]

Lacritus disclaimed responsibility for the debt on the ground that he was not Artemon's heir, but Androcles brushes this argument aside, perhaps too readily, pointing out that Lacritus has in fact been administering Artemon's estate.[6] However, the question whether Lacritus ought to pay Artemon's debts was one for a straight trial, not for a counter-indictment, which should be about the legal procedure. The ground for the counter-indictment must therefore have been that there was no written agreement between Androcles and Lacritus; a mercantile case had to be based on a written agreement. That is why Androcles actually has the agreement between him and Artemon read out twice in the course of his speech (in 35.10–13 and again in 35.37), to emphasize that a written agreement existed. But whether an agreement with a deceased person counted for this purpose as an agreement with the heir of the deceased was a question which may never have arisen before the present case (since the mercantile laws were a recent innovation). Lacritus was not a merchant, and may well have argued that an action against him should not be tried by the mercantile procedure. We do not know what the jury decided.

Androcles probably sensed that the jury's answer to this legal question was uncertain. So he devotes much of his speech to saying that Lacritus, as the elder brother of the two young men, was really responsible for what they did, or failed to do, in carrying out the terms of the agreement, and that the terms were in fact not carried out properly. They pledged the same goods as security for a second loan; they failed to purchase a return cargo in Bosporus; they lent some of the money to another Phaselite; they failed to bring the ship back into the

---

[5] On mercantile cases and counter-indictments, see pp. 12–14.

[6] No details of Phaselite law are known, but it was probably normal in Phaselis, as in Athens, for the property of a man who died childless to pass to his brother, if he had one. However, Lacritus may have said that Apollodorus was Artemon's heir.

port at Piraeus; and so on. Some of these allegations are confirmed by the testimony of witnesses. Some are not, and we cannot be sure that they are all true; but there does seem to be sufficient truth in the account to justify the conclusion that the terms of the agreement had not been fulfilled. In any case, the details of the story give us a vivid picture of the conditions of overseas trade in Demosthenes' time.

Another lively feature of this oration is the characterization of Lacritus and Androcles. At the beginning of the negotiations Lacritus presented himself as "a big shot, a pupil of Isocrates," who was ready to arrange everything (35.15–16). Androcles several times calls him a sophist and his tricks sophistries (35.2, 22, 39–40, 56). The implication is that he knows how to make false statements appear true, and the jury therefore should not believe anything he says. Androcles by contrast is a plain, blunt man, as he declares with an unusually strong oath: "As far as I'm concerned—by Zeus the Lord and all the gods!—I've never made any objection or criticism, men of the jury, if anyone wants to be a sophist and pay cash to Isocrates; I'd be crazy to bother about that" (35.40). Thus he hopes to convince the jury that he is not a liar. He uses some unusually strong language to attack the Phaselites in general at the start of the speech, and Lacritus and his brothers throughout. If this is skillful presentation of Androcles' bluff character, perhaps we should be cautious about following those scholars who say that the speech is not good enough to have been written by Demosthenes.

35. AGAINST LACRITUS' COUNTER-INDICTMENT

[1] It's nothing new that the Phaselites[7] are doing, men of the jury; it's what they usually do. They are the most terrible men for borrowing money in the port, and then, after they get it and draw up a maritime agreement, they immediately forget about written agreements and laws and the need to repay what they received. [2] They think that, if they pay it, it's like losing some of their own personal money, and to avoid paying they devise sophistries and counter-indictments and excuses. They're the most dishonest scoundrels in the world. Here's proof of it: although many men come to your port, both Greeks and

---

[7] Phaselis was a city on the east coast of Lycia in southern Asia Minor (near modern Kemer).

foreigners, the Phaselites by themselves always have more lawsuits than all the rest put together.

[3] That's the sort of men they are. I, men of the jury, lent money to Artemon, the brother of this man Lacritus, in accordance with the mercantile laws for a voyage to the Pontus[8] and back to Athens. He died without having repaid my money, and so I've brought this case against Lacritus in accordance with those same laws under which I made the contract, [4] because he is Artemon's brother and has possession of all his property, both what he left at Athens and what he had at Phaselis, and is heir to the whole of his estate. He cannot point to a law which gives him the right to hold his brother's property and to have administered it as he thought fit, and yet not to repay other men's loans but to say now that he's not the heir and disclaims it. [5] That's the nature of this man Lacritus' offense. Now I ask you, men of the jury, to listen favorably to what I say about this business, and, if I demonstrate that he has done wrong both to us, the lenders, and equally to you, give us the support we deserve.

[6] I had no knowledge at all of these men myself, men of the jury, but Thrasymedes son of Diophantus—the well-known man of Sphettus[9]—and his brother Melanopus are friends of mine, and we get together as often as we can. They came to me with this man Lacritus, having become acquainted with him somehow or other (I don't know how), [7] and asked me to lend money to Artemon, this man's brother, and Apollodorus[10] for a voyage to the Pontus, to set them up in business. Thrasymedes was equally unaware of their dishonesty, men of the jury; he thought they were respectable people, as they claimed and asserted they were, and he believed they would carry out all that this man Lacritus promised and undertook that they would. [8] So he was utterly deceived and quite failed to realize what beasts these men were with whom he was dealing. As for me, because I was convinced by Thrasymedes and his brother, and this man Lacritus un-

---

[8] The Black Sea.

[9] Diophantus was a politician, mentioned also in Dem. 19.86, 19.198, 19.297, 20.137, and Is. 3.22; no political activities of Thrasymedes are known to us. Sphettus was a deme, about nine miles southeast of Athens, to which Androcles himself also belonged.

[10] Apollodorus was another brother of Lacritus and Artemon (as is clear from 35.8, 35.15, and 35.31), probably the youngest of the three.

dertook that his brothers would deal honestly with me, I lent 30 silver minas jointly with a friend of ours from Carystus.[11] [9] Now, men of the jury, I want you first to hear the written agreement, under which we lent the money, and the witnesses who were present when the loan was made. Then I shall tell you the rest of what happened, to show you what robbers they were concerning the loan. [*To the clerk*] Read out the written agreement, and then the testimonies.

[10] [WRITTEN AGREEMENT] *Androcles of Sphettus and Nausicrates of Carystus lent to Artemon and Apollodorus of Phaselis 3,000 drachmas of silver for a voyage from Athens to Mende or Scione,[12] and from there to Bosporus,[13] and, if they wish, on the left-hand side as far as the Borysthenes,[14] and back to Athens, at 225 a thousand[15]—and if they sail after Arcturus[16] out of the Pontus towards Hierum,[17] at 300 a thousand—on security of 3,000 Mendaean jars of wine,[18] which will be shipped from Mende or Scione in the twenty-oared ship skippered by Hyblesius. [11] They[19] pledge these, not owing any money to anyone else on this security, nor will they obtain any further loan on it. They will convey back to Athens in the same boat all the goods from the Pontus purchased with proceeds from the outward cargo.*

---

[11] A city in the south of Euboea. The friend is named as Nausicrates in the agreement.

[12] Two cities, only about seven miles apart, on the coast of Pallene, the western promontory of Chalcidice. If weather or other circumstances made it difficult to put in to Mende, the ship might put in to Scione instead.

[13] See 34.2n.

[14] Along the coast of the Black Sea as far as the river Borysthenes (modern Dnieper, in Ukraine), near which the city of Olbia was situated.

[15] At interest of 22.5 percent.

[16] The rising of the star Arcturus (in September) marked the end of the usual sailing season. After that, the weather deteriorated, and the voyage would be more risky.

[17] This would be their departure from the Black Sea towards Athens. Hierum was the name of a promontory on the Asiatic side of the Thracian Bosporus strait, where it joins the Black Sea. A temple of Zeus stood there, and it was a regular meeting-place point for ships; cf. Dem. 20.36, 50.17.

[18] A quotation from the comic dramatist Cratinus (Fr. 195) implies that Mendaean was a highly esteemed white wine.

[19] Artemon and Apollodorus.

If the goods reach Athens safely, the borrowers will pay the accruing money to the lenders in accordance with the agreement within twenty days of their arrival at Athens in full—apart from any jettison which the fellow-voyagers vote to make jointly and any enemy exaction from them,[20] *but otherwise in full. They will place the security intact under the control of the lenders until they pay the accruing money in accordance with the agreement.*

[12] *If they do not pay within the agreed time, the lenders shall be permitted to pledge the pledged goods*[21] *and to sell them at the prevailing price; and if the proceeds fall short of the amount which ought to accrue to the lenders according to the agreement, the lenders, both singly and together, shall be permitted to exact it from Artemon and Apollodorus and from all their property, both on land and at sea, wherever it may be, in the same way as if judgment had been given against them and they had defaulted in payment.*

[13] *If they do not enter the Pontus, after waiting in the Hellespont*[22] *for ten days after the Dog-star,*[23] *they shall unload in any place where Athenians are not liable to seizure of goods,*[24] *and after sailing back from there to Athens, they shall pay the amount of interest written in the agreement in the previous year.*[25] *If any ship in which the*

---

[20] To save a ship in a storm it might be necessary to lighten it by throwing part of the cargo overboard. This would be done not by decision of the skipper alone but after a vote of the merchants on the ship, who would share the loss in proportion to the amount of goods they had on board. Similarly, they would share the loss if enemies or pirates attacked the ship and seized part of the cargo.

[21] To use the goods as security for another loan.

[22] "The Hellespont" here means not only the Dardanelles strait but the whole stretch of water between the Aegean and the Black Sea.

[23] The Dog-star (Sirius) rises in late July. If bad weather or other circumstances delayed the ship's arrival in the Black Sea beyond early August, not enough time would remain before the end of the sailing season for a worthwhile trading visit to Bosporus.

[24] This implies that in some cities, unfriendly to Athens, the authorities permitted individuals who had suffered loss or damage by Athenian action to seize in compensation any Athenian goods which were landed there.

[25] These words may refer to a previous agreement. Yet it is strange if the amount of interest payable is stated only by reference to another document. Alternatively, the meaning may be that, although a new year will by then have begun (at midsummer), the amount of interest payable when the goods have been

goods are being conveyed suffers irreparable loss but the pledged goods are saved, the lenders shall share what is preserved.[26] *On these matters nothing else is to prevail over the written agreement.*

Witnesses: Phormion of Piraeus,[27] *Cephisodotus of Boeotia, and Heliodorus of Pithus.*[28]

[14] Read out the testimonies also.

[TESTIMONY] *Archenomides son of Archedamas of Anagyrus*[29] *testifies that written terms were deposited with him by Androcles of Sphettus, Nausicrates of Carystus, and Artemon and Apollodorus of Phaselis, and the agreement is in his keeping still.*

Read out also the testimony of those who were present.

[TESTIMONY] *Theodotus an equal-tax man,*[30] *Charinus son of Epichares of Leuconoeum,*[31] *Phormion son of Ctesiphon*[32] *of Piraeus, Cephisodotus of Boeotia, and Heliodorus of Pithus testify that they were present when Androcles lent 3,000 drachmas of silver to Apollodorus*

---

merely unloaded and not sold is still to be the same as the amount specified in *this* document.

[26] The pledged goods (the 3,000 jars of wine, or the return cargo, or whatever is left of them) are to be shared equally between the lenders and the borrowers. This clause makes an exception to the usual rule that, if a ship was lost, the borrowers need repay nothing to the lenders.

[27] Probably the same man as the Phormion in Dem. 36.

[28] These two men are not otherwise known. Pithus was an Athenian deme, but its location is unknown.

[29] The mention of a daughter (named Democrateia) of Archedamas of Anagyrus in an inscription (*Inscriptiones Graecae* 2² 7277.10–11) reassures us that he was a real person, and thus that this testimony is a genuine document. Anagyrus was a deme on the coast halfway between Piraeus and Sunium, but this does not mean that the contract was kept there; no doubt Archenomides had a house in Athens.

[30] See 34.18 with note.

[31] A fifth-century inscription (*Inscriptiones Graecae* 1³ 696) mentions two brothers named Epichares and Charinus, who were probably earlier members of the same family. The location of the deme Leuconoeum is uncertain.

[32] The manuscripts here give Cephisophon as the name of Phormion's father, but an inscription (*Inscriptiones Graecae* 2² 1623.247) shows that Ctesiphon is correct.

and Artemon, and that they know that they deposited the written
agreement with Archenomides of Anagyrus.

[15] It was in accordance with that written agreement, men of the
jury, that I lent the money to Artemon, this man's brother. It was this
man who urged me to lend it, and undertook that everything would
be done for me honestly and in accordance with the agreement under
which I made the loan; and it was this man who actually wrote it, and
joined in sealing it after it was written. For his brothers were still quite
young, just lads, whereas this man was Lacritus of Phaselis, a big shot,
a pupil of Isocrates. [16] He was the man who arranged it all and told
me to listen to him. He said he would stay in Athens and do everything for me honestly, while his brother Artemon would make the
voyage in charge of the goods. At that time, men of the jury, when he
wanted to get the money from us, he declared that he was both the
brother and the partner of Artemon, and he spoke in a wonderfully
convincing manner. [17] But as soon as they got control of the cash,
they divided it between them and did what they liked with it. They
did nothing, large or small, in accordance with the maritime agreement under which they got the money, as the actual events showed.
And this man Lacritus was the ringleader of it all. On each clause in
the written agreement I shall prove that their actions have been utterly
dishonest.

[18] First, it is written that they borrowed the 30 minas from us on
security of 3,000 jars of wine, on the basis that they already had security of another 30 minas,[33] so that the cost of the wine amounted to a
talent of silver, including the expenses incurred in procuring the
wine;[34] and these 3,000 jars were to be taken to the Pontus in the
twenty-oared ship skippered by Hyblesius. [19] That's what is written
in the agreement, which you have heard, men of the jury. But these
men, instead of the 3,000 jars, didn't put even 500 jars on board the
boat. Instead of having purchased the correct quantity of wine, they

---

[33] The meaning is that Artemon and Apollodorus already possessed 30 minas
to contribute to the total cost of 60 minas (= 1 talent) of the wine which would
be the security for the loan.

[34] This shows that one jar of Mendaean wine cost somewhat less than 2 drachmas. However, the size of a jar (*keramion*) is uncertain.

did what they liked with the money, and they had no thought or intention of putting the 3,000 jars on board the boat in accordance with the written agreement. [*To the clerk*] To show that I'm telling the truth, take the testimony of the men who sailed with them in the same boat.

[20] [TESTIMONY] *Erasicles testifies that he was the helmsman of the ship skippered by Hyblesius, and he knows that Apollodorus*[35] *conveyed in the boat 450 jars of Mendaean wine and no more, and that Apollodorus conveyed no other wares in the boat to the Pontus.*

Hippias son of Athenippus of Halicarnassus testifies that he also sailed in Hyblesius' ship as the ship's commander,[36] *and that he knows that Apollodorus of Phaselis conveyed in the boat from Mende to the Pontus 450 jars of Mendaean wine, and no other cargo.*

He gave his testimony out of court to the following:[37] *Archiades son of Mnesonides of Acharnae, Sostratus son of Philippus of Hestiaea,*[38] *Eumarichus son of Euboeus of Hestiaea, Philtades son of Ctesias of Xypete,*[39] *Dionysius son of Democratides of Cholleidae.*

[21] So that was what they actually did with regard to the quantity of wine which they were required to put on board the boat; they began straightaway to depart from the first clause of the agreement and not to do what is written in it. Next, it's in the written agreement that they pledge these goods free from encumbrance and owing nothing to anyone, and that they will not obtain any further loan from anyone on this security. That is written explicitly, men of the jury. [22] And what

---

[35] Artemon seems to have ceased to be active in the business. Possibly he began to be affected by an illness which eventually caused his death.

[36] The exact function of this officer is not clear, but he evidently ranked below the skipper.

[37] Hippias is not present in court to confirm his testimony (no doubt because he is abroad on another voyage), but the five men listed confirm that he confirmed it previously in their presence. All five are shown by their demes to be Athenian citizens.

[38] Another son of Philippus of Hestiaea is attested in an inscription (*Inscriptiones Graecae* 2^2 1666.A5).

[39] The father of Philtades is named as Ctesicles in 35.34. There must be a scribal error either here or there.

did these men do? They ignored what is written in the agreement and borrowed money from a certain young man;[40] they lied to him that they owed nothing to anyone. They cheated us, by obtaining a loan on the security of our goods without telling us, and they lied to that young man, the lender, that they were borrowing on the security of unencumbered goods. Such is the evil-doing of these men.[41] And all these are sophistries devised by this man Lacritus. To prove that I'm telling the truth and they did obtain a further loan, contrary to the written agreement, the testimony of the lender himself will be read to you. [23] [*To the clerk*] Read out the testimony.

> [TESTIMONY] *Aratus of Halicarnassus testifies that he lent to Apollodorus 11 minas of silver on the security of the merchandise which he was conveying in Hyblesius' ship to the Pontus, and of the goods purchased there with the proceeds; and that he did not know that he had borrowed money from Androcles, or he would not have lent Apollodorus the money himself.*

[24] Such are the villainies of these people. Next, it's written in the agreement, men of the jury, that, after selling in the Pontus what they have brought, they are to use the proceeds to make further purchases as a return cargo and convey the return cargo to Athens, and after reaching Athens they are to repay us in good silver within twenty days; until they pay, we are to have control of the goods, and they are to hand these over intact until we receive payment. [25] This is written quite exactly in the agreement. But in this matter especially, men of the jury, these men displayed their own insolence and shamelessness, and they showed that they took not the least notice of what was written in the agreement, but considered the agreement to be just stuff and nonsense. They neither made any purchases with the proceeds in the Pontus nor loaded a return cargo to take to Athens; and because they arrived from the Pontus without it, we, the lenders of the money, had nothing to lay our hands on and take under our control until we

---

[40] Named as Aratus of Halicarnassus in the testimony which follows.

[41] This sentence makes a line of iambic verse. The writer may have had a poetic passage (such as Aeschylus, *Seven Against Thebes* 649) at the back of his mind, but the context does not suggest that he is deliberately quoting.

obtained what belonged to us, for they didn't import anything at all into your harbor. [26] What has happened to us is quite extraordinary, men of the jury: in our own city, though we've done nothing wrong and haven't been condemned to pay them any penalty, we've been robbed of our property by these men, who are Phaselites—as if Phaselites had been granted rights of seizure against Athenians! For, since they refuse to repay what they received, what else can one call such men but violent misappropriators of other men's possessions? I've never even heard of any action more wicked than the one these men have perpetrated against us, even though they admit receiving the money from us. [27] Whereas any disputed points in contracts require a trial, men of the jury, the points that are accepted by both parties, and are written in maritime agreements, are considered by everyone to be valid, and it's right to abide by the documents. Yet they have done nothing at all in accordance with the agreement, but right from the beginning they were plotting to swindle and defraud; that's proved quite plainly, both by the testimonies and by their own statements.

[28] But you must hear the most terrible thing of all that this man Lacritus did—for he was the one who arranged all this. When they arrived here, they didn't put in to your port but anchored in Thieves' Cove,[42] which is outside the boundary signs of your port.[43] Anchoring in Thieves' Cove is like anchoring at Aegina or Megara; you can sail off from that harbor wherever you wish and whenever you like. [29] The boat lay at anchor there for more than twenty-five days, while these men walked around in the sample-market,[44] and we approached them and spoke to them, telling them to make sure we got our money

---

[42] Thieves' Cove (*Phōrōn Limēn*) was a creek somewhere along the coast to the west of Piraeus, near modern Perama (Strabo 395 = 9.1.14). It was used by traders who wanted to evade the customs duties or harbor dues at Piraeus. Isager and Hansen (1975: 171–172) plausibly suggest that the Phaselite captain of the ship put in there because he was conveying to Chios (cf. 35.52–53) a cargo of grain which he would have been compelled to unload if he had put in at Piraeus (cf. Arist. *Ath. Pol.* 51.4).

[43] The boundary of the port was marked by inscribed stones, two of which have been found (*Inscriptiones Graecae* I³ 1101).

[44] An area of the port at Piraeus where samples of ships' cargoes were displayed to prospective purchasers. It is mentioned also in Dem. 50.24.

as soon as possible. They agreed and said that was just what they were arranging. We kept on approaching them, and at the same time we were watching to see if they were unloading anything from a boat anywhere or paying the two-percent tax.

[30] When they had been in Attica for a good many days, and we found that nothing whatever had been unloaded or taxed in their name, we then began to press them harder with our demands. And when we were badgering them, this man Lacritus, Artemon's brother, answered that they wouldn't be able to pay, but all the goods were lost; and Lacritus said he could give a good explanation of that. [31] We became annoyed at what he said, men of the jury, but we didn't gain anything by our annoyance, because they didn't care in the least. Nonetheless, we asked them how the goods had been lost. This man Lacritus said the boat was wrecked while sailing along the coast from Panticapaeum to Theodosia,[45] and when the boat was wrecked, his brothers lost the goods which were in the boat at the time. It contained salt fish, Coan wine,[46] and some other things, and they said that all these were the return cargo which they intended to convey to Athens, if they hadn't been lost in the boat. [32] That's what he said; but it's worth hearing what disgusting liars these people are. They had no agreement concerning the boat that was wrecked,[47] but it was someone else who had lent money on the security of the freight from Athens to the Pontus and of the actual boat; the lender's name was Antipater, a Citian by birth.[48] The Coan plonk[49] was eighty jars of wine which had gone off, and the salt fish was being transported for a farmer in the boat from Panticapaeum to Theodosia for the use of his farm laborers. So why do they make these excuses? They're irrelevant.

[33] [*To the clerk*] Please take first Apollonides' testimony that it was Antipater who lent on the security of the boat, and the shipwreck

---

[45] Panticapaeum was the principal city in Bosporus, at the eastern extremity of what is now called the Crimea, and Theodosia was about 70 miles further west.

[46] Wine from the island of Cos in the southeast Aegean.

[47] The meaning is that no loan had been obtained on the security of the ship for the return journey (but merely for the outward journey).

[48] Citium was a city in Cyprus.

[49] The Greek word used here for the wine seems to be disparaging.

was of no concern to these men; and then Erasicles' and Hippias' testimony that only eighty jars were being transported in the boat.

[TESTIMONIES] *Apollonides of Halicarnassus testifies that he knows that Antipater, a Citian by birth, lent money to Hyblesius for a voyage to the Pontus on the security of the ship skippered by Hyblesius and the freight to Pontus; and that he himself shared ownership of the ship with Hyblesius, and his own slaves sailed on the ship; and that, when the ship was damaged, his own slaves were there, and they reported it to him; and that the ship was empty*[50] *when it was damaged while sailing along the coast to Theodosia from Panticapaeum.*

[34] *Erasicles testifies that he sailed with Hyblesius as helmsman of the ship to the Pontus, and that he knows that, when the ship was sailing along the coast to Theodosia from Panticapaeum, the ship was sailing empty, and that there was in the boat no wine belonging to Apollodorus himself, the defendant in this case,*[51] *but about eighty Coan jars of wine were being conveyed for one of the men from Theodosia.*

Hippias son of Athenippus of Halicarnassus testifies that he sailed with Hyblesius as the ship's commander,[52] *and that, when the ship was sailing along the coast to Theodosia from Panticapaeum, Apollodorus put on board the ship one or two bags of wool, eleven or twelve jars of salt fish, and some goat-skins—two or three bundles—but nothing else.*

He gave his testimony out of court to the following:[53] *Euphiletus son of Damotimus of Aphidna, Hippias son of Timoxenus of Thymaetadae, Sostratus son of Philippus of Hestiaea, Archenomides son of Straton of Thria, Philtades son of Ctesicles of Xypete.*

[35] Such is the shamelessness of these people. But just think to yourselves, men of the jury, whether you know or have heard that any

---

[50] "Empty" evidently means "without a full cargo," not contradicting the statement that there was on board some salt fish, Coan wine, and other things (35.31).

[51] This testimony (and perhaps also those in sections 20 and 23) seems to have been given originally for Androcles' prosecution of Apollodorus, but it is read out here as being relevant to the present case too.

[52] See 35.20n.

[53] See 35.20n.

people ever imported wine to Athens from the Pontus by way of trade
—especially Coan! Quite the contrary, surely: wine is exported to the
Pontus from our part of the world—from Peparethos[54] and Cos, Tha-
sian[55] and Mendaean and every sort of wine from various other cities—but the goods imported here from the Pontus are different.

[36] We held on to them and pressed them to say whether any of
the goods were saved in the Pontus. This man Lacritus replied that
100 Cyzicene staters[56] were saved, and his brother had lent that gold
in the Pontus to a Phaselite skipper, a fellow-citizen and friend of his
own, and was unable to recover it, so that this too was as good as lost.
[37] That's what this man Lacritus said. But it's not what the written
agreement says, men of the jury. It instructs these men to purchase a
return cargo and bring it back to Athens, not to lend our property in
the Pontus to anyone they like without our consent but to produce it
intact for us in Athens until we get back all the money we lent. [*To the
clerk*] Please read the written agreement again.

[WRITTEN AGREEMENT][57]

[38] Does the written agreement, men of the jury, instruct these
men to lend our money—and that to a person we don't know and
have never seen—or to purchase a return cargo and bring it to Athens and produce it for us and hand it over intact? [39] The agreement
lays down that nothing is to prevail over what is written in it, and no
law or decree or anything else is to be brought to bear against the
agreement. But right from the beginning these men didn't care about
this agreement, but used our money as if it were their own; they're
such criminal sophists and dishonest people. [40] As far as I'm concerned—by Zeus the Lord and all the gods!—I've never made any
objection or criticism, men of the jury, if anyone wants to be a sophist and pay cash to Isocrates; I'd be crazy to bother about that. But, by
Zeus, I don't think that conceited people who think themselves clever

---

[54] One of the Sporades islands in the northwest Aegean (modern Skopelos).

[55] Thasos is an island in the north Aegean.

[56] See 34.5n. If the rate of exchange was 28 Athenian drachmas = 1 Cyzicene
stater, the sum of 100 staters was not a great deal less than the whole amount
which Androcles and Nausicrates had lent.

[57] The document read out in 35.10–13 is now read out again.

should covet other people's property and deprive them of it, relying on making a speech. That's what a rascally damned sophist does.

[41] This man Lacritus, men of the jury, has come to this trial not relying on the justice of his case but well aware of what they've done with regard to this loan. He believes that he's clever and will easily find words for talking about dishonest activities, and he thinks he'll mislead you in any way he wishes. He claims to be clever at this; he charges money and takes pupils because he claims to give training on this very subject. [42] And first of all he gave his own brothers this training—you can see it's wicked and dishonest, men of the jury—training them to obtain maritime loans in the port and misappropriate them and not repay them. How could there be anyone wickeder than either the teacher or the learners of such skills? Anyway, since he is clever and relies on his speaking and on the 1,000 drachmas which he paid his tutor, [43] tell him to explain to you either that they did not receive the money from us, or that since receiving it they have repaid it, or that written maritime agreements should not be valid, or that it's right to make any other use of the money than the ones for which they received it according to the written agreement. Let him convince you of whichever of those he prefers, and I myself concede that he's a very clever man if he convinces you who give judgments concerning mercantile contracts. But I know very well that he can't explain or convince you of any of those things.

[44] Apart from that, tell me this, by the gods, men of the jury: if the opposite had happened—if it had not been this man's dead brother who owed me money, but I had owed his brother a talent or 80 minas or more or less—do you think, men of the jury, that this man Lacritus would be using the same words as the ones he's been throwing about now, saying that he's not the heir and disclaims his brother's estate? Wouldn't he be relentlessly demanding payment from me, as he has from all the other people who owed anything to his dead brother either in Phaselis or anywhere else? [45] And if any of us, when prosecuted by him, had dared to bring a counter-indictment claiming that the case was not admissible, I'm quite sure he would have been indignant, and he would have protested to you that it was outrageous and illegal treatment if his case, which was a mercantile one, was voted to be inadmissible. Then, Lacritus, if that seems just for you, why won't it be just for me? Don't we all have the same inscribed

laws and the same rights with regard to mercantile cases? [46] But he's such a disgusting person, he beats everyone at dishonesty: he's attempting to persuade you to vote that this mercantile case is not admissible, although you are trying mercantile cases at this time.[58]

What is it you're demanding, Lacritus? That it should not be sufficient to deprive us of the money we lent you, but that we should also be thrown into prison by you if we fail to pay the penalty which we incur in addition?[59] [47] Surely it would be dreadful and scandalous and a disgrace to you, men of the jury, if men who make maritime loans in your port and are defrauded were taken off to prison by the borrowers who defraud them. That, Lacritus, is what you are urging to the jury.

Where else should justice concerning mercantile contracts be obtained, men of the jury? Before which official, or at what time?[60] Before the Eleven?[61] But they bring into court burglars and thieves and other malefactors liable to the death penalty. [48] Before the Archon?[62] The Archon, though, is instructed to look after heiresses and orphans and parents. Well, someone might say, before the Basileus.[63]

---

[58] During the winter; see 33.23 with note.

[59] Whichever litigant lost in the trial of a counter-indictment was required to pay to his opponent a penalty amounting to one-sixth of the sum in dispute (*epōbelia*, 1 obol per drachma). In any mercantile case, a litigant who was required to make a payment could be imprisoned until he paid (cf. 33.1); otherwise it might have been too easy for a skipper or merchant to slip away from Athens without paying.

[60] The series of suggestions and answers which follows, with the speaker conducting virtually a dialogue with himself, is a striking example of the figure of speech called *hypophora*. It is intended to show that the present case has correctly been brought before the Thesmothetae, because no other magistrates would be appropriate for it.

[61] Eleven citizens were selected annually by lot to supervise the prison and executions. They also, as this passage shows, arranged and presided at trials for certain crimes.

[62] The Archon (*epōnymos*, the principal of the nine Archons) was responsible especially for trials concerning family and inheritance disputes.

[63] The Basileus or King-Archon was responsible for trials concerning religious matters, including festivals and also homicide cases.

But we aren't gymnasiarchs,[64] nor are we prosecuting anyone for impiety. Well, the Polemarch will bring us into court.[65] Oh yes, for defection and lack of a sponsor![66] Then the generals are left.[67] But they appoint trierarchs;[68] they never bring a mercantile case into court. [49] I am a merchant, and you are the brother and heir of one of the merchants, who received the mercantile loan from us. Where, then, ought this case to come into court? Tell us, Lacritus—only say something that's just and in accordance with law. But there's no human being clever enough to justify that sort of behavior.

[50] That's not the only dreadful treatment I've had from this man Lacritus, men of the jury. Besides being defrauded of the money, I would have fallen into a very dangerous position as a result of his activities, if my written agreement with these men hadn't protected me by attesting that I lent the money for a voyage to the Pontus and back to Athens. You know, men of the jury, how severe the law is on any Athenian who imports grain to any place other than Athens or lends money for trade to any port other than the Athenian port, and what heavy and fearful penalties there are for those offenses. [51] [*To the clerk*] You'd better read them the actual law, to inform them more exactly.

---

[64] A gymnasiarch supported the runners in a torch-race at a festival.

[65] The Polemarch (no longer a military commander at this period) was responsible for certain trials involving those who were not Athenian citizens.

[66] These were accusations which could be brought only against metics (resident aliens). A case of defection (*dikē apostasiou*) was probably one in which a slave who had been freed and given metic status was accused of failure to observe the conditions laid down by the owner who had freed him. A case of sponsorlessness (*graphē aprostasiou*) was one in which a metic was accused of not having an Athenian citizen as his sponsor (*prostatēs*).

· [67] The generals (*stratēgoi*), besides commanding in war, were responsible for arranging trials and taking various decisions concerning military and naval matters.

[68] A trierarch maintained and captained a trireme in the navy, or paid a deputy to do so. At this point, most of the manuscripts add the words "bringing them into the court." Those words are deleted by Dindorf and other editors, because the routine appointment of trierarchs did not take place in a court. If the words are retained, the reference must be to cases in which an appointment was disputed.

[LAW] *And it is not to be permitted for any of the Athenians or the met-ics residing in Athens or those whom they control*[69] *to advance money for any ship which is not going to bring grain to Athens*—and the other provisions about each of them.[70] *If anyone does advance money in contravention of this, there may be showing* (phasis) *and listing* (apographē)[71] *of the money to the supervisors* (epimelētai),[72] *in the same way as has been specified concerning the ship and the grain.*[73] *He may not raise an action to recover any money which he advances for any destination other than Athens, nor may any magistracy bring an action into court for it.*

[52] That's how strict the law is, men of the jury. But these men—the wickedest men in the world!—although it was explicitly written in the agreement that the money was to come back to Athens, allowed what they borrowed from us in Athens to be taken to Chios.[74] The Phaselite skipper wanted to borrow a further sum in the Pontus from a Chian man, and because the Chian man refused to lend it unless he was given as security the whole of what the skipper had on board with the consent of the previous lenders, they did consent that this money of ours should become security for the Chian and gave him control of everything. [53] On those terms they sailed away out of the Pontus with the Phaselite skipper and with the lender from Chios, and they anchored at Thieves' Cove,[75] without anchoring in your port. And now, men of the jury, the money lent in Athens for a voyage to the Pontus and back from the Pontus to Athens has been transported to

---

[69] This expression covers women, children, and slaves. Here the reference must be primarily to slaves used as agents.

[70] The words following the dash seem to mean that the text here omits a part of the law which is not relevant to the present case. But the wording is strange, and there may be some corruption in the text.

[71] *Phasis* and *apographē* were two procedures for initiating prosecution in pub-lic cases.

[72] Ten supervisors of the port (*epimelētai emporiou*) were appointed by lot each year.

[73] This may refer to something in the omitted portion of the law.

[74] Chios is an island in the eastern Aegean. There had long been friendly rela-tions between the Chians and the Phaselites (cf. Plut. *Cimon* 12).

[75] See 35.28n.

Chios by these men! [54] So, as I stated at the beginning of my speech, you are victims just as much as we who lent the money. Just consider, men of the jury: aren't you victims, when someone attempts to get the better of your laws, and makes written maritime agreements invalid and void, and has dispatched to Chios the money borrowed from us? Isn't such a man doing wrong to you too?

[55] My case, men of the jury, is against these men, because it was to these men that I lent the money. It will be for them to proceed against that skipper from Phaselis, their own fellow-citizen, to whom they say they lent the money, without our consent and contrary to the written agreement. We don't know what dealings they had with their own fellow-citizen, but they know that themselves. [56] That's what we consider to be just. We ask you, men of the jury, to support us, who are wronged, and to punish those who use tricks and sophistries, as these men do. If you do that, you will have voted for what is advantageous to yourselves, and you will get rid of all the crimes of these wicked people, crimes which some men commit concerning maritime contracts.

36. FOR PHORMION

❖❖

INTRODUCTION

Seven speeches in the Demosthenic corpus (Orations 45, 46, 49, 50, 52, 53, and the main part of 59) are composed for delivery by Apollodorus son of Pasion, and most or all of them are now generally believed to have been written by him. The speech *For Phormion*, on the other hand, is a speech against Apollodorus and enables us to see his affairs from an opposing point of view.

Pasion had been a slave working in a bank in Piraeus owned by Antisthenes and Archestratus. Eventually he was given his freedom, took over the bank, became a wealthy man, and in return for benefactions to Athens was given Athenian citizenship. In his turn, he owned a slave named Phormion (not the same man as the Phormion in Oration 34), who was a cashier or manager in the bank, was given his freedom as a reward for good service, and later (in 361/0) became an Athenian citizen. Pasion and his wife Archippe had two sons. By the time of Pasion's death in 370/69 the elder son, Apollodorus, was already adult, but the younger son, Pasicles, was only about ten years old. Pasion therefore left a will appointing Phormion and a man named Nicocles as guardians. (He did not make Apollodorus a guardian of his young brother, probably because he regarded him as unreliable.) The guardians were to look after the whole of Pasion's property, which besides the bank included a shield-factory and other buildings, and also substantial sums which he had lent to various men and which were due to be repaid. The property was not to be divided between the sons until Pasicles came of age. Meanwhile Phormion was to hold a lease of the bank and the shield-factory, arranged by Pasion before his death. Phormion also married Pasion's widow Archippe, and in due course had children by her.

During the next two years, we are told, Apollodorus spent lavishly from the not-yet-divided property. The guardians began to be afraid that much of it would be gone before Pasicles came of age and received his share; so they decided to disregard the will in this respect and divide the property immediately, giving Apollodorus his share and retaining responsibility only for Pasicles' share during the rest of his minority. Phormion also kept the bank and the shield-factory on lease until Pasicles came of age. Then Apollodorus, as the elder, was allowed to choose between those two items, and he chose to have the factory. Pasicles thus received ownership of the bank, but subsequently the bank and the factory were both leased out again for ten years to four other men, Xenon, Euphraeus, Euphron, and Callistratus.

It was not until after the end of that second lease that Apollodorus accused Phormion of failure to return all that was lent to him under the earlier lease. There had already been another dispute between them at the time of Archippe's death (in 361/0), when Apollodorus claimed some of her possessions and Phormion reluctantly gave in to most of his demands. But now Apollodorus asserted that, when Phormion took the lease of the bank, he had also received a sum of money as working capital to finance the bank's operations and had never returned it. Phormion denied that he had ever received any such sum. Apollodorus prosecuted him for the alleged debt, claiming 20 talents, but Phormion blocked the prosecution by a counter-indictment[1] on the ground that it was illegal to reopen the matter after Apollodorus had, many years before, released Phormion by a formal declaration that all his obligations under the lease had been fulfilled.

The speech which we have belongs to the trial of this counter-indictment. It is composed for delivery not by Phormion himself but by a supporter. From the first sentence it appears that Phormion was unable to make a speech, either because of his poor command of the Greek language or because of illness or old age; he was nevertheless present in the court. The speech is skillfully written, presenting Phormion as an honest and conscientious servant of Athens, and Apollodorus as dishonest and profligate. It has never been seriously doubted that Demosthenes was the author, but many scholars have considered that it was probably not delivered in court by Demosthenes himself

---

[1] On the procedure of counter-indictment (*paragraphē*), see pp. 12–13.

but by some other friend of Phormion. Dinarchus, however, does say that Demosthenes spoke for Phormion in a trial, and presumably he is referring to this case.[2] The date is probably 350/49.[3]

This is one of the few Athenian speeches for which we also have some information about the opponent's case and the result of the trial. Apollodorus subsequently alleged that one of Phormion's witnesses, named Stephanus, had lied. He prosecuted Stephanus for false witness, and we have the texts of two speeches (Orations 45 and 46) which he delivered against Stephanus. There he describes the trial of Phormion's counter-indictment in the following way.

> First he brought a counter-indictment that the case was not admissible. Then he produced false witnesses that I had released him from the charges, and testimony of a lease, which was fabricated, and of a will, which had never existed. He was able to speak before me, because it was a counter-indictment and he was not facing a straight trial, and by reading these,[4] and by the other lies which he considered were to his advantage, he so influenced the jurors that they refused to listen to a single word of ours. So I incurred the *epōbelia*[5] and wasn't even given a hearing. I don't know if any other person has ever been so insulted, men of Athens, and I went away indignant and upset. (45.5–6)

Thus Apollodorus claims that much of Phormion's evidence, including the texts which he produced of Pasion's will and of the lease of the bank to Phormion, was false, and that he himself was shouted

---

[2] Din. 1.111. Another passage adduced by some scholars is probably not relevant here: Aes. 2.165 says that Demosthenes was paid to write a speech for Phormion when he was prosecuted by Apollodorus on a capital charge. If the statement is true, it must refer to a different case from our one, which is merely a prosecution for debt.

[3] For discussion of the evidence for the date, see Trevett 1992: 48. It is apparently more than twenty years since Phormion took the lease of the bank (36.26), and yet the news of Callippus' death has not yet reached Athens (36.53).

[4] Having the testimonies read out by the clerk of the court.

[5] The payment (1 obol per drachma) required from the losing party in a counter-indictment.

down by the jury and not given a fair hearing. We cannot now establish the truth or falsehood of the evidence for certain,[6] but it is notable that Apollodorus does not produce any alternative texts of the lease and the will, and he does not explain convincingly why he waited so many years before prosecuting Phormion.

36. COUNTER-INDICTMENT FOR PHORMION

[1] You can all see for yourselves, men of Athens, Phormion's inexperience in speaking and his weakness.[7] It's necessary for us, his friends, to speak and explain to you the facts that we know because we've often heard him relating them, so that, once you know what is right and have understood it from us correctly, you may give the right verdict in accordance with your oath.

[2] Our purpose in bringing the counter-indictment in the case was not to put it off and cause delay, but that, if he proves he's not guilty of anything, he may obtain from you an authoritative discharge from the business. Phormion here has done everything which, in the eyes of other people, is satisfactory and convincing without needing a trial in your court: he has done much to benefit this man Apollodorus; [3] he has paid and handed over honestly all of Apollodorus' assets which were left in his hands; and subsequently he was released from all charges. Nevertheless, as you see, since Apollodorus cannot bear him, he has maliciously raised this action against him for 20 talents. So I'll try to tell you from the beginning as briefly as I can everything that Phormion has done with regard to Pasion and Apollodorus. From this I'm sure it will become clear that Apollodorus' accusation is malicious, and at the same time you'll realize when you hear it that the action is inadmissible.

[4] So first he[8] will read to you the terms on which Pasion leased the bank and the shield-factory to Phormion. [*To the clerk*] Please take the terms, the challenge, and those testimonies.

---

[6] On this question, see especially Trevett 1992: 46–48.

[7] Phormion, a former slave, spoke bad Greek (cf. 45.30), and besides he was by now an old man.

[8] The clerk of the court.

[TERMS,⁹ CHALLENGE,¹⁰ TESTIMONIES¹¹]

So those, men of Athens, are the terms on which Pasion leased the bank and the shield-factory to Phormion, who was by then independent;¹² and you must hear and understand in what way Pasion came to owe the further sum of 11 talents in connection with the bank.¹³ [5] The reason why he owed it was not a lack of resources but a wish to make use of them. Pasion's landed property was worth about 20 talents, and in addition he had more than 50 talents in cash out on loan. Of those 50 talents, 11 talents which were invested came from deposits in the bank. [6] When Phormion took a lease of the bank's actual business and deposits, seeing that, if he did not yet have Athenian citizenship, he would be unable to recover the sums which Pasion had lent on security of land and buildings,¹⁴ he preferred to have Pasion himself as the debtor for this money, rather than the other men to whom he had lent it. So for that reason it was written into the lease that Pasion owed 11 talents in addition, as has been testified to you.

---

⁹A document purporting to be this lease contract is preserved in 45.31, but it is probably spurious.

¹⁰Before a trial was held, a litigant could challenge his opponent to produce some evidence which he had under his control, such as a document or a slave having knowledge of the facts. If the opponent refused to do so, a written record of the challenge and the refusal could be read out at the trial in an attempt to influence the jury against the opponent who had withheld evidence. In the present case, Phormion must have challenged Apollodorus to produce some evidence concerning the lease, which Apollodorus withheld.

¹¹From 36.7 it appears that one of these testimonies was given by the manager of the bank.

¹²Previously Phormion had been Pasion's slave.

¹³Phormion is clearly anxious to convince the jury that the sum of 11 talents mentioned in the lease is not a sum which Pasion handed over to Phormion as working capital for the bank and which Phormion should therefore have repaid to Apollodorus and Pasicles on the expiration of the lease. Actually, the sum which Apollodorus claimed was 20 talents (36.3); the explanation of that figure may be that he demanded not only the alleged capital sum of 11 talents but also 9 talents as interest for the years during which Phormion had kept the capital.

¹⁴Athenian law permitted land and buildings to be owned only by citizens. Thus Phormion, who was not yet a citizen, would be unable to take possession of the security for an unpaid debt secured in this way.

[7] The manner in which the lease was made, then, has been attested for you by the manager himself.[15] Later, when Pasion's health grew worse, notice what he put in his will. [*To the clerk*] Please take the copy of the will and this challenge and these testimonies.

[WILL,[16] CHALLENGE,[17] TESTIMONIES[18]]

[8] When Pasion had died after making this will, this man Phormion married his wife in accordance with the will and became a guardian of the boy.[19] But when Apollodorus started purloining and thinking he should spend large sums from the property which belonged to them both, the guardians reckoned to themselves that if, as the will re-

---

[15] The manager or supervisor was presumably Pasion's employee, who carried on the everyday business of the bank.

[16] Pasion died in 370/69. A document purporting to be his will is preserved in the first speech *Against Stephanus,* as follows. "Pasion of Acharnae made this will. I give my wife Archippe to Phormion, and I give with Archippe as dowry a talent due at Peparethos, a talent due here at Athens, a building worth 100 minas, some female slaves, the gold jewelry, and everything else which she has in the house, all these I give to Archippe" (45.28). This cannot be the complete document, but may be an authentic extract from it. Apollodorus, however, denied that this document was Pasion's will.

[17] This challenge is discussed in 45.8–26. It appears that, when Phormion produced his copy of Pasion's will, Apollodorus said it was not genuine; Phormion therefore challenged Apollodorus to open another document said to be the will, but Apollodorus did not. So now a record of the challenge is read out to support the claim that Phormion's copy is accurate.

[18] Texts, possibly authentic, of these testimonies are preserved in the first speech *Against Stephanus.* "Stephanus son of Menecles of Acharnae, Endius son of Epigenes of Lamptrae, and Scythes son of Harmateus of Cydathenaeum testify that they were present before the arbitrator, Teisias of Acharnae, when Phormion challenged Apollodorus, if he denied that the document which Phormion put into the jar [containing evidence for presentation to the jury] was a copy of Pasion's will, to open Pasion's will submitted to the arbitrator by Amphias, brother-in-law of Cephisophon; that Apollodorus refused to open it; and that the present document is a copy of Pasion's will" (45.8). "Cephisophon son of Cephalion of Aphidna testifies that his father left him a document labeled 'Will of Pasion'" (45.19).

[19] Pasion's younger son, Pasicles. For a will providing that a guardian should marry the testator's widow, cf. 27.5.

quired, before dividing the rest between the two, they should make a deduction equivalent to everything that Apollodorus spent from the property belonging to both, there would be nothing left. So they decided to carry out the division of the property, to safeguard the boy. [9] They did divide the rest of the property, except for what Phormion had leased, and from that part they gave half of the income[20] to Apollodorus. So, up to that time, how can he make any accusation about the lease? Objections ought to have been made straightaway at the time, not now. And he can't say he hasn't received the subsequent payments of rent either. [10] [*To Apollodorus*] Otherwise, when Pasicles came of age and Phormion's lease ended, you would never have released him from all charges; you would have been demanding payment at once of anything further that he owed you. [*To the clerk*] To prove that what I'm saying is true, and Apollodorus shared with his brother, who was still a boy, and they released Phormion from the lease and from all other charges, take this testimony.

[TESTIMONY][21]

[11] As soon as they had released Phormion from the lease, men of Athens, they shared between them the bank and the shield-factory, and Apollodorus, having the choice,[22] chose the shield-factory in preference to the bank. But if Phormion had had some personal capital attached to the bank,[23] why would Apollodorus ever have chosen the factory rather than the bank? The income was not greater, but smaller: the factory brought in a talent, but the bank 100 minas. Nor was the factory a more attractive possession, if there was some personal money attached to the bank. But there was not. That's why Apollodorus was sensible to choose the shield-factory. It is a possession free from risk,

---

[20] The rent paid by Phormion for the bank and the shield-factory.

[21] In 45.5 Apollodorus asserts that this testimony that he released Phormion from all charges was false.

[22] Apollodorus was allowed to choose between the shares because he was the elder brother.

[23] "Some personal capital" means some of Pasion's own money used as working capital to finance the bank's operations. Phormion denies that any such capital sum existed; the bank's operations were financed only by the proceeds of its lending and borrowing activities.

whereas the bank is an operation with a risky income based on other people's money.

[12] One could mention and point out many proofs that Apollodorus' accusation about a capital sum is malicious. But I think the strongest evidence of all that Phormion received no capital for this purpose is that it is written in the lease that Pasion owed money to the bank, not that he had given Phormion any capital; and secondly that at the time of the division it is clear that Apollodorus made no accusation; and thirdly that, when he[24] later leased this same business to other men for the same price, it will be clear that he didn't lease any personal capital in addition. [13] Yet, if he had been defrauded by Phormion of a capital sum provided by his father, he ought himself in that case to have given to those men a sum procured from some other source.[25] To prove that what I say is true and that he later leased it to Xenon, Euphraeus, Euphron, and Callistratus[26] and did not hand over any personal capital to them either, but they took a lease on the deposits and the investment of the deposits only, [*To the clerk*] please take the testimony about these matters—and also that he chose the shield-factory.

[TESTIMONY]

[14] So testimony has been given to you, men of Athens, that they leased it to those men too without handing over any personal capital, and being very satisfied with the way they had been treated, they set them free[27] and raised no action at that time either against them or

---

[24] After the property left by Pasion was divided between his sons, the bank belonged to Pasicles. How then was Apollodorus able to lease it out? Presumably he was acting as an agent for his young brother; cf. "they leased it" in 36.14.

[25] The meaning is that, since the price of the later lease was the same as the price of the lease to Phormion, the terms (including any capital sum provided) ought also to have been the same.

[26] These four men are mentioned again in 36.37. Euphraeus is also mentioned in 49.44, from which it appears that he had previously been an employee in the bank.

[27] This implies that the four lessees were slaves. Some scholars find it incredible that slaves could hold a lease of a bank, and they therefore interpret the words as meaning "they declared them free of obligation," but it is doubtful whether

against Phormion. Throughout the lifetime of his mother, who had an accurate knowledge of all this business, Apollodorus never brought any charge against this man Phormion. But when she died,[28] he started his malicious accusations, bringing claims for 3,000 drachmas in cash, as well as the 2,000 which she had given to Phormion's children,[29] and some little tunic,[30] and a female slave. [15] Even then he mentioned none of the claims he's making now, as will become clear. He entrusted the arbitration[31] to his wife's father,[32] his brother-in-law,[33] Lysinus, and Andromenes.[34] They persuaded Phormion here to hand over as a gift[35] the 3,000 drachmas and the additional amount, and to be friends with Apollodorus rather than become his enemy on this account. Thus Apollodorus obtained 5,000 altogether; and after going into Athena's temple[36] and releasing him from all charges a second time, [16] he is prosecuting again, as you see, concocting every accusation and—worst of all—charges from the whole of the past which he never made before. [*To the clerk*] To prove that what I'm say-

---

they can mean that. Cf. Harrison 1968–1971, vol. 1: 176; Cohen 1992: 76; Todd 1994: 137.

[28] Archippe died in 361/0.

[29] Presumably these were Archippe's own children by Phormion, but Apollodorus regarded certain of Archippe's possessions as having been part of Pasion's property, of which he was the heir.

[30] The wording is contemptuous, but the clothing in question must really have been of some value.

[31] On private arbitration, see p. 96. Despite "He entrusted," Phormion also must have agreed to the arrangement.

[32] Deinias son of Theomnestus of Athmonon. He was the father of the Theomnestus who was the speaker of the first part of Dem. 59.

[33] The husband of Apollodorus' wife's sister. He is named as Nicias in 36.17, but it is uncertain whether he is to be identified with any other Nicias known in this period.

[34] Lysinus and Andromenes are otherwise unknown. Probably they were nominated as arbitrators by Phormion.

[35] This means that Phormion did not concede that Apollodorus' claim was legally justified.

[36] The Parthenon on the Acropolis. A temple was considered a suitable place for any solemn pronouncement.

ing is true, please take the verdict which was delivered on the Acropolis and the testimony of those who were present when Apollodorus released him from all the charges upon receiving that money.

[VERDICT, TESTIMONY]

[17] You hear the verdict, men of the jury, which was delivered by Deinias, whose daughter Apollodorus has married, and Nicias, her sister's husband.[37] Now, after receiving that payment and releasing him from all the charges, he dares to raise and bring a prosecution for such a huge sum—as if either those people were all dead, or the truth would not become obvious!

[18] You have heard everything from the beginning, men of Athens —how Phormion has acted towards Apollodorus and how he has been treated. But I suppose this man Apollodorus, having no justification to give for his charges, will say what he had the audacity to say before the arbitrator,[38] that his mother was persuaded by Phormion to make away with the records,[39] and because they have been destroyed, he has no way of proving his case in detail. [19] Well, with regard to those statements and that accusation, consider what strong arguments can be brought forward to show that he's lying. In the first place, men of Athens, who would have taken his share of his father's possessions without obtaining records from which he would know what property had been left? No one, surely. [To Apollodorus] And yet it's eighteen years since you took your share, and you can't show that you ever brought any charge about the records. [20] Secondly, at the time when Pasicles came of age and was receiving the accounts of the guardianship,[40] who, if he was reluctant to accuse his mother of destroying the

---

[37] The verdict must have been given by Lysinus and Andromenes too, but here the speaker wishes to emphasize that Apollodorus is ignoring the decision of his own relatives.

[38] The public arbitrator to whom the case was referred before proceeding to trial by jury.

[39] Pasion's records of sums owed to or by him.

[40] When the young man reached the age of eighteen, his guardians had to hand over his property to him, providing accounts of the income and expenditure during the time when they had controlled it.

records himself, wouldn't have pointed it out to Pasicles, so that the facts might be established through him?[41] Thirdly, what records were the basis for your initiation of prosecutions? [*To the jury*] Apollodorus has prosecuted a great many of the citizens and has made them pay a great deal of money by writing in the charges "So-and-so committed damage[42] against me by not paying me the money which my father left him owing, according to the records." [21] But if the records had been made away with, what records were the basis for his initiation of prosecutions? To prove that what I'm saying is true, you have already heard about the share he took, and testimony about it has been given to you. Now he'll read you the testimonies about those initiatory statements. [*To the clerk*] Please take the testimonies.

[TESTIMONIES]

So by those initiatory statements he has admitted receiving his father's records; for he wouldn't say that he was prosecuting without justification, or for money which the people didn't owe.

[22] I think, men of Athens, that, of many strong indications from which it can be seen that Phormion here is not guilty, the strongest of all is that Pasicles, who is the brother of this man Apollodorus, has neither raised an action nor brought any of the charges which Apollodorus is bringing. [*To Apollodorus*] But surely, since Pasicles was a child when he lost his father, Phormion, who had been left in control of his property as guardian, would not have refrained from defrauding him and yet have defrauded you, who were then twenty-four years old and would easily have claimed your rights immediately if you had been wronged. That's not possible. [*To the clerk*] To prove that what I'm saying is true and Pasicles is bringing no charge, please take the testimony of this fact.

---

[41] Since Pasicles was at that time inspecting the accounts of what had happened to Pasion's property since his death, it would not have seemed invidious for him at the same time to inquire into the accounts of Pasion's property before his death.

[42] A prosecution for damage (*dikē blabēs*) was a regular way of claiming an unpaid debt.

[TESTIMONY]

[23] Now, on the specific point of the inadmissibility of the case, you should recall, men of Athens, from what has already been said the facts which you now need to consider. Because there had been a reckoning and a release from the lease of the bank and the shield-factory, and because there had been an arbitration and a second release from all obligations, and because the laws forbid raising actions for matters from which release has once been given, [24] and because Apollodorus was making malicious accusations and prosecuting illegally, we have brought in accordance with law a counter-indictment claiming that the case is inadmissible. To help you understand the question on which you will be casting your votes, he will read you this law and the individual testimonies of those who were present when Apollodorus released Phormion from the lease and from all the other charges. [*To the clerk*] Please take those testimonies and the law.

[TESTIMONIES, LAW[43]]

[25] You hear, men of Athens, that among the other matters for which there are not to be actions the law includes those from which release or discharge has been granted. That's quite reasonable: if it's right that no second prosecution should be allowed for cases which have once been tried, all the more is it right that there should be no trials of those who have been released. A man who has lost a case in your court may perhaps say you were misled; but when a man has openly decided against himself, by granting both release and discharge, what reason could he have had for accusing himself that would justify his prosecuting for the same matters subsequently? None, surely. That's why the legislator included in the first place among the matters for which there are not to be actions those from which release or discharge has been granted. Phormion has been given both of these, for Apollodorus granted both release and discharge; and testimony has been given to you that I am speaking the truth, men of Athens.

[26] [*To the clerk*] Now please take also the law of limitation.

---

[43] This law, forbidding prosecution after the accuser has declared his opponent free of obligation to him, is read out also in 37.18 and 38.4.

[LAW]⁴⁴

So the law, men of Athens, defines the time quite clearly. But this man Apollodorus, after the passing of more than twenty years,⁴⁵ is asking you to set his malicious accusation above the laws in accordance with which you are sitting as sworn judges. But you are expected to attend to all the laws, and not least to this one, men of Athens. [27] It seems to me that Solon⁴⁶ enacted it for no other purpose than to protect you from malicious accusations. He considered that the period of five years was sufficient for victims to obtain redress. He believed that time would provide the surest refutation of liars, but he also realized that it was impossible for contracting parties and witnesses to live forever, and so he enacted this law to replace them and to be a witness of justice for those who have no one to support them.⁴⁷

[28] I wonder, men of the jury, what argument there is which this man Apollodorus will attempt to use in reply to this. He can't have assumed that, though you saw he had not been defrauded of money, you would condemn Phormion because he married his mother. He's aware of the fact, which is known both to him and to many of you, that Socrates the well-known banker, after being released by his masters just as Apollodorus' father had been, gave his own wife in marriage to Satyrus, who had once been his slave. [29] Socles was another banker who gave his own wife in marriage to his former slave Timodemus, who is still alive to this day.⁴⁸ This is the practice of men engaged in that busi-

---

⁴⁴This law, setting a limit of five years, is read out also in 38.17.

⁴⁵This is an exaggeration. Although it was probably more than twenty years since the start of the lease, which was granted to Phormion before Pasion's death in 370/69, it was not until the end of the lease eight years later that Phormion (even if Apollodorus' accusation was true) was due to make repayment.

⁴⁶It is common for an Athenian orator to attribute an established law to Solon, even if he does not know that Solon was the actual proposer of it.

⁴⁷If more than five years have elapsed since payment was due under a contract or guardianship and the witnesses to it have died meanwhile, the alleged debtor can adduce the law to support his argument that the creditor would have made his claim sooner if the money had really been still owed.

⁴⁸Socles the banker may have been the father of Blepaeus, the banker mentioned in 21.215 and 40.52; cf. MacDowell 1990: 417. Timodemus the banker is

ness not only here, men of Athens, but in Aegina Strymodorus gave his wife to his slave Hermaeus, and after her death he went on to give him his daughter.[49] Many such instances could be mentioned. [30] It's quite reasonable: for you who are citizens by birth, men of Athens, it is not honorable to prefer any amount of money to good birth, but for those who have received citizenship as a gift either from you or from any other state, and who, thanks originally to luck, have been thought worthy of those same privileges because they have made money and acquired more than other men, those assets must be protected. [*To Apollodorus*] That's why your father Pasion, who was not the first nor the only man to do this, and was not thereby humiliating either himself or you, his sons, but saw that he would safeguard his business only if he bound Phormion in relationship to you, gave his own wife, your mother, to him in marriage. [31] If you examine the beneficial effects of this, you'll find that his plan was a good one; but if your regard for family pride leads you to reject Phormion as a stepfather, take care that your assertion doesn't become ridiculous. For if someone asked you what sort of a man you consider your father was, I'm sure you would say a good man. Then do you think that you yourself or Phormion more closely resembles Pasion in character and life in general? I'm sure you would say Phormion. So if this man, who resembles your father more than you do, has married your mother, do you reject him? [32] It was by your father's gift and instruction that this was done, as can not only be seen from his will, men of Athens,[50] but as you yourself have attested; for at the time when you demanded your share of your mother's property, and Phormion here had children by her, you conceded then that she had been married legally because your father's giv-

---

mentioned again in 36.50. The other bankers referred to in this passage are not mentioned elsewhere.

[49] Probably in all three cases (Socrates, Socles, and Strymodorus), as in the case of Pasion, what is meant is that the husband gave his wife to another husband in his will, not that she left him during his lifetime. If that is right, we must assume that Strymodorus' wife died after he had made his will but before he himself died, and he then decided to give his daughter to Hermaeus.

[50] If the text is correct, the speaker turns briefly to the jury in the middle of a passage addressed to Apollodorus.

ing of her was valid. If Phormion had taken her illegally, with no one giving her to him, the children were not heirs, and if they were not heirs, they were not entitled to share her property.[51] [*To the jury*] To prove that what I'm saying is true, testimony has been given that he accepted one quarter and granted release from all charges.[52]

[33] Having no justification to offer on any point, men of Athens, he was bold enough to produce quite shameless arguments before the arbitrator, and it's better that you should hear about them in advance.[53] One is that no will whatever was made, and the document is a complete fiction and fabrication. A second is that his reason for going along with all this and not prosecuting previously was that Phormion was willing to pay him a substantial rent and promised to go on paying it; "but now that he's not doing that," he says, "I'm prosecuting." [34] To see that both of those assertions, if he makes them, will be lies, and he'll be contradicting his own actions, consider the following points. When he denies the will, ask him in what manner he obtained the privilege[54] of owning the building[55] in accordance with the will. He can't say that the parts of the will which his father wrote in his favor are valid, and the other parts are invalid. [35] And when he says he was led on by Phormion's promises, remember that we have

---

[51] Only legitimate children could inherit. They were legitimate only if their mother had been duly given in marriage to their father—normally by her father, but this passage shows that her previous husband had the right to give her to a new one.

[52] If Archippe's children by Phormion had not been legitimate, Apollodorus would have been entitled to receive half of her property, sharing it only with Pasicles. His acceptance of a quarter implies that Archippe also had two legitimate sons by Phormion. The testimony was given in 36.16.

[53] The speaker presumes that Apollodorus will repeat to the jury the same arguments as he used to the public arbitrator.

[54] The Greek word (*presbeia*) strictly means "privilege of the eldest." But in the present instance (according to the speaker) Apollodorus did not claim possession of the building by a right of primogeniture (which did not prevail in Athenian law) but because it was bequeathed to him in his father's will.

[55] The Greek word (*synoikia*) implies a tenement-house, occupied by more than one family. The one mentioned here seems to be a different building from the one said to have been mentioned in Pasion's will as forming part of Archippe's dowry (45.28, quoted in the note on 36.7).

provided as witnesses for you the men who became their lessees of the bank and the shield-factory for a long time after Phormion had given them up.[56] When Apollodorus gave the lease to those men, that was when he ought to have brought charges against Phormion immediately, if the accusations were true on which he is prosecuting him now after releasing him then. [*To the clerk*] To prove that I'm telling the truth, and he took the building as his privilege in accordance with the will, and he not only did not think fit to bring charges against Phormion but thanked him, take the testimony.

[TESTIMONY]

[36] He wails about being hard up and having lost everything; so listen while I tell you briefly, men of Athens, how much money he has from rents and from debts owed to him. From the debts he has collected 20 talents altogether, in accordance with the records his father left, and he retains more than half of that; for in many cases he defrauds his brother of his share. [37] From the rents, in the eight years for which Phormion held the bank, he got 80 minas a year, half of the total rent, making 10 talents and 40 minas; in the ten years after that, for which they later gave a lease to Xenon, Euphraeus, Euphron, and Callistratus, he got a talent a year.[57] [38] Besides those, for about twenty years there has been the income of the property which was divided at the start and which he looked after himself,[58] more than 30 minas. If you put it all together—the amount he received as his share, the amount he collected from debtors, and the amount he has received in rent—you'll see that he's received over 40 talents, not counting what Phormion has given him,[59] and what he inherited from

---

[56] This testimony was given in 36.13.

[57] See 36.11–13, where it is said that the later lease was at the same rent as the lease to Phormion, and that the annual rent of the bank was 1 talent 40 minas, and the rent of the shield-factory was 1 talent. During Phormion's lease Apollodorus received half of these two sums combined, but during the later lease, after the properties had been distributed between the two brothers, Apollodorus received only the rent of the factory.

[58] Apollodorus' share of his father's property other than the shield-factory and the bank.

[59] See 36.15.

his mother, and 2½ talents 600 drachmas which he has had from the bank and doesn't repay.

[39] [*To Apollodorus*] Oh, but, you'll say, the city has been given that, and after spending a great deal on liturgies, you've been treated disgracefully.[60] But the amount you paid for liturgies while your money was held in common was spent by you and your brother jointly, while what you paid later is not equivalent to an income—I won't say of 2 talents,[61] but even of 20 minas. So don't blame the city, and don't say the city has been given those of your assets which you have shamefully squandered. [40] To show you, men of Athens, the amount of money he's received and the liturgies he's performed, they'll be read to you one by one. [*To the clerk*] Please take this document and this challenge and these testimonies.

[DOCUMENT, CHALLENGE, TESTIMONIES]

[41] So he has received all that money, and he also has debts amounting to many talents due to him, some of which are being paid voluntarily, and some he is recovering by lawsuits. Those are additional to the lease of the bank and the rest of the property left by Pasion; they are debts which were owed to Pasion and have now been taken over by these people. He has then spent on liturgies the amount you heard—not even a tiny fraction of the income, much less the capital. Yet he'll still boast and talk about trierarchies and chorus-productions. [42] I have already shown that he will not be telling the truth about this. But I suppose that, even if what he says were absolutely true, it would be better and more just for Phormion to perform liturgies for you out of his own funds, rather than for you to give his funds to Apollodorus and then get only a small share of the total amount yourselves, while seeing Phormion in the utmost poverty and Apollodorus indulging himself and squandering it in his usual way.

[43] [*To Apollodorus*] As for his "affluence" and his acquiring it from your father's property, and the questions you said you'd ask

---

[60] See Dem. 50 on the large sums which Apollodorus claimed to have expended as a trierarch.

[61] The total income of 40 talents in twenty years (36.38) was an average annual income of 2 talents.

about where Phormion has acquired his property, you're the one person in the world who can't talk about that. Pasion, your father, also acquired his wealth not by a windfall or by inheritance from his father, but he came to be trusted in the house of his masters, the bankers Antisthenes and Archestratus,[62] because he showed himself to be honest and reliable. [44] To people working in commercial finance, it's a marvelous thing for the same man to be found industrious and also to be honest. That wasn't something passed on to Pasion by his masters; he was honest by his own nature. Likewise, your father didn't pass it on to Phormion; he'd have preferred to make *you* honest, if it had been in his power! If you don't understand that trustworthiness is the best of all foundations for making money, you won't understand anything. Apart from that, Phormion has been useful in many ways to your father and to you and to your business in general. But as for your greedy character, could anyone match it?

[45] I'm surprised you don't reflect on the fact that Archestratus, your father's former owner, has a son in Athens, Antimachus, who is less successful than he deserves to be. He's not prosecuting you or complaining of unfair treatment because you wear a fine woolen cloak, and you've bought the freedom of one mistress and given away another in marriage—all the time having a wife as well—and you go around with three slaves attending you, and your self-indulgent way of life is noticeable even to people who meet you in the street, while Antimachus himself is in want. [46] Nor is he unaware of Phormion's position. Yet if you think you have a claim on Phormion's property on the ground that he once belonged to your father, Antimachus has a stronger claim on it than you; for your father belonged to those men, so that both you and Phormion now belong to Antimachus, according to that argument. But you are so far gone in stupidity that you yourself compel people to say things which you might be expected to hate anyone for saying. [47] You insult yourself and your deceased parents; you abuse the city; and instead of guarding and enhancing the benefits[63] your father, and afterwards Phormion, gained from enjoying the kind-

---

[62] Archestratus the banker is mentioned also in Isoc. 17.43, but Antisthenes has not been identified elsewhere.

[63] Athenian citizenship.

ness of these gentlemen,[64] in order to bring the utmost credit both to those who bestowed them and to your family who received them, you make public and display and demonstrate and all but denounce the kind of man you are—whom they made an Athenian! [48] Even now, when we are claiming that, since Phormion was released, no account should be taken of his having once belonged to your father, you are so far gone in lunacy—what else could one call it?—that you don't realize that our argument favors you, and that, when you claim that Phormion should never be on equal terms with you, you are arguing against yourself. Whatever claims you make for yourself against him, the very same claims can be made against you by your father's original owners. Indeed, to prove that Pasion too belonged to owners and then was released in the same manner as Phormion was released by your family, [To the clerk] please take these testimonies that Pasion belonged to Archestratus.

[TESTIMONIES]

[49] So Phormion originally guarded the business and made himself useful to Apollodorus' father in many ways, and has done Apollodorus himself all the good turns which you have heard about—and then Apollodorus thinks he should get him convicted in this serious case and turn him out unjustly![65] [To Apollodorus] For there's nothing else you could accomplish. If you look closely at his possessions, you'll discover whom they belong to, if—heaven forbid!—the jury is misled.[66] [50] Look at Aristolochus son of Charidemus.[67] He once owned

---

[64] The jury, here regarded as representative of the city of Athens.

[65] This is not a reference to exile, which would not be imposed for debt. The meaning is rather that, since Phormion could not pay 20 talents in cash, Apollodorus, if he won the case, would be entitled to take possession of Phormion's house and other property.

[66] If the jury is so misguided as to give a verdict against Phormion, the money at present in his possession will have to be returned to those who deposited it in the bank, and Apollodorus will get none of it.

[67] The financial ruin of Aristolochus the banker is mentioned again in 45.63–64. He may have been identical with Aristolochus of Erchia, who is known to have been a trierarch several times.

some land. Now it's owned by a number of people, because he was in debt to a number of people when he acquired it. Look at Sosinomus and Timodemus[68] and the other bankers who were all turned out of their possessions when they had to settle with their creditors. But you don't think it necessary even to consider any of the plans which your father, a far better and more sensible man than you, made to meet all contingencies. [51] Zeus and the gods! He considered Phormion to be so much more valuable, both to you and to him and to your business, that, even though you were a grown man, he left Phormion, not you, as guardian of half of his estate[69] and gave him his wife and respected him as long as he lived. Quite rightly, men of Athens; [*To Apollodorus*] for the other bankers, though they were not paying rent but were working solely for themselves, were all ruined, whereas Phormion, while paying rent of 2 talents 40 minas, also preserved the bank for you. [52] Pasion was grateful to him for that, whereas you take no account of it; in opposition to the will and the curses in it,[70] written by your own father, you harass, you accuse, you prosecute. My good sir—if it's possible to call you that—won't you stop it? Won't you realize that honesty is more profitable than wealth? In your own case, if you're telling the truth, after receiving so much money you've lost it all, you say. But if you were a good man, you'd never have spent it.

[53] But I declare, by Zeus and the gods, however I look at it I can't see any reason for the jury to believe you and convict Phormion. Why should they? Because you're charging him while the offenses are recent? But you're making your accusations long years afterwards. Because you were avoiding litigation during that time? Everyone knows how much of it you were continually carrying on, not only bringing private cases just as serious as this one, but making malicious public accusations and putting one and all on trial. Didn't you prosecute Timomachus? And Callippus, the man now in Sicily? And Menon too? And Autocles?[71]

---

[68] Timodemus is mentioned earlier, in 36.29. Sosinomus is not known.

[69] The half to be inherited by Pasicles.

[70] Pasion's will evidently invoked divine punishment on anyone who contravened its provisions.

[71] Autocles, Menon, and Timomachus were successively generals commanding the Athenian fleet in the north Aegean in the years 362/1 and 361/0, and Cal-

And Timotheus?[72] And lots of others? [54] Yet how does it make sense that a man like you, Apollodorus, should have sought justice for public offenses, of which only a part affected you, before the private ones for which you're now bringing charges, especially when they're so serious, as you allege? Why then did you prosecute those men and leave Phormion alone? Because he wasn't doing you any wrong; your accusation now is surely a malicious one.

So I consider, men of Athens, that it's above all relevant to provide witnesses of these facts; for if a man is continually bringing malicious accusations, what are we to think he's doing now? [55] And, by Zeus, I think myself, men of Athens, that it's also relevant to tell you everything that is evidence of Phormion's character and of his honesty and kindness. For a man who was regularly dishonest might very well turn out to be defrauding Apollodorus too; but if a man has never defrauded anyone but has voluntarily helped many people, what could his character be that would be likely to make him defraud Apollodorus and no one else? So if you listen to these testimonies, you'll understand the characters of both of them.

[TESTIMONIES]

[56] And now the testimonies of Apollodorus' dishonesty too.

[TESTIMONIES]

Is Phormion like that? Just consider. [*To the clerk*] Read them out.

---

lippus held some subordinate command under Timomachus. Apollodorus was one of the trierarchs in that fleet, and his personal disputes with Timomachus and Callippus are described in his speech *Against Polycles* (Dem. 50). After his return to Athens in 360, he prosecuted (or supported the prosecution of) each of the four on various charges of treacherous or incompetent conduct during the campaign; for discussion of the political significance of these prosecutions, see Trevett 1992: 131–138. Callippus escaped to Sicily, where he became a supporter of Dion of Syracuse and eventually succeeded him for a short time, but was killed in about 350.

[72] Timotheus, the well-known general, was one of Pasion's debtors whom Apollodorus prosecuted to recover the money after Pasion's death. Apollodorus' speech for the case survives (Dem. 49). (Since the speaker has just mentioned private cases as well as public ones, it may be unnecessary to suppose that Apollodorus also brought an otherwise unknown public prosecution against Timotheus.)

[TESTIMONIES]

Read also all the public services which Phormion has done for the city.

[TESTIMONIES]

[57] Phormion, men of Athens, has done all those services for the city and for many individuals among you. He's never done anyone any harm in either private or public matters—nor has he defrauded this man Apollodorus. So he asks and entreats and claims that he should be acquitted, and we, his friends, join in this request.

There's something else that you should hear. According to the testimonies read to you, men of Athens, Phormion has procured for you larger sums than either he or anyone else possesses. But then he has credit with those who know him for such large sums and for far greater ones, and that enables him to provide both for himself and for you. [58] Don't sacrifice all this, and don't allow that scoundrel to upset it. Don't set a disgraceful example, showing that horrible malicious accusers are permitted by you to take the money of men who work and are content to live modestly. That money is much more useful to you in Phormion's hands. You see for yourselves and you hear from the witnesses what his attitude is to those who ask for help; [59] and he hasn't done any of those things for the sake of financial profit, but from the kindness and goodness of his heart. It's not right, men of Athens, to sacrifice such a man to Apollodorus, nor to sympathize with him only when it will be no use to him. You should sympathize now, when it's in your power to protect him. I don't see at what other time you might be of more assistance to him.

[60] Most of what Apollodorus will say you should consider to be just malicious talk. Tell him[73] to show either that this will was not made by his father, or that there is some other lease apart from the one which we are bringing to your attention, or that he had not made a reckoning and released Phormion from all the charges, in accordance with his father-in-law's verdict and his own consent,[74] or that the laws

---

[73] A jury could not give formal instructions to a speaker, but might shout and heckle if he failed to speak to the point.

[74] See 36.15–17.

allow one to prosecute for matters that have been dealt with in this way or to raise anything of the kind. [61] But if he can do nothing but utter accusations and slanders and abuse, pay no attention. Don't be taken in by his shameless bawling, but be careful to keep in mind what we've told you. If you do, you will be keeping your own oath and you'll justly acquit Phormion. He deserves it, by Zeus and all the gods!

[62] [*To the clerk*] Take and read to them the law and these testimonies.

[LAW, TESTIMONIES]

I don't know why I need say any more. I think you have understood everything that has been said. Pour out the water.[75]

---

[75] The last sentence is addressed to the attendant in charge of the water-clock (*klepsydra*). It signifies that the speaker does not need the remainder of his allocation of time. Oration 38 has the same conclusion.

37. AGAINST PANTAENETUS

INTRODUCTION

The speech *Against Pantaenetus* is written for delivery by a man named Nicobulus. Neither Nicobulus nor Pantaenetus is otherwise known, but it appears from the speech that both were Athenian citizens, not metics. The original agreement between them was made in the spring of 347 BC (37.6), after which Nicobulus went off on a trading voyage to the Black Sea, and the dispute arose after his return; thus the date of the speech is probably 346. There is no reason to doubt that it was written by Demosthenes.

The Athenian silver mines were owned by the state and let out on lease. Pantaenetus was the lessee of a mine, and he had a workshop with thirty slave workmen for processing the silver ore obtained from it. However, he could not afford to buy the workshop and workmen outright, and so he held them on an arrangement which is sometimes called "sale with a view to release" or "sale with right of redemption." [1] This was much like a lease by which the lessee paid a monthly rent to the lessor, but with the difference that the agreement gave Pantaenetus the right to buy the property at the original price if he wished to do so within a stated period of time. The terminology used for such an arrangement is confusing, because either the debtor or the creditor is liable to be spoken of as the owner of the property: sometimes the man whom we may call the debtor or lessee (such as Pantaenetus) is

---

[1] The Greek expression *prasis epi lysei* is not actually used in this speech or in any Athenian text, but selling *epi lysei* is recorded on a number of *horoi,* stones marking ownership of pieces of land; cf. Harris 1988.

said to have bought the property with money lent to him by the other party; sometimes the creditor or lessor is said to have bought it; thus the monthly payments made by Pantaenetus may be called either interest or rent.

According to Nicobulus' account the course of events was as follows. The workshop and workmen were bought by Mnesicles from a previous owner named Telemachus for 105 minas, of which 45 minas was contributed by two other men, Phileas and Pleistor. The agreement was that Pantaenetus was to have the use of them, with the right of redemption, for a rent of 105 drachmas a month. After a while Mnesicles wished to sell the property, and so it was bought by Nicobulus and his friend Euergus[2] at the same price of 105 minas, of which Nicobulus paid 45 and Euergus 60 minas. They made an agreement with Pantaenetus on exactly the same terms as his previous agreement with Mnesicles: he was to pay rent of 105 drachmas a month, of which we may assume 45 drachmas was to go to Nicobulus and 60 drachmas to Euergus.

However, the figure of 105 minas seems to need further explanation, because we are told that the property was later sold for 3 talents 2,600 drachmas (37.31), equivalent to 206 minas. Granted that the value of property may vary over time, it is strange if the workshop and workmen almost doubled in value over a short period. It has therefore been suggested that Mnesicles, Phileas, and Pleistor did not pay the whole of the price, and the difference was made up by Pantaenetus. That may be correct; but, I suggest, it produces a more economical hypothesis if we bring into the account at this point the other men who later claimed to have lent money to Pantaenetus (37.7). They seem to have been friends of his, but their names are not given; since they claimed to be creditors but their claim was disputed, I shall call them the "creditors" in quotation marks. My suggestion is that the "creditors" did lend approximately 101 minas, while Mnesicles, Phileas, and Pleistor provided 105 minas, enabling the workshop and workmen to be bought for approximately 206 minas for Pantaenetus' use. Then what Mnesicles later sold to Nicobulus and Euergus, though they prob-

---

[2] It is not known whether this Euergus is the same man as the one in Oration 47.

ably did not realize it at the time, was not really full ownership but only a partial or encumbered ownership of the workshop and workmen, which served also as security for the "creditors."

Nicobulus then left Athens on a trading voyage (an unsuccessful one, he says) to the Black Sea, and on his return he found that events had taken an unexpected turn. According to what Euergus told him, Pantaenetus had failed to pay the rent, and Euergus had therefore repossessed the workshop and workmen. That was what he was entitled to do if Pantaenetus had indeed defaulted on the agreement. Pantaenetus, however, made various objections, which might well be clearer to us if we possessed his speech; as it is, they do not emerge clearly from Nicobulus' hostile account. Apparently Pantaenetus asserted that Euergus was transgressing the agreement when he repossessed the property. He brought forward the "creditors"; and, if my hypothesis about them is correct, he will have said that Euergus and Nicobulus were not entitled to take sole possession of the property because about half of its value was security for the money put up by the "creditors."

He also said that Euergus was to blame for his (Pantaenetus') failure to pay the rent due to the state treasury for the mine. This incident involved a slave named Antigenes, who belonged to Nicobulus; Pantaenetus alleged that his own slave had been carrying the money which was to be paid to the treasury, but Antigenes took it away from him. If this happened while Nicobulus was in the Black Sea, Antigenes can hardly have been carrying out a specific order from him; but probably Nicobulus left Antigenes in Athens with general instructions to carry out orders given by Euergus. Possibly Pantaenetus' slave was confused; he may have thought that the money he was carrying was intended by Pantaenetus to be the rent for the workshop and workmen rather than the rent for the mine, and so he may have handed it over when Antigenes came to collect the rent for the workshop and workmen. That might be the reason why Pantaenetus said that Euergus had no right to repossess the workshop and workmen, having actually received a payment. But we do not possess enough evidence to be sure of the facts of this incident. Whatever the truth of it, Pantaenetus went on to prosecute Euergus, won the case, and was awarded the sum of 2 talents in compensation.

The trial of Euergus may not yet have been held when Nicobulus arrived back in Athens, for he found Euergus still in possession of the workshop and workmen. He did not want to get involved himself in the processing of silver ore, but a way out of his difficulty was then offered to him by the "creditors." They pointed out that the workshop and workmen were actually worth much more than the sum of 105 minas which Nicobulus and Euergus had paid for them, so that Nicobulus and Euergus were not entitled to keep them as their own property while denying the "creditors" their rights. They made alternative offers to Nicobulus and Euergus: either they should repay to the "creditors" the amount which the "creditors" had lent to Pantaenetus, and then keep the workshop and workmen; or they should accept from the "creditors" the sum of 105 minas which they had originally paid, and give up the workshop and workmen to the "creditors." (If my hypothesis about the money originally put up by the "creditors" is correct, these alternative offers were essentially a fair proposal.) Nicobulus chose, and persuaded Euergus to accept, the latter alternative, to recover their money and be rid of the whole business. After some delay the money was paid over to them, and thus Nicobulus formally sold the workshop and workmen (or rather his and Euergus' share of them) for 105 minas to the "creditors," who subsequently sold the entire property to some other purchaser for 206 minas.[3]

Nicobulus then, so he claims, obtained from Pantaenetus a formal release and discharge, acknowledging that he was under no further obligation. So he was astonished when Pantaenetus subsequently prosecuted him for "damage" (*blabē,* in the sense of causing him financial loss). Much of the charge is quoted in the surviving speech. The following were apparently the principal accusations.

1. Nicobulus ordered his slave Antigenes to seize the money which was to have been taken to the state treasury to pay the rent for Pantaenetus' mine, thus causing Pantaenetus to incur an additional payment as a debtor to the treasury.

2. Nicobulus sent Antigenes to repossess the workshop and workmen.

---

[3] Although Nicobulus says to Pantaenetus in 37.31 that the property was sold by "you," the same passage makes clear that Pantaenetus was not formally the vendor.

3. Nicobulus told the workmen to stop working for Pantaenetus.

4. Nicobulus took over the ore in the workshop and kept the silver extracted from it.

5. Nicobulus sold the workshop and workmen to other purchasers, in contravention of the agreement giving Pantaenetus the right to buy it.

6. There were other accusations involving "assault and insolence and offenses of violence and against heiresses" (37.33), but details of these are not given.

For all these Pantaenetus claimed compensation of 2 talents. Nicobulus in his speech denies the truth of the accusations, declaring that he was actually abroad when some of the acts were alleged to have been committed. He also points out that Pantaenetus has already been awarded compensation of 2 talents to be paid by Euergus. But presumably Pantaenetus maintained that Euergus and Nicobulus were jointly responsible for what had happened, so that he should receive compensation from both of them. No doubt that point would have been argued in a straight trial of the case.

Nicobulus, however, is trying to prevent the case from going to a straight trial by bringing a counter-indictment.[4] He states correctly that according to law a prosecution is inadmissible if the prosecutor has previously released his opponent, and he calls witnesses to testify that Pantaenetus did release him (37.17). If those witnesses were telling the truth, this argument for the counter-indictment seems to be conclusive as far as the accusations about the workshop and workmen are concerned, but it does not deal with the other accusations (nos. 1 and 6 in the list given above). As a secondary argument, he also maintains that some of Pantaenetus' accusations were ones which should have been taken to different magistrates, not to the Thesmothetae, who were the magistrates responsible for mining cases. That too seems to be a sound argument, but it would have been valid against only some, not all, of the accusations.

---

[4]On the procedure of counter-indictment (*paragraphē*), see pp. 12–13.

37. COUNTER-INDICTMENT AGAINST PANTAENETUS

[1] Since the laws, men of the jury, permit a counter-indictment for any matters for which a person brings a prosecution after granting release and discharge, and I received both of those in relation to this man Pantaenetus, I have brought a counter-indictment, as you heard just now, that the case is not admissible. I did not think that I should give up this right,[5] nor that, when I demonstrate that, besides everything else, he has granted me release and ended his dealings with me, it should be open to him to say that I am not telling the truth and to argue that, if any such thing had been done, I would have brought a counter-indictment against him; I thought I should bring this plea into court and demonstrate both facts to you, that I have done him no wrong and also that his prosecution of me is illegal.

[2] If Pantaenetus had suffered any of the things of which he's now accusing me, he would have come forward to prosecute me straightaway, at the time when we had the contract with each other. These cases are monthly,[6] and we were both in Athens, and all men are usually indignant at the actual time of an offense rather than after some time has elapsed. But when a man has not suffered any wrong—as I'm sure you'll agree when you hear the facts—but brings a malicious accusation because he's been buoyed up by his success in his case against Euergus, I can only try to protect myself in your court, men of the jury, by showing that I've done nothing wrong at all and providing witnesses for my statements.

[3] I am going to make a moderate and just request of you all: to listen to me favorably on the subject of my counter-indictment and to give your attention to the whole affair. There have been many prosecutions in this city, but I think it will be clear that no one has ever brought a more shameless or more malicious prosecution than the one which this man has dared to initiate and bring into court. I'll explain to you everything that happened from the beginning as briefly as I can.

[4] Euergus and I lent 105 minas, men of the jury, to this man Pan-

---

[5] By allowing the case to go directly to a straight trial.
[6] See 33.23n.

taenetus on security of a workshop in the workings at Maroneia[7] and thirty slaves. Of the sum lent, 45 minas belonged to me and 1 talent to Euergus. The situation was that Pantaenetus owed 1 talent to Mnesicles of Collytus[8] and 45 minas to Phileas of Eleusis and Pleistor.[9] [5] The vendor[10] of the workshop and the slaves to us was Mnesicles; he had bought them for Pantaenetus from Telemachus, the previous owner. Pantaenetus rented them from us for the amount of interest accruing on the money, 105 drachmas a month.[11] We drew up terms of agreement, in which the rent was specified and also Pantaenetus' right of redemption from us within a stated period.

[6] When all this had been done in the month Elaphebolion in the year when Theophilus was Archon,[12] I immediately sailed off to the Pontus,[13] but Pantaenetus and Euergus were in Athens. What dealings they had with each other while I was abroad, I can't say. Their accounts are not consistent with each other, and Pantaenetus is not always consistent with himself: sometimes he says he was evicted from the lease by Euergus by force, contrary to the terms; sometimes he says Euergus was to blame for his being inscribed on the treasury list;[14] sometimes he says anything else he likes. [7] Euergus says simply that, since he did not receive the rent and Pantaenetus was not carrying out

---

[7] A district in the silver-mine area of Laurium in southeast Attica.

[8] Mnesicles of the deme Collytus is named in the naval records as having been appointed by the Council in 346/5 as a supervisor of naval equipment (*Inscriptiones Graecae* 2² 1622.420).

[9] Phileas of the deme Eleusis is named in the records of the Poletae as lessee of a mine in about 340 (*The Athenian Agora,* 19: p. 120, no. P27, line 87). Pleistor is unknown.

[10] I keep the literal translation of *pratēr* as "vendor," though some scholars prefer to translate it as "warrantor" because the vendor would have to guarantee that the property being sold was free from other liabilities or debts. It seems that Mnesicles gave this guarantee when he was not entitled to do so, for other creditors later turned up (37.7).

[11] The interest payable was 1 drachma per mina per month = 12 percent per annum.

[12] Approximately March 347.

[13] The Black Sea.

[14] As a debtor to the state, having failed to pay the rent for the mine.

any of the other terms of the agreement, he went and recovered his property from Pantaenetus with his consent; after that, Pantaenetus went away and came back with the men who were going to make claims on it,[15] but Euergus did not give way to them, although he was content for Pantaenetus to keep possession of what he had rented as long as he fulfilled the agreed conditions. That's what they tell me. [8] But one thing I'm sure of: if Pantaenetus is telling the truth and has been treated disgracefully by Euergus, as he claims, he has received compensation at his own valuation. For he came to your court and got him convicted; and it's surely not right for him to obtain compensation for the same offense both from the man responsible and from me, when I wasn't even in Athens at the time. But if Euergus is telling the truth, he is the victim of a malicious accusation, it seems, and in that case too it would be unreasonable for me to be prosecuted for the same offense. To prove that I'm telling the truth about this, first of all, I'll provide the witnesses of it for you.

[WITNESSES]

[9] So you hear from the witnesses, men of the jury, that the vendor of the property to us was the man who had originally bought it, and that the workshop and slaves were our property when Pantaenetus rented them in accordance with the terms, and that I was not present at the subsequent dealings between him and Euergus and wasn't in Athens at all, and that he brought a case against Euergus and never brought any charge against me.

[10] After I returned—having lost nearly everything I had when I set out—I was told and discovered that Pantaenetus had given up the property we had bought, and Euergus was in possession and control of it. I was exceedingly upset when I saw the strange turn that the affair had taken. I needed either to share the business and operations with Euergus, or to have Euergus as my debtor in place of Pantaenetus and to draw up a new lease and make a contract with him; but I didn't want to do either of those things. [11] Being unhappy with the circumstances I have mentioned, when I saw Mnesicles, who had been

---

[15] Men who claimed that they had made loans to Pantaenetus on the security of this same property.

the vendor of this property to us, I went and complained to him, telling him what sort of a man he'd introduced to me; and I asked him about the claimants and what it was all about. When he heard about the claimants, he laughed. He said that they wanted to meet me, and that he would bring us together and advise Pantaenetus to do all that was right for me, and he thought he would persuade him. [12] When we met—what need is there to give the details? The men who arrived asserted that they had made loans to Pantaenetus on the security of the workshop and slaves which we purchased from Mnesicles; and there was nothing straightforward or honest about them. When it was proved that their statements were all lies and Mnesicles confirmed our claim, they issued a challenge to us, expecting that we would not accept it: either to take the whole amount of money from them and withdraw, or to settle the amounts they claimed—because they alleged that the property we were holding was worth much more than the money we had paid for it. [13] When I heard that, I immediately, without even thinking about it, agreed to take the money and persuaded Euergus to do so. But when the time came for us to be paid it, and the affair had reached that point, those men, who had previously offered to pay it, then refused to do so unless we became vendors[16] of the property to them. In that respect at least they were sensible, men of Athens, because they saw how we were being maliciously accused by Pantaenetus. [*To the clerk*] To prove that what I say is true, please take these testimonies too.

[TESTIMONIES]

[14] So that was where the matter stood: the money was not forthcoming from the men Pantaenetus had brought in, while we quite properly appeared to be in control of the property we had bought. He begged, entreated, and implored us to become the vendors;[17] and

---

[16] See 37.5n. The point here is that the prospective purchasers were not willing to trust Pantaenetus' word as warrantor that the property was not subject to other liabilities or debts.

[17] Pantaenetus was keen that the sale should go ahead, probably because he expected that the new purchasers would then allow him to continue in occupation and use of the workshop and workmen.

since he asked me and begged me repeatedly and I don't know what he didn't do, I submitted to that too. [15] Seeing that he was a vicious person, men of Athens, at first denouncing Mnesicles to us, and next quarreling with the man with whom he had been especially friendly, Euergus, and when I first returned from my voyage asserting he was glad to see me, but later being surly towards me when he had to honor his obligations, and being everyone's friend until he secured and obtained what he wanted, but afterwards becoming hostile and disagreeable—[16] I thought it best to be reconciled and assist him by becoming the vendor and thus reach a settlement, being discharged and released from all the accusations. When this had been agreed, he released me from everything, and as he asked I became the vendor of the property on the same conditions as I had myself bought it from Mnesicles. After getting back my money and doing Pantaenetus no wrong whatever, I thought, by the gods, that, whatever happened, he would never prosecute me.

[17] Those, men of the jury, are the facts which will be the subject of your vote and which have given rise to my counter-indictment that this malicious case is inadmissible. After producing as witnesses men who were present when I was released and discharged by him, I shall show that according to the laws the case is not admissible. [*To the clerk*] Please read out this testimony.

[TESTIMONY]

Please read out the purchasers' testimony too, [*To the jury*] to make clear to you that I sold it at his request to the men he requested.

[TESTIMONY]

[18] I have not only these men as witnesses that I have been released and am now being accused maliciously, but Pantaenetus himself as well. For when he brought his case against Euergus and took no action against me, he was testifying then that he had no remaining claim against me; for surely, if the offenses were the same and he had similar claims against us both, he wouldn't have let one of us go and prosecuted the other. Now, the laws do not permit a subsequent prosecution concerning what has been done in this way, as I think you know even without my telling you; but still [*To the clerk*] read this law out to them too.

[LAW]¹⁸

[19] You hear, men of the jury, the law says explicitly that for matters from which anyone grants release and discharge there are to be no further prosecutions. And in fact both of those things have been granted to me by Pantaenetus, as you heard from the testimonies. Now, all prosecutions forbidden in the laws should be avoided, but these most of all. What the treasury has sold, someone might be able to say it has sold unjustly and improperly;¹⁹ [20] and when the court has given a verdict, it's possible to say that it was deceived when it did so; and in each of the other cases in the law there might reasonably be some argument. But when a man has himself been convinced and has granted release, it's surely not possible for him to argue and accuse himself of doing it unjustly. Men who prosecute in infringement of those other rules are ignoring other people's verdicts, but a man who grants release and subsequently brings a case is ignoring his own. That's why those men especially deserve condemnation.

[21] So I've shown that he granted me release from everything when I became the vendor of the slaves, and you've just heard from the law which was read that the laws forbid prosecutions in these cases. But I don't want any of you, men of Athens, to think that I'm resorting to this plea because I'm guilty on the actual facts of the case; so I want to go through each of his charges and show that he's lying. [22] [*To the clerk*] Read out the actual charge which he's bringing against me.

[CHARGE] *Nicobulus caused me damage*²⁰ *by scheming against me and my property: he ordered his slave Antigenes to take away from my slave the cash which he was bringing as payment to the city for the mine which I had purchased for 90 minas, and he was responsible for my being listed as owing double to the treasury*²¹—

---

¹⁸ The same law is read out in 36.24 and 38.4.

¹⁹ The reference is primarily to property confiscated from an offender as a penalty and then sold to raise money for the public treasury. The offender may complain that he was wrongly convicted and punished.

²⁰ "Damage" (*blabē*) here as often means simply financial loss.

²¹ The penalty for failure to pay on time was a doubling of the amount due. Until that payment was made, the debtor to the treasury automatically suffered disfranchisement (*atimia*).

· [23] Stop there. All those charges which he has now brought against me, he previously brought against Euergus, and won the case. Testimony has also been given to you at the beginning of my speech[22] that I was abroad when their disagreements with each other began, and anyway that's clear from this charge. For he has nowhere written that I've done any of these things myself, but, putting in that I schemed against him and his property, he says that I instructed my slave to do them—which is a lie; how could I have instructed him, since at the time when I set off on my voyage, I obviously knew nothing whatever of what was going to happen in Athens? [24] And what stupidity, when saying that I was scheming to disfranchise him and inflict the utmost harm, to have written that I instructed a slave to do these things, which not even a fellow-citizen could do![23] What is the point? I suppose that, as he could not in any way attribute any of these actions to me because of my absence abroad and yet he wanted to bring a malicious accusation, he wrote in the charge that I gave instructions; for if he didn't do that, he did not have a word to say. [25] [*To the clerk*] Read out what follows.

[CHARGE]—*and after I incurred the payment to the treasury, he posted his slave Antigenes at my workshop at Thrasymus*[24] *to take charge of my property, although I forbade it*—

Stop there. All this too will be proved by the actual facts to be lies. He has written that I posted a slave and that he forbade it. That's impossible, because I wasn't here. I didn't post a slave because I was in the Pontus, and he didn't forbid me because I wasn't here; how could he? [26] So what compelled him to write it in this way? I suppose Euergus, at the time when he was committing the transgressions for which he has paid a penalty, since he was my friend and knew me well, took the slave from my house and posted him to keep guard at his premises. If Pantaenetus had written the truth, it would have been ridicu-

---

22 At the end of 37.8.

23 Disfranchisement could be imposed only by law, not by an individual.

24 The manuscripts give Thrasyllus here and in Aes. 1.101. This has been corrected to Thrasymus, which the inscribed records of mining leases show was a place in the mining area. Evidently it was near Maroneia, so that Pantaenetus' mine could be referred to by either name; cf. 37.4.

lous; if Euergus posted the slave, how am I guilty? To avoid that, he was compelled to write the charge as he did, so as to direct it against me. [*To the clerk*] Read out what comes next.

[CHARGE] —*and then he persuaded my slaves*[25] *to sit down in the* kenchreōn,[26] *to my detriment*—

[27] This point, now, is utterly shameless. It's obviously a lie, as is clear not only from his refusal to hand over those slaves[27] when I challenged him but from the whole situation. Why should I have wanted to persuade them? "In order to get possession of them." But when I was given a choice between keeping them and recovering my money, I chose to recover the money, and testimony of that has been given. [*To the clerk*] Nevertheless, read out the challenge.

[CHALLENGE]

[28] He didn't accept that challenge, but avoided it; and look what he puts in the charge immediately afterwards! [*To the clerk*] Read out the succeeding words.

[CHARGE] —*and he worked the silver ore which my slaves had mined, and has kept the silver from that ore*—

[*To Pantaenetus*] Again, how is it possible that that was done by me, when I wasn't here, and when you successfully prosecuted Euergus for it? [29] [*To the clerk*] Read out to them what comes next.

[CHARGE] —*and he sold my workshop and slaves, contrary to the terms of the agreement he had made with me*—

Stop there. This goes far beyond everything else. In the first place, he says "contrary to the terms of the agreement he had made with me." What are these terms? We leased our own property to Pantaene-

---

[25] Although Pantaenetus calls them "my slaves," they formed part of the rented property; cf. 37.4.

[26] The meaning of *kenchreōn* is uncertain, but it was presumably some part of the workshop area. When the slaves sat down there, that probably just means that they stopped working for Pantaenetus; less probably, they sat as suppliants to beg for transfer to a different owner.

[27] For interrogation under torture. See p. 48.

tus for the amount of the accruing interest, and that was all. It was Mnesicles who had been the vendor to us, in the presence of Pantaenetus and at his request. [30] Afterwards we sold it to others in the same way, on the conditions on which we ourselves had purchased it; he not only requested but begged us to, because nobody was willing to accept him as vendor. [*To Pantaenetus*] So what is the relevance of the terms of the lease? Why did you write that in the charge, you utter villain? But to prove that we resold it at your request and upon the conditions on which we ourselves had purchased it, [*To the clerk*] read out the testimony.

[TESTIMONY]

[31] [*To Pantaenetus*] You testify to it yourself too; for the property bought[28] by us for 105 minas was later sold by you for 3 talents 2,600 drachmas, but who would have paid a single drachma if you had simply[29] been the vendor? [*To the clerk*] To prove that what I say is true, please call the witnesses of this.

[WITNESSES]

[32] So he has the price he agreed to accept for his property, and he asked me to be the vendor to the extent of the cash I had contributed—and then he prosecutes me for 2 talents in addition! And the rest of the charges are even worse. [*To the clerk*] Please read out the rest of the charge.

[CHARGE]

[33] There he makes a large number of serious charges against me all at once: assault (*aikeia*) and insolence (*hybris*) and offenses of violence (*biaia*) and against heiresses (*epiklēroi*). But actions for each of these are distinct. They don't go to the same magistracy or involve

---

[28] Some manuscripts say "sold." That makes little difference to the argument, since Nicobulus and Euergus both bought and subsequently sold the property at the same price.

[29] There is doubt about the interpretation of the word here translated "simply" (*kathapax*). It may mean "if you had sold it outright (unencumbered)" or it may mean "if you had been the sole seller (with no one else to warrant that it was unencumbered)." The latter suits the context better.

the same penalties. Assault and offenses of violence go to the Forty,[30] prosecutions for insolence to the Thesmothetae, and all those regarding heiresses to the Archon.[31] The laws allow initiation of counter-indictments also for prosecutions for which they are not the introducing magistrates.[32] [*To the clerk*] Read this law out to them.

[LAW]

[34] Now, along with the rest of my counter-indictment I added this objection: "and because the Thesmothetae are not the introducing magistrates for the matters for which Pantaenetus is initiating prosecution." But it has been erased and is not included in the counter-indictment. How that happened, I leave you to consider.[33] It makes no difference to me at all, as long as I can refer to the law itself; for he won't be able to erase the knowledge and understanding of justice from your minds.

[35] [*To the clerk*] Take the mining law also. From this too I think I can show that the case is not admissible and that I deserve gratitude rather than a malicious accusation. Read it out.

[LAW]

This law clearly defines the proper subjects for mining cases. The law, then, makes liable to prosecution anyone who excludes anyone

---

[30] The Forty consisted of four citizens picked by lot from each of the ten tribes (*phylai*). Each group of four handled the trial arrangements for members of their tribe prosecuted in various kinds of private cases.

[31] "The Archon" means the chief of the nine Archons (*archōn epōnymos*). The Thesmothetae were six of the others, concerned mainly with the trial arrangements for many kinds of cases.

[32] The meaning is that, if the would-be prosecutor has brought his prosecution before magistrates who are not the correct ones to introduce that type of case to a court for trial (and if they have mistakenly accepted it; we must remember that the magistrates were not professionals and did not necessarily have much knowledge of law), the defendant can object by counter-indictment (*paragraphē*). Pantaenetus has brought his prosecution before the Thesmothetae; Nicobulus objects that those are not the right magistrates to handle accusations of assault or violence or concerning heiresses.

[33] The implication is that Pantaenetus by bribery or other improper means has got the document altered.

from his workings; but I, so far from excluding him myself, have given him control of what someone else was keeping from him, and handed it over to him, and acted as vendor at his request.³⁴ [36] "Yes," he says, "but prosecutions can be brought also for other offenses concerning the mines." Quite right, Pantaenetus, but what are they? Causing smoke; attacking with weapons; cutting a mine through the limits.³⁵ Those are the other offenses, and surely I haven't committed any of them against you—unless you consider that creditors recovering their money from you are armed attackers! If you think that, you can bring mining cases against all men who lend you their money. But that's not right. [37] Tell me, will every man who buys a mine from the state ignore the general laws, under which everyone should be brought to justice or obtain it, and have his case tried among the mining cases, if he obtains a loan from someone? Or if he is slandered? Or if he is assaulted? Or if he brings a charge of theft? Or if he does not recover *proeisphora*?³⁶ Or anything else at all? [38] [*To the jury*] I don't think so. I think mining cases are for those who are partners in a mine, and those who have bored another mine into their neighbors', and in general those who work the mines and do any of the things mentioned in the law. But I don't think a man who has lent money to Pantaenetus, and has got it back from him with difficulty and ado, should have to face a mining case in addition; by no means!

[39] So anyone who considers these points can easily understand that I have done him no wrong and the case is inadmissible according to law. Having not a single just argument on any of his charges, and having made false statements in his written charge, and prosecuting for matters for which he had granted release, last month, men of Athens, when I was about to go into the trial, after the courts had already been

---

³⁴ After Euergus had excluded Pantaenetus from the workshop, Nicobulus persuaded Euergus to join in selling it, enabling Pantaenetus to obtain a lease from the new owners.

³⁵ Extending the mine beyond the area leased from the state.

³⁶ *Proeisphora* was an advance made by a rich man from his own resources, equal to the total amount of *eisphora* (property tax) due from a number of people. He then attempted to collect the sums due from the individuals. If any of them failed to pay up, he might prosecute them to recover his money.

allocated, he stepped forward, surrounding himself with his friends, his gang of supporters, and did an outrageous thing. [40] He read me a long challenge, calling for the questioning of the slave[37] who, he said, had knowledge of these matters; if they were true, the case was to be decided in his favor with a fixed penalty,[38] and if false, Mnesicles as the questioner was to assess the value of the slave.[39] He received guarantors[40] of these terms from me, and I sealed[41] the challenge—not because I considered it fair; [41] how could it be fair that the imposition of a penalty of 2 talents on me or the exemption of the malicious accuser from punishment should depend on the body and life of a slave?—but I agreed to it because I wanted to win the case with plenty of fairness.[42] After that he issued a fresh summons to me, as soon as he had recovered his deposits;[43] that's how quick he was to show that he didn't even abide by the trial procedure he himself had specified![44] [42] When we went to the questioner, instead of opening up the challenge, displaying the written terms, and proceeding to do in accor-

---

[37] Antigenes, mentioned in the charge (37.22 and 37.25).

[38] Nicobulus was to pay the amount of compensation which Pantaenetus had proposed (2 talents).

[39] On the questioning of slaves under torture, see p. 48. The present passage shows how such questioning would be preceded by an agreement between the litigants about the questions to be asked and the action to be taken in consequence of the answers. Pantaenetus, it appears, proposed that Mnesicles should conduct the questioning. If the slave's evidence supported Nicobulus, Mnesicles should also decide the amount of compensation to be paid to Nicobulus by Pantaenetus for any damage done to the slave in the process; if the slave's evidence supported Pantaenetus, no such compensation would be payable.

[40] Men who undertook to pay the amount due from Nicobulus, if Nicobulus failed to pay it.

[41] Nicobulus put his seal (equivalent to a modern signature) on the document to show that he agreed to its terms.

[42] Nicobulus means that the agreement, though not fair to himself, was more than fair to his opponent.

[43] A deposit (*parakatabolē*), to be forfeited if he lost the case, must have been paid by Pantaenetus on initiating his prosecution, but the reason for the use of the plural here is obscure.

[44] Pantaenetus abandoned the prosecution for which he had originally applied.

dance with them whatever seemed right—because of the hubbub at the time and the imminent calling of the case,[45] it went like this: "I issue this challenge to you." "I accept it." "Let's have your ring."[46] "Take it." "Who is the guarantor?" "This man." I didn't make any copy or anything of that sort—instead of proceeding in the way I have mentioned, he came with another challenge, demanding to question the man himself; he took hold of him, manhandled him, and subjected him to all kinds of bullying. [43] And I thought to myself, men of the jury, what an advantage it is to have concealed[47] one's way of life. It seemed to me that I was suffering this treatment because I was despised for living in a straightforward manner, in accordance with my nature, and in putting up with this I was being very heavily penalized. But anyway, to prove that I was compelled to issue a counter-challenge along the lines I considered fair, and offered to hand over the slave, and to prove that what I am saying is true, [*To the clerk*] read out the challenge.[48]

[CHALLENGE]

[44] Since he rejected this, and also rejected the challenge which he himself made at first, I wonder what on earth he'll say to you. But so that you may know who it is who, he says, treated him outrageously, look at him![49] This is the man who turned Pantaenetus out; this is the man who overpowered Pantaenetus' friends and the laws! For I wasn't in Athens, nor does he charge me with it.

[45] I want to tell you also the means by which he misled the previous jury and got Euergus convicted, to show you that now too there's no impudence or lying that he won't resort to. Besides, you'll find that his accusations against me now can be rebutted in the same ways—

---

[45] The area around the courts was thronged with people.

[46] A signet ring for sealing the document.

[47] "Concealed" (more literally "plastered over") is an emendation of the manuscripts' "shocked," which makes no sense.

[48] Nicobulus' own challenge, not Pantaenetus'. Evidently this was a challenge to Pantaenetus to accept the slave for questioning under different conditions from those he had proposed.

[49] Here Nicobulus beckons Antigenes forward to stand before the court. Presumably he was small or weak, perhaps old.

which is a very cogent proof that Euergus then was accused maliciously. He accused Euergus, in addition to everything else, of going to his house in the country and bursting in on the heiresses[50] and his mother, and he brought the laws about heiresses to the court. [46] To this day, he has never presented himself before the Archon, whom the laws make responsible for such matters and before whom the offender faces a decision on the penalty or compensation he must pay, while the prosecutor obtains a remedy without risk of punishment,[51] and he has never prosecuted[52] either me or Euergus for the offense; he made these accusations in the court[53] and won a case for 2 talents. [47] If Euergus, in accordance with law, had known in advance the accusation on which he was being tried, I think it would have been easy for him to give a true and just explanation and get acquitted. In a mining case, however, it was difficult on the spur of the moment to refute the slander about matters which he would never have expected to be brought up against him; and the anger of the jurors, when they were misled by Pantaenetus, condemned Euergus in the case on which they were voting. [48] But do you think that the man who misled those jurors will hesitate to mislead you? Or that he comes into court relying on the facts, rather than on his speech and his gang of witnesses— that dirty scoundrel Procles, the big man, and Stratocles, the most plausible villain in the world[54]—and his readiness to weep and wail without restraint or shame?

[49] [*To Pantaenetus*] Yet, so far from being worthy of any pity, you deserve to be loathed more than anyone else for your dealings. When

---

[50] The identity of the heiresses (*epiklēroi*) is not explained. Probably they were not Pantaenetus' own daughters (who could not be heiresses before his death) but daughters of his deceased brother or other relative, so that he was their guardian until they were married.

[51] A case of maltreatment of an heiress was not subject to the rule that the prosecutor was punished if he obtained less than one-fifth of the jury's votes.

[52] The Greek verb used here indicates that such a prosecution was called *eisangelia*.

[53] The court of the Thesmothetae, trying Pantaenetus' mining case against Euergus.

[54] Procles and Stratocles were both common names, and it is uncertain whether Pantaenetus' supporters were identical with any other known holders of them.

you owed 105 minas and were not able to pay it, you not only cheated on your actual contracts with the men who jointly supplied the money and were responsible for your fulfilling your obligations to the original contributors,[55] but you seek to disfranchise them as well![56] Other borrowers can be seen giving up their possessions; in your case, that's happened to your creditor,[57] and for lending a talent he's been maliciously accused and condemned to pay 2 talents. [50] I personally lent 40 minas[58] and am facing this prosecution for 2 talents. And for property on which you were never able to borrow more than 100 minas, and which you've sold outright for 3 talents 2,000 drachmas,[59] you have, it seems, been cheated of 4 talents! Who did this to you? My slave, you say. [To the jury] And what citizen would give up his money to a slave? Or who would say that my slave ought also to be held to account for acts for which Pantaenetus has already prosecuted Euergus and got him convicted? [51] And apart from that, Pantaenetus has himself released him from all such accusations. He should not have been raising them now, or inserting them in the challenge in which he asked for him to be handed over for questioning; he should have initiated the case against the slave and proceeded against me as the owner. Instead, he has initiated it against me and is accusing him. That's not allowed by law. Who ever initiated a case against the master and then accused the slave of the acts as if he were the owner?

[52] When anyone asks him, "What justification will you be able to give for accusing Nicobulus?" he says, "The Athenians hate money-lenders. Nicobulus is unpopular; he walks quickly, he talks loudly, and he carries a cane. All these things," he says, "are in my favor." He's

---

[55] Nicobulus and Euergus enabled Pantaenetus to pay off Mnesicles, Phileas, and Pleistor.

[56] For certain of the offenses of which Pantaenetus accused Euergus and Nicobulus (insolence, wronging an heiress) the penalty would usually have been a fine payable to the state treasury, and the offenders would have suffered disfranchisement (*atimia*) until they paid it.

[57] Euergus.

[58] Actually 45 minas: either Nicobulus is just giving an approximate round number here, or the word for "five" has been lost from the text.

[59] These too seem to be approximate round numbers. Pantaenetus borrowed 105 minas, and the property was sold for 3 talents 2,600 drachmas; cf. 37.31.

not ashamed to say this, and he thinks people who hear him don't realize that this is the argument of a malicious accuser, not of a victim of wrongdoing. [53] In my opinion, none of the moneylenders are criminals, but it's reasonable for you to dislike some of them, who have made a profession of the business and are not concerned with sympathy or anything else but gain. Because I have often been a borrower also, and have not merely lent to Pantaenetus myself, I too am not unacquainted with them, and I'm not fond of them; but I certainly don't defraud them, by Zeus, or accuse them maliciously. [54] A man who has been a trader, as I have, making voyages and taking risks, and having made a little money has lent it, and wants to do a favor but doesn't want his money to leak away unnoticed—why should he be classed with them? [*To Pantaenetus*] Unless you say that anyone who lends to you should be regarded as a public enemy! [*To the clerk*] Please read out the testimonies about the kind of person I am in my dealings with those who make loans and those who ask for them.

[TESTIMONIES]

[55] That, Pantaenetus, is the sort of man I am, the quick walker; and that's the sort you are, the leisurely one! But as for my manner of walking or talking, men of the jury, I'll tell you the whole truth quite frankly. I have not failed to realize, and I'm well aware, that I am not one of the people who are well endowed in those respects, to their own advantage. If I annoy some people by conduct which is of no use to me, surely that's my bad luck, as far as that's concerned. [56] What do I deserve, then? To lose a law case too, just because I lend money to So-and-so? Certainly not. Pantaenetus won't prove against me any wickedness or wrongdoing, and not one of you in this large gathering knows of any. But in those other respects, each of us, I suppose, has the nature he happens to have. It's not practicable to fight against one's nature—otherwise we'd all be alike—but it's easy for someone else who sees it to recognize it and criticize.

[57] But what has all this to do with my dealings with you, Pantaenetus? You've been treated very badly? Well, you've obtained compensation. Not from me? That's because I didn't do you any wrong. Otherwise you would never have released me or let me go when you chose to initiate a case against Euergus, and you would not have asked a man who had treated you very badly to undertake to be a vendor for

you. Besides, how could I have done you any wrong when I wasn't here and wasn't in Athens? [58] [*To the jury*] Even if one granted him that the greatest possible wrongs have been done and that his speech about them now will be entirely true, I think at least you'd all agree that some people before now have suffered many wrongs more serious than financial ones. Acts of unintentional homicide and insulting treatment of what is sacred and many other such things occur. Nevertheless, for all these, release by consent is laid down as a limit and settlement for the victims. [59] This principle is so strong among all people that, if one has obtained a conviction for unintentional homicide and has clearly shown that the offender is impure,[60] but afterwards pardons and releases him, one no longer has authority to banish the same man.[61] And if the victim himself, before dying, releases the perpetrator from the homicide, none of the surviving relatives is permitted to take proceedings; those who are required by law to be banished and to live in exile, if convicted, and to be put to death, are freed from all danger, if they have once been released by that pronouncement. [60] Then, when release possesses such strength and permanence with regard to life and the most important matters, will it be powerless with regard to money and lesser charges? Certainly not. The most serious thing of all will not be if I fail to obtain justice in your court, but if you now subvert in our day a rule of justice determined from the beginning of time.

---

[60] Homicide was believed to cause religious pollution.

[61] Exile was the standard penalty for unintentional homicide.

38. AGAINST NAUSIMACHUS
AND XENOPEITHES

✧✧

INTRODUCTION

Some passages of *Against Nausimachus and Xenopeithes* are almost identical with passages of *Against Pantaenetus:* 38.1 with 37.1, and 38.21–22 with 37.58–60. That makes it likely that this speech was written by Demosthenes around the same time as that one, about 346 BC, and he saved himself a little trouble by using some of the same material in both. There is no other evidence of the date of this speech.

Nausicrates was a rich man who died about thirty-eight years earlier, and thus probably around 384. He left two sons named Nausimachus and Xenopeithes, who were only about two years old. They seem to have been close together in age, perhaps twins.[1] Until they came of age, they and Nausicrates' property were looked after by guardians. One of the guardians was Aristaechmus. His relationship to the family is never stated in the text, but it has been reasonably suggested that he was the boys' uncle, the brother of their mother.[2] Their other uncle, also named Xenopeithes, the brother of their father, was probably also a guardian initially, but he too died before they came of age, so that his property also passed to them. There was a third guardian (as is clear from 38.7), but his identity is not known.

Nausicrates and his brother, the elder Xenopeithes, left a house with some furniture and slaves, but the greater part of their property

---

[1] See 38.6n.

[2] An inscription records as trierarchs Aristaechmus of Cholleidae and Xenopeithes of Paeania (*Inscriptiones Graecae* 2² 1609, lines 98 and 117). If those are the persons who appear in our speech, the difference of demes shows that Aristaechmus did not belong to the family of the boys' father.

consisted of money invested in the form of loans due to be repaid with interest at later dates. The guardians duly collected some of these debts and used the proceeds to buy some land and buildings. When the boys came of age, the guardians were slow to render accounts of their guardianship and hand over the property, and after a few years (perhaps when the five-year limit on such prosecutions was about to expire) Nausimachus and Xenopeithes began taking steps to prosecute them. At first they demanded the huge sum of 80 talents, but eventually they agreed to accept 3 talents without a trial, and gave Aristaechmus formal release and discharge from his liabilities to them. If the figures in 38.6 are correct, it was now eight years since they had come of age.

Aristaechmus died only three or four months later; the other guardian is not mentioned again and may also have died by this time. Aristaechmus left four young sons, who in their turn had guardians, including one named Demaretus, until they came of age. And then, about thirty-eight years after Nausicrates' death, Nausimachus and Xenopeithes decided to take further action to recover what they claimed. First, they successfully prosecuted a man named Aesius for some amount. Next, they took steps to prosecute the sons of Aristaechmus, claiming that the money from a debt repaid by a man named Hermonax had not been handed over to them. The sum repaid by Hermonax is said to have been 100 Cyzicene staters. Nausimachus and Xenopeithes each claimed 30 minas (half a talent) from each of the four sons of Aristaechmus. The speaker of the surviving speech asserts that this means they were demanding 4 talents in total. However, 100 staters can hardly have been worth more than about 30 minas,[3] and it would clearly have been unreasonable for them to demand eight times that amount if Hermonax' payment was the only one they were claiming. Possibly they were unsure which of Aristaechmus' sons had the money, and so prosecuted them all, expecting to be successful in only one of the cases.

To prevent the trials from going ahead, the sons of Aristaechmus brought a counter-indictment (*paragraphē*)[4]—strictly, perhaps, eight

---

[3] For the approximate rate of exchange, see 34.23.
[4] On counter-indictments, see p. 12–13.

counter-indictments, each of the four sons against each of Nausimachus and Xenopeithes. The surviving speech is written for delivery by one of the sons, perhaps the eldest. The verdict in his counter-indictment would no doubt be accepted as decisive for the others.

There are two grounds for the counter-indictment. One is that Nausimachus and Xenopeithes gave Aristaechmus release and discharge from their claims against him, and so should not be permitted to reopen them. The other is that the law prescribes a time-limit of five years for claims by wards against their guardians, and that limit is long past. However, although the speaker naturally does not present his opponents' arguments clearly, it appears that they maintained that the debt owed to Nausicrates by Hermonax, and recorded by Aristaechmus as not yet paid, had been paid after Aristaechmus' death to Demaretus, who had passed the money on to Aristaechmus' sons, who had kept it. If that was true, Nausimachus and Xenopeithes may have been able to argue plausibly that laws restricting their right to prosecute their former guardian were irrelevant, because Aristaechmus had not handled this particular debt and their dispute was only with Aristaechmus' sons; thus the counter-indictment should fail. But when it comes to the facts of the dispute, we now have no means of discovering who was telling the truth about the money repaid by Hermonax. Indeed, the rather weak arguments from probability in 38.9–13 suggest that the speaker, who after all had been only a child at the time of the alleged repayment, may not really have known the facts himself.

38. COUNTER-INDICTMENT AGAINST NAUSIMACHUS AND XENOPEITHES

[1] Since[5] the laws, men of the jury, permit a counter-indictment for any matters for which a person goes on to bring a prosecution after granting release and discharge, and our father received both of those in relation to Nausimachus and Xenopeithes who have initiated cases against us, we have brought a counter-indictment, as you heard just now, that the case is not admissible.

---

[5] The beginning of this speech is almost the same as 37.1.

[2] I am going to make a moderate and just request of you all: first, to listen to my speech favorably; then, if it seems that I am being wrongfully prosecuted on an inappropriate charge, to give me the support I deserve. The assessment[6] you have heard for the case is 30 minas, but the money for which we are being prosecuted is 4 talents. For the two of them have brought four cases against us, all for the same sum, 3,000 drachmas each,[7] for damage;[8] 30 minas is now written on the charge, but we are standing trial for that large amount of money. [3] The maliciousness of their accusation, and how treacherously they have proceeded against us, you shall learn from the actual facts. First, he will read you the testimonies, that they released our father from their charges concerning the guardianship; for it's on this ground that we have brought the counter-indictment that the case is not admissible. [*To the clerk*] Please read out these testimonies.

[TESTIMONIES]

[4] So you hear from the testimonies, men of the jury, that they initiated cases for the guardianship and then gave them up, and have accepted the agreed amounts of money. The laws do not permit a subsequent prosecution concerning what has been done in this way, as I think you all know even without my telling you anything about it; but still I want him to read you the actual law too. [*To the clerk*] Read out the law.

[LAW][9]

[5] You hear, men of the jury, the law specifying each of the things for which there are not to be prosecutions. One of them, just as valid as the others, is that one is not to prosecute for matters for which one has granted release and discharge. Now, although release has been granted in that way before a large number of witnesses, and the law clearly exonerates us, they have sunk to such a depth of brazen shamelessness [6] that, after an interval of fourteen years since they released

---

[6] The compensation or damages demanded by the prosecutor.

[7] 3,000 drachmas = 30 minas = half a talent.

[8] "Damage" (*blabē*) here as often means simply financial loss.

[9] The same law is read out in 36.24 and 37.18.

our father, and twenty-two since the time when they were registered,[10] and after the deaths both of our father, with whom their settlement was made, and of the guardians who took charge of our affairs after his death, and of their own mother, who knew all about these matters, and of the arbitrators and witnesses and practically everyone, they considered that our inexperience and inevitable ignorance of the facts was a godsend for them; so they brought these prosecutions against us, and they have the impudence to say what is neither just nor reasonable. [7] They say that they did not relinquish their father's estate for the money they received, and did not give up the property, but that all that was left to them in the form of debts[11] and furniture and money in general belonged to them. But I know, because I've been told, that Xenopeithes and Nausicrates left all their property in the form of debts and possessed little visible property. When the debts had been collected and some furniture sold, and also some slaves, the guardians bought the land and buildings which they handed over to these men. [8] If there had been no dispute about this previously, and no prosecution for not administering the estate properly, it would be a different story; but after these men brought charges about the whole of the guardianship, initiated prosecutions, and obtained money, release was given for all this at that time. After all, these men were not pursuing their cases for the sake of the word "guardianship," but for the money; and their opponents weren't paying for the word with the money they handed over, but for the accusations.

[9] So I think you have all understood well enough from the actual laws and the release that, because they have granted a discharge, they

---

[10] A young man of citizen birth was registered in his deme at the age of eighteen. If the figure of twenty-two is correct for both Nausimachus and Xenopeithes, that means that they either were twins or were born within a year of each other. Alternatively, the speaker uses the figure loosely, and one brother was really registered a year or two later than the other. Some manuscripts, instead of "they were registered," have "they prosecuted him by *graphē*" (or possibly "they wrote their charge"); but that is unlikely to be correct, because *graphē* was not the procedure used for guardianship cases, and because it is hardly credible that eight years elapsed between the initiation of prosecution and the settlement of the case.

[11] Loans to other people, to be repaid with interest in due course.

have no case against us for any of the debts which our father collected before the discharge, or in general for any of the money which he received because of the guardianship. Now, I want to show that that money cannot have been recovered later; that's a misleading fabrication by these men. [10] They would not claim that our father received it, for he died three or four months after his settlement with them; and I shall also show that it's impossible that Demaretus, who was left as our guardian, received it—for they have included his name in the charge too. [11] They themselves are our best witnesses of that, because they clearly never brought a case against Demaretus during his lifetime; besides, observation and scrutiny of the actual facts will show that he not only did not receive it, but he couldn't have received it. The debt was owed in Bosporus,[12] and Demaretus never visited that place; so how could he have collected it? "He would have sent someone to recover it," someone might say. [12] But look at it this way. Hermonax owed them 100 staters,[13] which he'd obtained from Nausicrates. Aristaechmus was their guardian and protector for sixteen years. The money which Hermonax repaid personally after they had grown up was not repaid by him when they were minors; for he would not have paid the same debt twice. Now, is there any human being so odd as to evade payment for such a long time to those with authority to receive it, and then voluntarily hand it over to someone who had no authority[14] because he'd sent a letter? I don't think so. [13] But to prove that I'm telling the truth, and that our father died immediately after the settlement, and these men never brought a case against Demaretus for that money, and Demaretus did not go abroad or make any voyage there at all, [*To the clerk*] take the testimonies.

[TESTIMONIES]

[14] So it has been made clear to you from the dates and from the testimonies that our father did not collect the money after the release, and no one would have given it voluntarily to someone sent by Demaretus, and he did not make the voyage or travel there himself. Now,

---

[12] See 34.2n.

[13] See 34.5n.

[14] Demaretus had no authority to receive payments due to Nausimachus and Xenopeithes, because he had not been their guardian.

I want to show that their account of the whole matter is entirely false. In the charge they're now pursuing, they have written that we owe them the cash because our father recovered it, and he passed this debt on to them as still owed in his account of the guardianship. [*To the clerk*] Please take and read out the actual charge.

[CHARGE]

[15] You hear that it's written in the charge, "Aristaechmus passed the debt on to me in his account of the guardianship." Now, when they were prosecuting our father for his guardianship, their written charge was the opposite of this; for it's clear that at that time they charged him with not rendering an account. [*To the clerk*] Read out the actual charge which they brought against our father at that time.

[CHARGE]

[16] So in what account are you now charging that he passed it on, Xenopeithes and Nausimachus? At that time you were bringing prosecutions and demanding money on the ground that he hadn't rendered one. If you're going to be able to make malicious accusations on both grounds, and at one time you obtained money because he did not pass the debt on but at another time you're prosecuting because he did pass it on, there's nothing to stop you looking for a third reason later, for which you'll prosecute again. But the laws don't say that; they say there are to be prosecutions only once against the same person for the same acts.

[17] To show you, men of the jury, that not only are they not the victims of any wrong now, but also their prosecution of us violates all the laws, I also want to cite to you this law which says explicitly that, if five years have elapsed without their prosecuting, orphans are no longer allowed to prosecute on charges arising from the guardianship. He'll read you the law.

[LAW] [15]

[18] You hear, men of the jury, that the law says explicitly that, if they don't prosecute within five years, there is to be no prosecution. "We did initiate a case," they may say. Yes, and you made a settlement,

---

[15] The same law is read out in 36.26.

so that you can't prosecute again. It would be truly terrible if, when the law does not allow orphans to bring prosecutions after five years against guardians who have not been released for the original offenses, you were to carry through now, in the twentieth year,[16] a prosecution against us, guardians' sons, for matters for which you did release them.

[19] I hear they are going to avoid any justification concerning the actual facts and the laws, and are prepared to say that a large amount of money was left to them and they've been deprived of it, and they'll use as evidence of this the size of the claims they originally made, and bewail their orphanhood, and go through the account of the guardianship; that and suchlike is what they're relying on, and what they think will enable them to deceive you. [20] But in my opinion the size of the claims that were made at that time is stronger evidence for us, that the accusations against our father were malicious, than for them, that they were deprived of a large amount. No one who was able to prove a claim of 80 talents would have accepted 3 talents as a settlement, whereas no one who was being prosecuted for guardianship for so much money would have refused to pay 3 talents to buy off the risk and the advantages which these men naturally possessed at that time. For they were orphans and young, and their character was not known; and everyone says those considerations weigh more with you than strong arguments.

[21] I think I can also show that it would be reasonable for you not to tolerate a word from them on the subject of the guardianship. Even if[17] one granted them that the greatest possible wrongs have been done and that their speeches about them now will be entirely true, I think at least you'd all agree that some people before now have suffered many wrongs more serious than financial ones. Acts of unintentional homicide and insulting treatment of what is sacred and many other such offenses occur. Nevertheless, for all these, release by consent is laid down as a limit and settlement for the victims. [22] This principle is so strong among all people that, if one has obtained a conviction for uninten-

---

[16] This number is not explained. Possibly it is just an approximation for the twenty-two years mentioned in 38.6.

[17] The passage from here to the end of 22 is repeated almost verbatim from 37.58–60.

tional homicide and has plainly shown that the offender is impure, but afterwards pardons and releases him, one no longer has authority to banish the same man. Then, when release possesses such strength and permanence with regard to life and the most important matters, will it be powerless with regard to money and lesser charges? Certainly not. The most serious thing of all will not be if I fail to obtain justice in your court, but if a rule of justice determined from the beginning of time is now subverted.

[23] "They did not lease our property," perhaps they'll say. [*To Nausimachus and Xenopeithes*] No, because your uncle Xenopeithes did not wish it: when Nicides revealed it, he persuaded the jurors to let him administer it.[18] That is known to everyone. "They stole a great deal from us." Well, for that you've got from them the compensation to which you agreed, and you surely ought not to receive any more from me. [24] To show you there's nothing in this: it's obviously not fair, after reaching a settlement with those responsible, to make accusations against those who know nothing about it, but still, Xenopeithes and Nausimachus, if you do believe that these claims of yours are amazingly strong, you should pay back the 3 talents before going ahead with them. Since you were paid such a large sum of money to give up your accusations, it's right that you should say nothing until you pay it back, and not make accusations while keeping it; that really is going too far.

[25] [*To the jury*] Possibly they'll also talk about trierarchies, and how they've spent their assets in support of you.[19] That they'll be lying, and after squandering most of their assets on themselves, with the city getting only a small share, they'll be asking you for gratitude

---

[18] This means that Nicides (whose identity is unknown) brought a legal action in support of the young Nausimachus and Xenopeithes, to have their property let out on lease until they came of age, so that they would receive the income from it; but when the action came to trial their uncle Xenopeithes persuaded the jury that it was better for him to administer it. The verb translated "revealed" indicates that the legal procedure was *phasis,* but it is not clear why; the problem is considered by MacDowell 1991: 196–197.

[19] They may claim that they have spent large amounts of money on the maintenance of ships in the navy, and that this was a great service to Athens.

which is not deserved or due—I'll say nothing about that.[20] But my own request to you, men of the jury, is that some gratitude should be shown by you to all who perform liturgies for you. And which of them deserve most? The ones who carry out a useful part of the city's policy, while avoiding action that everyone would call shameful and disgraceful. [26] So men who, besides performing liturgies, have wasted their own possessions bequeath disrepute to the city rather than service—for no one ever blames himself, but he alleges that the city has ruined him.[21] But men who readily carry out all your instructions, while preserving their property by their moderation in other expenditure, not only are likely to surpass the others in their past and future service but do so without bringing disgrace on you. You'll see that's the sort of men we all are towards you; for them, I'll say nothing, in case they say I'm slandering them.

[27] I shouldn't be surprised if they also try to weep and make you pity them. I therefore ask you all to bear in mind that it's a shameful thing, or rather quite unjust, for them to have shamefully misspent their money on gourmandizing and getting drunk with Aristocrates and Diognetus[22] and other men of that sort, and now to weep and wail so as to get hold of other people's. [*To Nausimachus and Xenopeithes*] What you should have been weeping over are your own actions. But now is not the time to weep, but to show that you did not grant release, or that you can prosecute again for matters for which you granted it, or that it's right to initiate a case in the twentieth year[23] when the law has prescribed five years as the time-limit; those are the issues the jury is trying. [28] [*To the jury*] If they are unable to show

---

[20] A striking instance of paralipsis, the rhetorical device of mentioning something while professing to omit it.

[21] The meaning is that, if a man squanders his money and then claims that performing liturgies, not his own extravagance, has made him poor, Athens will get a bad reputation for extorting money, and this will outweigh the usefulness of the liturgies that he has performed.

[22] This Aristocrates may be the one who is mentioned in 54.39, or possibly the one who is the opponent in Oration 23. Diognetus is unknown.

[23] The reference to the twentieth year depends on Reiske's restoration of the text. The manuscripts say "still," with some unintelligible variants. For the number, see 38.18.

those things—as they will be—we request you all, men of the jury, not to deliver us up to these men, and not to give yet a fourth inheritance to them when they have misused three others—the one the guardians handed over to them willingly, the one they exacted for their prosecutions, and the one they obtained from Aesius[24] the other day by winning a case—but to allow us to keep our own property, as is right. It's of greater assistance to you in our hands than in theirs, and it is surely more just for us than for them to possess our property.

I don't know why I need say any more. I think you have understood everything that has been said. Pour out the water.[25]

---

[24] This is probably the brother of Aphobus who appears in Oration 29. Presumably he had borrowed money from Nausicrates and never repaid it.

[25] See 36.62n.

BIBLIOGRAPHY FOR THIS VOLUME

Blass, Friedrich, 1893: *Die attische Beredsamkeit,* volume 3.1 (second edition). Leipzig.

Burke, Edmund M., 1998: "The Looting of the Estate of the Elder Demosthenes," *Classica et Mediaevalia* 49: 45–65.

Calhoun, George Miller, 1934: "A Problem of Authenticity (Demosthenes 29)," *Transactions of the American Philological Association* 65: 80–102.

Carawan, Edwin, 2001: "What the Laws Have Prejudged: Παραγραφή and Early Issue-Theory," in Cecil W. Wooten (ed.), *The Orator in Action and Theory in Greece and Rome* (*Mnemosyne* Supplement 225). Leiden: 17–51.

Carey, Christopher, 1997: *Trials from Classical Athens.* London.

Carey, C., and Reid, R. A., 1985: *Demosthenes: Selected Private Speeches.* Cambridge.

Cohen, Edward E., 1973: *Ancient Athenian Maritime Courts.* Princeton.

Cohen, Edward E., 1992: *Athenian Economy and Society: A Banking Perspective.* Princeton.

Cox, Cheryl Anne, 1998: *Household Interests: Property, Marriage Strategies, and Family Dynamics in Ancient Athens.* Princeton.

Davies, J. K., 1971: *Athenian Propertied Families, 600–300 B.C.* Oxford.

Doherty, F. C., 1927: *Three Private Speeches of Demosthenes.* Oxford.

Gagarin, Michael, 1996: "The Torture of Slaves in Athenian Law," *Classical Philology* 91: 1–18.

Garland, Robert, 1987: *The Piraeus.* London.

Garnsey, Peter, 1988: *Famine and Food Supply in the Graeco-Roman World.* Cambridge.

Harris, Edward M., 1988: "When Is a Sale not a Sale? The Riddle of Athenian Terminology for Real Security Revisited," *Classical Quarterly* 38: 351–381.

Harris, Edward M., 1993: "*Apotimema:* Athenian Terminology for Real Security in Leases and Dowry Agreements," *Classical Quarterly* 43: 73–95.

Harrison, A. R. W., 1968–1971: *The Law of Athens* (two volumes). Oxford.

Hunter, Virginia J., 1989: "Women's Authority in Classical Athens: The Example of Kleoboule and Her Son," *Echos du Monde Classique = Classical Views* 33 = n.s. 8: 39–48.

Hunter, Virginia J., 1994: *Policing Athens: Social Control in the Attic Lawsuits, 420–320 B.C.* Princeton.

Isager, Signe, and Hansen, Mogens Herman, 1975: *Aspects of Athenian Society in the Fourth Century B.C.* Odense.

Lambert, Stephen D., 2001: "Ten Notes on Attic Inscriptions," *Zeitschrift für Papyrologie und Epigraphik* 135: 51–62.

Lofberg, J. O., 1932: "The Speakers in the Case of Chrysippus v. Phormio," *Classical Philology* 27: 329–335.

McCabe, Donald F., 1981: *The Prose-rhythm of Demosthenes.* New York.

MacDowell, Douglas M., 1978: *The Law in Classical Athens.* London.

MacDowell, Douglas M., 1989: "The Authenticity of Demosthenes 29 (Against Aphobus III) as a Source of Information about Athenian Law," in Gerhard Thür (ed.), *Symposion 1985.* Cologne: 253–262.

MacDowell, Douglas M., 1990: *Demosthenes: Against Meidias (Oration 21).* Oxford.

MacDowell, Douglas M., 1991: "The Athenian Procedure of *Phasis,*" in Michael Gagarin (ed.), *Symposion 1990.* Cologne: 187–198.

Millett, Paul, 1991: *Lending and Borrowing in Ancient Athens.* Cambridge.

Mirhady, David C., 1996: "Torture and Rhetoric in Athens" (with a response by G. Thür), *Journal of Hellenic Studies* 116: 119–134.

Mirhady, David C., 2000a: "Demosthenes as Advocate," in Ian Worthington (ed.), *Demosthenes: Statesman and Orator.* London: 181–204.

Mirhady, David C., 2000b: "The Athenian Rationale for Torture," in Virginia Hunter and Jonathan Edmonson (eds.), *Law and Social Status in Classical Athens.* Oxford: 53–74.

Paley, F. A., and Sandys, J. E., 1896–1898: *Select Private Orations of Demosthenes* (two volumes, third edition). Cambridge.

Pearson, Lionel, 1972: *Demosthenes: Six Private Speeches*. Norman, Oklahoma.

Rosivach, Vincent J., 2000: "Some Economic Aspects of the Fourth-Century Athenian Market in Grain," *Chiron* 30: 31–64.

Thompson, Wesley E., 1980: "An Athenian Commercial Case: Demosthenes 34," *Tijdschrift voor Rechtsgeschiedenis* 48: 137–149.

Thür, Gerhard, 1972: "Der Streit über den Status des Werkstättenleiters Milyas (Dem., or. 29)," *Revue Internationale des Droits de l'Antiquité* 19: 151–177.

Thür, Gerhard, 1977: *Beweisführung vor den Schwurgerichtshöfen Athens: die Proklesis zur Basanos*. Vienna.

Todd, S. C., 1993: *The Shape of Athenian Law*. Oxford.

Todd, S. C., 1994: "Status and Contract in Fourth-century Athens," in Gerhard Thür (ed.), *Symposion 1993*. Cologne: 125–140.

Trevett, Jeremy, 1992: *Apollodoros the Son of Pasion*. Oxford.

Usher, Stephen, 1999: *Greek Oratory: Tradition and Originality*. Oxford.

Whitby, Michael, 1998: "The Grain Trade of Athens in the Fourth Century BC," in Helen Parkins and Christopher Smith (eds.), *Trade, Traders and the Ancient City*. London: 102–128.

Wolff, Hans Julius, 1966: *Die attische Paragraphe*. Weimar.

INDEX